Joseph Fisher

The Case of Ireland

Being an examination of the Treaty of union between Great Britain and Ireland; and

an inquiry into the manner in which it has been carried out: together with some

letters on the excessive taxation of Ireland

Joseph Fisher

The Case of Ireland
Being an examination of the Treaty of union between Great Britain and Ireland; and an inquiry into the manner in which it has been carried out: together with some letters on the excessive taxation of Ireland

ISBN/EAN: 9783337063405

Printed in Europe, USA, Canada, Australia, Japan

Cover: Foto ©Suzi / pixelio.de

More available books at **www.hansebooks.com**

THE

CASE OF IRELAND,

BEING AN EXAMINATION OF

THE TREATY OF UNION

BETWEEN

GREAT BRITAIN AND IRELAND;

AND AN ENQUIRY INTO THE MANNER IN WHICH
IT HAS BEEN CARRIED OUT:

TOGETHER WITH SOME

LETTERS ON THE EXCESSIVE TAXATION

OF

IRELAND.

BY

JOSEPH FISHER,

AUTHOR OF "HOW IRELAND MAY BE SAVED," "TAXATION OF IRELAND,"
"IRELAND, PAST AND PRESENT," ETC., ETC.

LONDON:
PUBLISHED BY RIDGWAY, PICCADILLY;
AND
SOLD BY MESSRS. W. H. SMITH AND SONS, DUBLIN & LONDON,
AND ALL BOOKSELLERS.
1863.

CONTENTS. 849545

AUTHORITIES.

The following authorities have been referred to in this work:—

ACTS OF PARLIAMENT.

28 Henry VIII.
10 Charles I., Cap. 21.
40 Geo. III , Cap. 34.
41 Geo. III., Caps. 3, 25, and 84.
42 Geo. III., Caps. 33 and 58.
43 Geo. III., Caps. 65, 68, and 113.
44 Geo. III., Caps. 47 and 48.
45 Geo. III., Caps. 12 and 38.
46 Geo. III., Caps. 32 and 47.
47 Geo. III., Caps. 28 and 46.
49 Geo. III., Caps. 69 and 78.
50 Geo. III., Cap. 68.
51 Geo. III., Cap. 62.
52 Geo. III., Cap. 70.
53 Geo. III., Cap. 61, 69, and 156.
54 Geo. III., Caps. 74 and 86.
56 Geo. III., Caps. 70, 89, and 98

PARLIAMENTARY PAPERS.

No. —, Session 1813.
No. 214, Session 1815.
No. 35, Session 1819.
No. 256, Session 1824.
No. 667, Session 1830.
No. 146, Session 1833.
No. 659, Session 1833.
No. 194, Session 1834.
No. 346, Session 1841.
27th April, Session 1841.
No. 305, Session 1842.
No. 361, Session 1842.
No. 443, Session 1849.
No. 417, Session 1858.
No. 423, Session 1858.
No. 303, Session 1862.
No. 355, Session 1863.
No. 356, Session 1863.

Journals of the Irish House of Lords.
Hansard's Parliamentary Debates.
Report of Finance Committee, 1814.
Report of the Finance Committee, 1815.
Report of the Lords' Committee on Ireland, 1825
Report of Irish Poor Committee, 1830.
Report of the Board of Trade, 1833.
Report of the Devon Commission, 1845.
Second Report of Poor Law Commission.

AUTHORS.

Vattel's Law of Nations.
Arthur Young's Travels in Ireland.
Edward Cooke, For and Against the Union.
The Annual Register.
Adam Smith's Wealth of Nations.
Sadleir, M. J., M.P., The Evils of Ireland and their Remedy.
Locke's Essay on Government.
Grove's System of Moral Philosophy.

Blackstone's Commentaries—Article Population.
Reece's Encyclopedia.
Plowden's History of England.
Jessop's Travels in Holland.
Addison's Travels in Italy.
Forsyth's Travels in Italy.
Chateauvieux's Travels in Italy.
Prior's List of Absentees.
Paley's Moral Philosophy.
Montesqueu's L'Esprit de Lois.
Report of the Case of John Jackson.
The Commercial Injustice of Ireland.
Encyclopædia Britannica.

SPEECHES OF

George III.
Lord Lieutenants.
  The Duke of Portland.
  The Duke of Rutland.
  The Marquis Cornwallis.
  Earl Fitzwilliam.
Marquis of Buckinghamshire.
Marquis of Lansdowne.
The Earl of Clare.
Earl Grey.
Earl of Rosse (Sir L. Parsons).
Earl of Carysford.
Lord Castlereagh.
Lord Plunket.
Lord Holland.
Lord Greville.
Lord Melville.
Lord Glenbervie.
Lord Powerscourt.
Lord Fitzgerald and Vesci.
Lord Althorpe.
Lord Monteagle (Mr. Spring Rice).
Lord Chief Justice Bushe.
Lord Justice of Appeal (Black burne).

The Hon. Justice Jebb.
The Hon. Baron Forster.
The Hon. Justice Day.
The Hon. Justice Fletcher.
The Right Rev. Dr. Doyle, R.C. Bishop of Carlow.
William Pitt.
Richard Brinsley Sheridan.
Charles J. Fox.
Henry Grattan.
John Forster, Speaker of the Irish House of Commons.
William Saurin.
Sir Robert Peel.
Sir John Newport.
Sir John Pakington.
Sir George Cornwall Lewis.
Henry Goulburn.
Nicholas Vansittart.
William Huskisson.
Colonel Dunne.
George Bennett, K.C.
William Gladstone.
Major Wilcocks.
Alexander Nimmo, C.E.

The Protest of the Irish Peers against the Union was signed by

Leinster.
Downshire.
Percy.
Meath.
Granard.
Ludlow.
Arran.
Charlemont.
Kingston.

Mountcashel.
Farnham.
Massey.
Enniskillen.
Kilmore.
Dillon.
Strangford.
Powerscourt.

De Vesci.
William Down and Connor.
Richard Waterford and Lismore.
Louth.
Lismore.
Sunderlin.

DEDICATION.

TO THE PEOPLE OF IRELAND.

IT is alike your interest, and your duty, to inquire into the covenants which were entered into with your forefathers, when Ireland surrendered her sovereignty as a Nation, and to ascertain whether those covenants have been fulfilled.

Having been asked by the Chamber of Commerce of this City to assist in preparing a case for the advice of Counsel, as to the legal rights of the Irish People under the Treaty of Union, I have been forced to examine the subject with more attention than I had previously given to it.

I have addressed this case to you, because it relates to the prosperity of Ireland, and I think I have shown, that the conditions of the Act of Union, and the dictates of public policy have been equally violated, in the conduct which has been adopted towards Ireland, since 1800.

I thank you for the attention you have given to my letters as they appeared week after week.

If they succeed in evoking that public spirit on which the welfare of this nation depends, I shall feel that I have not laboured in vain.

Your Faithful Servant,

JOSEPH FISHER

Waterford, March, 1863.

B

PREFACE.

It is necessary, in order to ascertain the true bearings of the Act of Union, between Great Britain and Ireland, upon the present position of both countries with regard to taxation, to examine somewhat minutely, into the laws of nations which govern such Unions, and thus discover the rights of the Parliament of each nation, to surrender its distinct nationality, and the power of the new Empire to alter or abrogate the Treaty and Acts which brought it into existence.

To aid in this inquiry, it also becomes absolutely requisite to discover the progress and condition of each nation previous to the Union, and to trace the course of those negociations by which separate pre-existing rights were secured and pre-served. The debates of the separate Parliaments of Great Britain and Ireland, shew what were the ideas of those who proposed and carried the Act of Union; and they have, therefore, an important bearing upon the construction which should be put upon the several clauses of that Act.

If it was intended that the Parliament of the United Kingdom should have had power to alter, change, or abrogate the conditions of the Treaty of Union, there was no occasion for such a treaty; the mere fact that there was a Treaty—that it gave the Parliament which it created power, under certain conditions, to do certain acts, and restricted it, under any conditions, from performing other acts, proves that it was intended, alike by the Parliament of Great Britain and the Parliament of Ireland, that the Parliament of the United Kingdom should not have the power of altering the Act of Union, or abridging the rights of the Irish people—the weaker of the parties—under it.

The competence of the Parliament of the United King-dom to deal with any legislation arising out of the Act of Union, was one of the subjects referred to the Finance Com-mitee of 1815, and upon their report was based the legisla-tion of 1816, under which the Exchequers of the United Kingdom were consolidated. I have given that report and the tables on which it was founded full consideration, and it appears to me that the preceding conditions not having been fulfilled, it was not competent for the Parliament of the United Kingdom to have swept away those rights, privileges, and immunities which were secured to the Irish Nation by the Act of Union.

The taxation imposed upon Ireland for twenty years after the Union—that is from 1801 to 1821—by the Act itself, was most onerous and oppressive; but Ireland paid its share of the burden, though, unfortunately, her trade, com-merce, and manufactures reeled and sank under that load. The Legislation of 1816 deprived her of the advantage which would have arisen in 1821 from a re-adjustment of those burthens. Since 1821, the taxation of Ireland has been far in excess of the proportion which she should contribute, and the effect of this excessive taxation, has been to retard her progress, and prevent her improvement; and thus, the Act of Union having been perverted from its original intention, it has failed of the object for which it was passed, which, as stated in the preamble, was " to secure and promote the essen-tial interests of Great Britain and Ireland."

The plain, obvious provisions of the Act of Union, that each country should continue to pay the interest of the debt due previous to the Union, has been systematically evaded or violated. Under that condition Great Britain should now raise, by special taxes in that island, a sum of *seventeen millions a year*, whereas the amount raised by special taxation in Great Britain, is not more than *three and a-half millions a year*; therefore Ireland is called on to pay the interest on the debt due by Great Britain previous to the Union, and this is done in direct opposition to the conditions of the Union, and also contrary to the recommendation of the Finance Committee of 1815.

The introductory letters on " Excessive Taxation" have obtained a large amount of publicity, and as they affect the question at issue, they are re-published.

Ireland's great need is industrial employment for her people. It was the policy of the Irish Parliament to foster and encourage every project which afforded that employment; that that policy was successful is shown by the manufactures in Ireland in 1800. The excessive taxation consequent upon the Union prevented the growth of capital, the competition with the manufactures of Great Britain affected the infant manufactures of Ireland; under the two-fold operation of these causes, but mainly from the excessive taxation, the growth of capital and enterprise were checked, and re-productive employment languished. One of the inducements held out to Ireland in 1800, was, that she would obtain the exclusive right to supply Great Britain with bread stuffs, and the exercise of that right afforded a good deal of employment to the agricultural population. That right was withdrawn by the legislation of 1846, which led to the extensive emigration of the Irish people, without securing any equivalent advantage to Great Britain.

Had the Union been equally advantageous to both countries, they would have progressed equally. In its original inception, it imposed on Ireland obligations which she was unable to discharge, and the effort to meet the payments forced upon her by the Act of Union ruined her. This is very fully proved by contrasting the amount raised in Ireland by taxation, in the ten years previous to the Union, with that raised during each of the ten years subsequent to it. The amounts were as follow :—

1791 to 1801 Revenue of Ireland,	£13,912,824
1801 to 1811 ditto ditto	47,237,360
1811 to 1821 ditto ditto	55,268,812

The legislation of 1816 prevented her deriving those advantages, from the re-adjustment of her fiscal burthens, which was intended, and thus her advancement has been retarded and her people injured; within the past seven years the principle of the Act of Union has been more grossly violated than at any previous epoch, and Ireland is now, like a patient struck down by repeated blows, in three successive bad harvests, and, while bleeding profusely from these wounds, is prescribed for by an ignorant quack, who, instead of affording nutriment and endeavouring to support the system, plunges the lancet into the arm, and draws away the life blood by undue taxation.

The attention of the Irish people is being awakened to the subject, and it is not improbable that the vicious system of Taxation may be altered and remedied, the attainment of which, is the object which the writer has in view.

INTRODUCTION.

EXCESSIVE TAXATION.

TO THE PEOPLE OF IRELAND.

FELLOW-COUNTRYMEN—

THERE are occasions on which humble individuals must abandon their privacy, and state openly and candidly their opinions as to the causes from which their country is suffering.

I believe the present crisis in the condition of Ireland is a sufficient excuse for so humble a person as I am venturing to claim your attention. I have done so at some length in a work I have just published;* but I have been asked to state, in a more condensed form, the conclusions at which I have arrived, and the *reasons on which they are based.*

That Ireland is suffering very much, there is abundant evidence—we read it in the continued disposition of her people to emigrate—in the increase of pauperism—in the decrease of the cattle, sheep, and live stock which depasture her fields—in the lessening traffic on her railways, and the diminished trade of her ports—in the decrease in the circulation of her banks, and the reduction in the amount invested in Government Securities. I shall now only bring forward two facts to prove the sad condition to which we are reduced, viz. :—

In 1859 the value of the live stock of Ireland was £35,368,259; and in 1862, it was £31,204,325; the reduction being £4,163,934.

1859, the amount invested in the Government Funds was £45,075,630; and in 1862, it was £40,985,687; the reduction being £4,089,943.

In these two items, there is a decrease in the capital of

---

* "How Ireland may be Saved." Ridgway, Piccadilly, London. W. H Smith and Son, Dublin.

Ireland of over eight millions, that is, *one-tenth* of the capital of this country has been lost; and can it be strange that, as a result, our profits from trade, nay, that trade itself, and all the employment that results from it, should be reduced?

Amongst the most striking causes of this decrease in the capital of Ireland must be reckoned the excessive and most unfair taxation which has been placed upon this country, and under which, the capital—I can hardly call it the wealth of Ireland, as Ireland never was wealthy—has been drained away.

Were I so disposed, I could show that this drain has been in defiance of the principles which guided those statesmen who framed the Act of Union between Great Britain and Ireland. I shall not go so far back, but will rest my argument on more recent legislation, on the principles affirmed by statesmen still living, and whose policy is within the memory of most of those who have not passed the prime of life.

That policy was based on a proposition so simple and so rational, that the meanest mind can appreciate its import, and it was this, that the two islands, Great Britain and Ireland, should contribute to the Imperial Revenue in proportion to their respective means; and I will take the amount of property assessed for the Property and Income Tax as the test of relative ability to pay taxes. It is as follows:—

	United Kingdom.	Ireland.
A. Land, &c.,	£131,680,497	£13,003,554
B. Occupation	33,128,296	2,773,644
C. Funded Property	27,480,840	1,174,536
D. Trade and profit	89,601,522	4,604,257
E. Profits of office	19,450,712	1,190,358
Total	£301,345,867	£22,746,344

The annual income of Ireland is £22,746,344, and the annual income of the United Kingdom is £301.345,867. The income of Ireland is about *one-fourteenth* of the whole. The above table is suggestive of the superior riches of Great Britain, because the income from funded property in Great Britain is *twenty-five* times as great as that of Ireland. The income from trades and professions is nearly *twenty* times as great in Great Britain as in Ireland, and the profits of office, that is government situations, is nearly *eighteen* times as much in Great Britain as in Ireland, while the land in Ireland is proportionably more heavily taxed with Poor Rates and Grand

Jury Rates than that in Great Britain. These rates in Ireland last year were £1,586,343, or over two shillings and sixpence in the pound on the income derivable from lands. But upon the whole, the income of Ireland is to that of the United Kingdom as *one* to *fourteen*.

In 1842 Sir Robert Peel came into office, and imposed the income tax on Great Britain; he did not extend it to Ireland, because Ireland was then paying her fair share to the finances of the Empire; and during the ensuing five years the public revenue which was raised in the United Kingdom was £258,392,012, of which Ireland paid £19,290,365, the proportion being 1 for Ireland, to 13¼ for Great Britain—this was the policy of Sir Robert Peel. At that time the population of Great Britain was 18,813,785 persons, and the annual contribution for each person was £2 12s. per annum; the population of Ireland was 8,175,124 persons, and the average contribution 9s. 6d. per annum for each person. This was the policy of Sir Robert Peel, under his sway Ireland was not called on to contribute more than one-thirteenth of the revenue of the Empire.

Now let us turn to the present. Mr. Gladstone (who professes to be a disciple of Sir Robert Peel) came into office in 1853, and during his career has loaded Ireland with taxes. He has imposed the Property and Income Tax upon lands and income—he has burthened trade and commerce with stamp duties—he has loaded property with legacy duties —he has increased the excise by nearly doubling the spirit duties—and even our very poverty is taxed! The deficiencies in our harvests oblige us to import grain, and the Customs' Duties are swelled by the tax on corn. During the past five years, the amount which the published returns admit was raised by taxes in Ireland, was £33,583,332; that is, £14,294,017 over what Sir Robert Peel raised in the five years, from 1841 to 1846. And instead of its being in the proportion of one to fourteen, as it ought to be, it is one to ten; this is a very great injustice.

The relative amounts which have been raised by taxation in Great Britain and Ireland, and the great increase which has taken place in the amount which Ireland has paid, are deserving of attention. Not only has she been very heavily taxed within the past seven years, but also the proportion which her contribution bears to that of the Empire has been seriously increased. The following is a statement of the payments in each period of five years since the Union, taken from official returns:—

Five years ending.	Great Britain.	Ireland.	Proportion of Ireland.
1806	... £213,903,759	£17,689,511	one-thirteenth.
1811	.. 306,835,611	22,925,431	one-fourteenth.
1816	... 337,878,839	28,924,312	one-thirteenth.
1821	... 272,936,110	24,861,134	one-twelfth.
1826	... 270,038,808	22,538,093	one-thirteenth.
1831	... 270,607,111	22,298,321	one-thirteenth.
1836	... 244,074,356	22,096,998	one-twelfth.
1841	... 242,422,560	22,668,098	one-twelfth.
1846	... 239,101,647	19,290,365	one-thirteenth.
1851	... 243,233,012	19,697,404	one-thirteenth.
1856	... 258,872,560	22,902,597	one-thirteenth.
1861	... 305,671,563	33,583,382	one-tenth.

It will be seen that a larger revenue has been raised from Ireland during the past five years than was raised during any previous five years, even when the Empire was engaged in the war. That it was in the past five years 50 per cent. higher then in the five years ending in 1846, under the Budgets of Sir Robert Peel—though the population has diminished 25 per cent., and the resources of the country have been reduced in the same proportion ; and it also appears that, while the revenue from Ireland exceeds by 20 per cent. that raised in the five years, ending in 1816, (the period in which the taxation of the Empire was greatest,) that of Great Britain was not as high by 10 per cent., though the population and resources of Great Britain had very largely increased.

The population of Great Britain is now more than double what it was in 1801, while there is hardly the shade of increase in that of Ireland. A comparison of population with taxation shews the following contrasts:—

GREAT BRITAIN.

	Population.	Taxation in five years.
1801	10,918,433 persons.	£213,903,755
1861	23,128,776 ,,	£305,671,563
Increase, 120 per cent.		Increase, less than 50 per cent.

IRELAND.

	Population.	Taxation in five years.
1801	5,395,456 persons.	£17,689,511
1861	5,764,443 persons.	£33,583,382
Increase, ¼ per cent.		Increase, nearly 100 per cent.

In the twenty years—from 1841 to 1861—the population

of Great Britain had increased to 23,423,776 persons, while that that of Ireland was nearly stationary, and was, 5,764,443. The average taxation of each person in Ireland has, in the twenty years, been increased 15s 6d. per annum, while the average taxation of each person in Great Britain has decreased about sixpence per annum. The payment in Ireland has increased from 9s. 6d per head, which it was in 1841, to 25s. per head, which we pay now; while, in Great Britain, it has fallen from £2 12s. per head, in 1841, to £2 11s. 6d., in 1861: thus showing the injustice which has been done to the people of Ireland.

The Irish Revenue Returns state our payments, in the past five years, were *thirty three millions and a-half*, but they do not include the receipts of the Irish Post-office, which were over a *million;* they do not include the receipts from Crown Lands in Ireland, which were nearly a *quarter* of a million; nor do they include customs paid in England on goods consumed in Ireland. If these items were added, it would make the Irish payments to the revenue in the past five years at least £36,000,000, and those of Great Britain £303,000,000, or, in other words, the average annual payments from Great Britain were £60,600,000, and from Ireland £7,200,000.

The equitable mode of adjustment would be, that each country should contribute in proportion to its income; nay, this very principle is affirmed in the income tax itself, for the income of £200 a-year pays the same poundage as that of £20,000. But when this principle is applied to Irish taxation, we see the grievous wrong which has been done to Ireland; and I shall make it plain in the following simple manner:—The annual income of Great Britain is £278,599,523, and her annual average Taxation £60,600,000, or at the rate of *four shillings and sixpence* in the pound. The annual income of Ireland is £22,746,344, and her average annual taxation £7,200,000, or at the rate of *six shillings and sixpence* in the pound; so that Ireland is paying to the Imperial Revenue at the rate of *two shillings* in the pound on her income more than Great Britain. This is not, and cannot be, just to Ireland.

Ireland has during the past five years contributed to the Imperial Exchequer two millions a year more than her fair proportion, and this is one of the causes, if not the principal cause, of her present depression.

The property and income tax in Ireland has been about £750,000 per annum; it is fifty per cent. more than the amount raised in Ireland under the poor law acts. The money raised as poor rate, is all spent in the country, the amount raised as income tax, is sent out of the country; every one who pays income tax has so much less to spend at home, and therefore the tradesman and artisan suffer, trade and commerce languish, and our country shews her retrogression.

I have shewn you that the capital of the country has diminished eight millions within the past three years, and I have also shewn you that during the same three years, we have been unfairly taxed, to the extent of at least that amount. I have shewn you the Imperial taxation is in Ireland equal to six shillings and sixpence in the pound on her income, while in Great Britain, it is only equal to four shillings and sixpence in the pound on her income. I have shewn you that the average contribution of the revenue has, since 1841, increased, at the rate of 15s. 6d. per head in Ireland, and that it has decreased nearly 6d. per head in Great Britain. It is for you to say if you consider this great increase of taxation in Ireland is right, just, and proper ?

Now for the remedy. If you think with me that Ireland is too heavily taxed, that she is drained of that capital which ought to be used to improve her system of tillage, to extend her trade and commerce, and to employ her people, you have legal and constitutional means of explaining your grievances and asking for redress; and the present juncture is particularly favourable. The Chancellor of the Exchequer has a large balance to his credit, as the revenue of last year exceeded the previous one. The Property and Income Tax was last session continued only for a year, and the whole financial system of the Empire must undergo revision. If you are satisfied with your condition—if you believe that Ireland is prosperous—if you consider she is fairly taxed, you have merely to sit still and do nothing. Should you decide on this course, and if any of your representatives try and obtain " justice for Ireland," the finance minister will quietly put him down by saying, " the people of Ireland are satisfied with their condition." But if you feel with me, that you have been unfairly taxed, and that our common country has been injured thereby, you are bound, by the claims of that country, you are urged by dictates of justice and right, to adopt every legal and constitutional way of expressing your opinions. I believe, in so doing, you will have the sympathy and support of a very large section of the

English people, who have, I am confident, no wish to save their own pockets at your expense; and who, if you represent your case to them, will not only admit the injury which has been done to you, but will aid you in obtaining redress.

You will have the support of the large landed proprietors and great commercial interests of your own country, who, lest the imputation of selfishness should have been imputed to them, have heretofore refrained from stating the grievances they suffered. It rests with you—the Irish people—to make a vigorous and combined effort to raise your country from the slough into which she has fallen. If you are calm, resolute, temperate, and combined—if you will resort to those means, which are legal and constitutional, of expressing your grievances—you may (and I fervently hope you will) succeed in bringing back to Ireland the sunshine of prosperity, and seeing her flourish under a more equitable system of taxation. If my feeble efforts but evoke in your bosoms the desire to improve the condition of Ireland, and to remove the incubus which presses upon her, I shall feel—what must to any of her sons be the highest reward—that I have tried at least to promote the prosperity of my native country.

Your faithful servant,
JOSEPH FISHER.

Waterford Mail Office, Waterford,
January 13, 1863.

THE CONDITION OF IRELAND.

TO THE EDITOR OF THE DUBLIN DAILY EXPRESS.

DEAR SIR—Since my return from Dublin my attention has been directed to your article of last Monday, on the condition of Ireland, in which you seem to allude to my work on Ireland; and I have little doubt you will feel pleasure in allowing me to say a few words on the subject of your article. It is quite evident from it that you feel a warm interest in the welfare of Ireland, and long to see her prosperous, and also that you look upon some of the returns as affording evidence of that prosperity which you patriotically wish was the condition of this country. I can assure you that I share in the same aspiration to the fullest extent. The desire which animated me in writing the letters on the condition of Ireland,

and prompted me to publish them in the collected form, was
the hope that I might benefit Ireland. No true Irishman
should, in alluding to the misery or suffering of his country,
do so with any motive save the wish to lift her from that
misery, and to alleviate that suffering. At least, I may say
that this has been my wish and desire.

The letters which have issued under the title of " How
Ireland may be Saved," were first published in the *Morning
Herald*, and they appeared at intervals during the first six
months of last year. In republishing them, the statistics have
been brought down to the latest date; but the work in its
complete form was issued before " Thom" for this year
appeared, so that it does not owe its inspiration (as you suppose) to that valuable repertory of information on Irish topics,
" Thom's Almanac." I have, however, just received the
volume for this year, and I have looked through it in the fond
hope that I might find in its pages those indications of returning prosperity which you seem to have discovered. I find
that the total value of the crops of Ireland were, in 1847,
£52,299,804; in 1860, they £42,621,918 ; and in 1861,
£36,776,326. The loss in 1861, as compared with 1847, was
fifteen millions and a-half sterling. It is not, therefore, surprising that our condition should be worse in 1861 than in
the former period. And when I look at the present state of
the country, I cannot see from what source our farmers are
to pay their next half-year's rent, nor what may be the condition of landowners, or those dependent on them if it be
not paid. You admit the falling off in the number of cattle,
horses, sheep, and pigs, between 1859 and 1862, in which
there has been a reduction of over £4,000,000 in the three
years. The export of grain from Ireland in '61, is slightly
in excess of that of 1851, but at the other side of the account,
the imports of corn were greater in 1861 than those of 1851.
In the two years, 1860 and 1861, the value of our exports of
grain was £4,152,694, while the value of our imports of
grain was £11,876,510; thus showing a balance against us
on this account of nearly £7,500,000 paid for cereals in cash.
This drain on our resources seems to have required Irish
capitalists to sell out the funds which they had invested; and
hence the reduction which has taken place in the investment
in the funds on Irish account, and which in the past three
years has been nearly four millions; and hence also the very
great excess which you notice in the number of ships, and

the tonnage, arriving at our ports with cargoes, over those which have left them loaded, and which you state correctly as being last year, *Inwards*—29,125 vessels; 4,306,770 tons; *Outwards*—15,046 vessels; 2,837,768 tons, so that 14,061 vessels of 1,469,002 tons came to our ports full, and went away empty, save that as we had no produce to ship, we had to pay for their cargoes in *cash*; this partly contributed to swell the Customs' Receipts; the principal item of increase in which has accrued from the duty levied on foreign grain; but this increase, so far from proving that Ireland is now more prosperous, shews the reverse—it is a tax on our poverty.

You refer to the increase in the Excise Duties as proving an improved condition, and indicating greater prosperity in this country. But the increase in the Excise is mainly owing to the advance in the duty on spirits. If you refer to Thom, page 779, you will see that, in 1851, the consumption of this article was 7,550,518 gallons ; in 1861, it has lessened to 5,022,891 gallons, though the duty has been enhanced by increased receipts to the extent of £1,504,687 !! So much for the Excise.

As to the circulation of the Banks—in Nov., 1860, it was £7,148,779 ; in Nov., 1862, it was £5,923,387. This hardly shews increased prosperity. Yet you will find (Thom, p. 96) that we have paid in 1861, as Income Tax, £715,269, and under the latter head you will see that the profits from trade in Ireland are less, in 1861, than they were 1860, though in Great Britain they are greater, in 1861, than they were the previous year. This hardly proves our increasing prosperity. If you turn to page 793, you will see that the Customs and Excise Receipts are both less than they were in 1859, thus shewing that our prosperity has not increased; and if you refer to page 748, you will find that the expenditure for support of the poor was, in 1859, £413,712; and in 1861, £516,769; the increase being about *twenty-five* per cent., and in page, 82, you will find the number receiving relief the first week in January, 1859, was, 44,816 persons; and in 1862, it increased to 59,541 persons.

As to crime, you will find that while the number of convictions, in 1860, bore the proportion of one to 2,014 of the population, it had increased, in 1861, to 1 in 1,762. If you see in these statements indications of greater prosperity, I am sorry to say I cannot agree with you. It seems to me that, materially and socially, Ireland is retrograding.

Were Ireland in a really prosperous condition—were her crops increasing, her land more productive, her flocks and herds becoming more numerous—were her people employed and contented—were pauperism and crime declining—were her exports in excess of her imports, and her investments gradually becoming greater, I should most gladly rejoice in her prosperity ; and in this happy state of things, I would not be disposed to press too far the question of unfair taxation, which has so greatly injured us; but when I see that Ireland is depressed, partly from the ungenial seasons with which it has pleased God to visit us, and partly from the effects of what seems to me to be vicious legislation ; and when I find that our taxation exceeds, by more then 50 per cent., the proportion which either in equity, by a comparison of our means, or by contract under that treaty which called the Parliament of the United Kingdom into existance, I cannot refrain from lifting my voice and using my pen, (feeble though their utterance may be,) to obtain for Ireland that relief from taxation to which she is, by equity and by contract alike, entitled.

I am, dear sir, yours, faithfully,
JOSEPH FISHER

Waterford Mail Office, Waterford,
January 23rd, 1863.

IRELAND'S BALANCE SHEET, 1862.

MESSRS. STURGE'S CIRCULAR.

THE valuable circular issued by this celebrated English firm, whose acquaintance with the grain trade is not surpassed by any of the eminent houses in this line of business, and who have for many years been in the habit of contributing very valuable statistical information of the imports and exports of corn into the United Kingdom; and also into Ireland, has just been published for the past year, and we are sorry to find that it reveals another phase in the downward course in which the agriculture of Ireland has ran for some years. It is surprising to find, that while the quantity of land under grass has been increasing, the quantity of stock, (the number of animals,) has been lessening.   It is somewhat sorrowful to have to notice, year after year, the increasing deficit in our home supply of grain, and the consequent increasing imports of corn. The balance sheet for 1860 shewed that the value of the imports of grain exceeded that of the exports by £3,539,776; in 1861 the excess in the value of imports over exports was £4,182,167, and in 1862, it was £5,693,712. The details are as follows, and it certainly affords us all ample food for reflection. Every thoughtful person will ask himself how is this drain to be met?

BALANCE SHEET FOR IRELAND FOR 1862.

CR. EXPORTS.

116,080 qrs.	wheat and fl ur, 55s. 5d.	£	319,471
57,979 ...	barley and malt, 35s. 1d.,		121,725
1,128,161 ...	oats and oatmeal 22s. 7d.,		1,373,882
23,766 ...	beans and peas, 40s.,	...	47,532
1,325,986	Total		£1,862,610
1,877,299	Deficiency ...		5,693,712
3,206,285			7,556,322

DR. IMPORTS.

1,770,780 qrs.	wheat and flour, 55s. 5d.,	£4,906,516
13,650 ...	barley,	35s. 1d.,	23,997
55 ...	oats,	22s. 7d.,	62
5,780 ..	beans, peas, and rye, 40s.,	11,560
1,413,020 ...	Indian corn,	37s.,	2,614,187
3,203,285	Total	£7,556,322

It is, indeed, sad to see a fine and fertile country like Ireland obliged, year after year, to import such large quantities of bread-stuffs—to note the consequently large sums paid away in cash from the coffers of a nation already so greatly impoverished; and this feeling of regret is greatly heightened when we remember that for a series of years we grew sufficient supplies of grain for our own consumption, and exported the surplus, and that surplus was on the average of the five years, from 1841 to 1846, as much as 2,622,825 qrs., the value of which was over £4,000,000. The loss on the grain trade is equal to *eight and a-half* millions sterling per annum, as we have lost our exports, which used to be £4,000,000 a-year; and we are now importing, on the average, corn to the value of £4,500,000 a year, which we have to pay for in cash. These two deficits make an annual loss of £8,500,000. No wonder that this country should be poor Ireland!!

C

THE CASE OF IRELAND.

LETTER I.

TO THE IRISH PEOPLE.

THE PRINCIPLES OF THE UNION—LAW OF NATIONS.

FELLOW-COUNTRYMEN—Since the publication, in a pamphlet form, of my letters on the condition of Ireland, which were addressed to his Excellency the Lord Lieutenant,* I have been repeatedly asked what is the position of Ireland with regard to the Treaty of Union? are its conditions in force? is its protection continued? or has it become a mere dead letter?

I have thus been forced, in a measure, into an examination of the subject. In order to appreciate the present position of Ireland, it is necessary to consider the circumstances antecedent to the first proposition for an union of Great Britain and Ireland—to take account of the ideas which were present in the minds of those who brought the proposal of the Union forward in the Houses of Parliament—to weigh the expressions which fell from them during the progress of the debates—to ascertain the conditions which were agreed to, and the reasons on which these conditions were based. I have therefore had to inquire into the manner in which the treaty was carried into effect—the influence it exercised upon both countries—and the subsequent legislation which, under the guise of " carrying into effect the provisions and purposes of the Act of Union," (I quote from the preamble to 58th Geo. III.,

* " How Ireland may be saved, or the Injurious Effects of the Present System of Agriculture on the Prosperity of Ireland and the Social Position of the Irish People." By JOSEPH FISHER. London ; Ridgway, Piccadilly. Dublin and London ; Messrs. W. H. Smith and Son. And all Booksellers.

chap. 98,) really annulled those acts, in some of their most important provisions; and I now lay before the public the result of my labours. It cannot be denied that if injustice has been done to either of the contracting parties the other would be a gainer to the extent of this loss; and, therefore, the question, whether an injustice has been done? becomes not a mere Irish question, it is one that affects Great Britain. If the sister country, having a larger numerical force in the Houses of Parliament, used that force to give effect to a policy which is neither wise nor equitable, then the British people incur the blame of being parties to a system which is unfair and unjust. A selfish policy, or one in which a nation secures to itself advantages over another nation— though it may, at the first blush, appear to be statesmanlike and advantageous—is, nevertheless, eventually not the best or wisest; and, if the true interests of every nation be found in the development of the industry and the resources of other countries, how much more is it the interest of the same nation, to secure the prosperity of all its constituent parts. It may appear to those whose minds are not sufficiently elevated, that the real welfare of Great Britain is promoted by an undue and forced taxation of Ireland, and that British interests are served, by raising two or three millions more from Ireland than she ought or can pay; and it may, perhaps, be thought that the relief which arises to the British tax-payer, from the transfer of his burthens to Irish shoulders, is so much clear gain. But the atrophy produced by excessive taxation has its effect beyond the nation which endures it; and the prostration of Ireland under so selfish a policy has been, and still is, the source of weakness to the whole Empire; thus proving that, in the body politic, as well as the body physical, "if one member suffer, the other members suffer with it," and that, with nations, as well as individuals, "Honesty is the best policy."

I do not think it is the wish of the British people, either to practise, or to perpetuate, an injustice towards Ireland; and if that nation appears to have done so, it has been either through ignorance of the facts, or through misapprehension of the results. The British people are, I believe, disposed to be honest and just, but they are too prone to be led astray by sophists and charlatans. Empiricism is not confined to medicine, but extends also to politics, and nostrums prevail in the regions of Parliament, as well as in the chemists shops.

It cannot be denied that, as far as taxation is concerned,

Ireland, when a separate nation, enjoyed many immunities which were not shared by England. The wars of William and of Anne, the continental contests of the early Sovereigns of the House of Hanover, the expensive war which Great Britain waged with America—in which the foolish conduct of Lord North lost England her American colonies, and involved Great Britain in an enormous debt—were not at all the policy of Ireland, nor did she adopt any of the debt or share in the liability so incurred. In 1790, the debt of Ireland was a little over *Two Millions*, while that of Great Britain was *Two Hundred and Forty Millions*. The Irish Parliament aided the Crown, in the French war for the re-establishment of the Bourbons, and increased the Irish debt at this period; but in 1800 the Irish debt, though it had increased over six fold in the ten years, stood (according to Parliamentary paper 443, Sess. 1858,) at *Thirteen and three-quarter Millions*,* while the debt of Great Britain had nearly doubled, and was *Four Hundred and Fifty-seven Millions;* but, notwithstanding this increase in the Irish debt, it was still less than a *thirtieth* of that of Great Britain, and the amount raised by taxation in each country was very different. Great Britain, though straining every nerve, and yielding about *sixteen* times as much to the Revenue as Ireland was paying, had, nevertheless, year by year, to increase her debt, and in the year 1800 she was forced to borrow twenty-seven millions. It was under this state of finances that the Union between two states was proposed—one lightly taxed and lightly encumbered with debt, the other heavily taxed, and enormously encumbered; and it was only natural to expect, that in the partnership arrangements, the partner who entered the concern with small outstanding liabilities, should refuse to be burthened with the liabilities of his partner, and also seek, that the immunity which was enjoyed in his separate state, should be continued under the partnership. The Act of Union was framed to preserve those immunities which Ireland enjoyed, and guaranteed to that nation, freedom from liability at foot of the English debt. In approaching the consideration of the Union, we must give due weight to the existing condition, the relative taxation, and the liabilities, of each country.

Ireland, previous to the Union, enjoyed a separate, inde-

* It is only fair to say, that according to a previous return, par paper of 1849, No. 423, the Irish debt of 1800, was stated at £27,792,975.

pendent existence. Her Parliament possessed the sole power
of making laws, and it was competent of it to reject the treaty
of Union which was offered, and even though it were carried
in the British Houses of Parliament, it would have had no
force in Ireland. In surrendering this independent condition, and becoming a small minority in the Parliament of the
United Kingdom, Ireland hoped to obtain in exchange for
what she gave up, equal social advantages with the English
people, and exemption from undue and unfair taxation. Ireland laid down the sovereignty which she enjoyed—she
descended from the rank of independent nations—her name
was erased from the list of independent European states—she
gave up those privileges dear to a nation, and surrendered
the right of making laws for her people, but she did not do
so unconditionally; she was offered, as an equivalent for her
abandoning her nationality, for those privileges and immunities
she was then enjoying, those rights and immunities which are
recited in the Act of Union.

History tells us that even after the Irish Parliament rejected
the Union, the British House of Commons proceeded to consider the principles on which it should be based, and recorded,
as resolutions, the offer which it made; and these resolutions
were the basis or foundation of that contract, the Act of Union,
it still remains in existence. Great Britian and Ireland were at
that time separate and independent nations—each possessed,
in right of its nationality, the power of passing laws for the
government of its own subjects—they held towards each other
a different relationship; as separate nations, they were subject
to that code of laws which is known as the Law of Nations,
and amongst which is the power of fettering their actions, by
the adoption of treaties, in which one country agrees to surrender rights and privileges, on the condition of acquiring
certain compensating rights and privileges in exchange. It
was under that law of nations that the two countries treated
with each other, and that treaty was the Union.

Great Britain wished to gain the advantage which arises
from a consolidation of power, and also the right to make
laws for Ireland; she also sought a partner in the heavy pecuniary engagements arising out of a Continental war; and
Ireland, though adverse to the change, was offered in exchange, equal political and social rights, and such an immunity
from taxation, as would prevent her being called on to pay
the interest on a debt, to which she was no party; or responsible

for expenditure, over the creation of which she had no control. It could not be expected that Ireland would waive or surrender her rights without a *quid pro quo.* The Parliament of England, omnipotent as it was supposed to be, could not, by an Act of Parliament, enforce the Union, her ministers therefore offered to Ireland that treaty which preceded the Act of Union. It was first submitted separately to the Parliament of each nation, by a message from the crown; and, though rejected in Ireland, in 1 '99, was considered in Britain; it was again offered to the Irish Parliament in 1800, and a treaty entered into; the treaty was subsequently brought up on an address to the Sovereign, and ratified by him, before any Act of Parliament was introduced to give it effect.

I cannot better describe the solemn manner in which this treaty was considered, agreed upon, and ratified, than by quoting from the Act of Union itself, the preamble says—

" Whereas, in pursuance of his Majesty's most gracious recommendation to the two Houses of Parliament in Great Britain and Ireland, respectively, to consider such measures as might best tend to strengthen and consolidate the connection between the two kingdoms, the two Houses of Parliament of Great Britain, and the two Houses of Parliament of Ireland, have severally agreed and resolved, that in order to promote and secure the essential interests of Great Britain and Ireland, and to consolidate the strength, power, and resources of the British Empire, it will be advisable to concur in such measures as may best tend to unite the two kingdoms of Great Britain and Ireland into one kingdom, in such manner, and on such terms and conditions as may be established by the acts of the respective Parliaments of Great Britain and Ireland.

" And, whereas, in furtherance of the said resolution, both Houses of the two Parliaments, respectively, have likewise agreed upon certain articles for effectuating and establishing the said purposes in the tenor following."

This is the preamble of the Irish Act, and the eight articles are then set out in the Act, the object of which was, as stated in the preamble, " to promote and secure the essential interests of Great Britain and Ireland"—not the advantage of one country, but of both. After reciting the eight articles which formed the treaty of Union, which had been agreed upon, the same clause of the Act declared—

" And, whereas, the said articles having, by address of the respective Houses of Parliament in Great Britain and Ireland, been humbly laid before his Majesty, his Majesty has been graciously pleased to approve the same, and to recommend it to his two Houses of Parliament in Great Britain and Ireland, to consider such measures as may be necessary for giving effect to the said articles. In order, therefore, to give full effect and validity to the same, be it enacted by the King's most excellent Majesty, by and with the consent of the Lords spiritual and temporal, and Commons, in this present Parliament assembled, and by the authority of the same, that the said foregoing recited articles, each and every one of them, according to the true intent and tenor thereof, be ratified, confirmed, and approved, and be, and they are hereby declared to be, the articles of the Union of Great Britain and Ireland, and the same shall be in force and have effect FOR EVER, from the first day of January, 1801, provided that before that period an act shall have been passed by the Parliament of Great Britain for carrying into effect the foregoing recited articles."

A treaty so inaugurated, so carried forward, and ratified, passes out of the category of mere statute law; it comes under the higher code—the LAW of NATIONS, and the rights so secured cannot be trampled on without violating the law of nations; so solemn is the trust reposed in the integrity of treaties, that Vattel, who is considered by jurists as the highest authority on international law, says, (page 228):—

" The faith of treaties, that firm and sincere resolution, that invariable constancy in fulfilling our engagements, of which we make a profession in a treaty, is, therefore, to be held sacred and inviolable between the nations of the earth, whose safety and repose it secures; and if mankind be not wilfully deficient in their duty to themselves, infamy must ever be the portion of him who violates his faith. He who violates his treaties, violates at the same time the law of nations; for he disregards the faith of treaties—that faith which the law of nations declares sacred, and, so far as depends on him, he renders it vain and ineffectual. Doubly guilty, he does an injury to his ally, he does an injury to all nations, and inflicts a wound on the great society of mankind."

The principles here so ably stated and laid down, are so important that I must dwell upon them, in order to show the

difference between rights secured by the law of nations and
those secured by act of Parliament; the one is permanent and
immutable, the other fleeting and transitory. Parliament
possesses the absolute right to make laws over its own subjects. That right lay in each of the separate Parliaments of
Great Britain and Ireland towards their own people; but
the Parliament of Great Britain had no power to make laws
for Ireland, nor could the Parliament of Ireland make laws
for Great Britain. That power was acquired by the Parliament of the United Kingdom, under treaty, and that treaty
is part of the higher code of laws referred to by Vattel; its
provisions are fixed and immutable. This writer further
elucidates his proposition thus—

" It is a settled point in natural law," says Vattel, page 196,
" that he who shall have made a promise to any one, has conferred upon him a real right to require the thing promised;
and, consequently, that the breach of a perfect promise is a
violation of another person's right, and as evidently an act
of injustice as it would be to rob a man of his property. . . .
As the engagements of a treaty, impose, on the one hand, a
perfect obligation, they produce on the other a perfect right.
The breach of treaty is, therefore, a violation of the perfect
right of the party with whom we have contracted, and this
is an act of injustice against him."

It is thus a settled point in natural law, that the engagements of a treaty produce a perfect right, and that to violate
that right is as gross an act of injustice as to rob a man of
his property. This natural or necessary law, which thus
protects rights secured by treaty, is thus defined by Vattel,
page 58:—

" We call that the necessary law of nations which consists
in the application of the law of nature and nations. It is
necessary, because nations are absolutely bound to observe it.
This law contains the precepts prescribed by the law of nature
to states, on whom that law is not less obligatory than on
individuals; since states are composed of men, their resolutions are taken by men, and the law of nature is binding on
all men, under whatever relation they act. This is the law
which Grotius, and those who follow him, call the internal
law of nations, on account of its being obligatory on nations
in point of conscience. Several writers call it the natural law of
nations. Since, therefore, the necessary law of nations con-

sists in the application of the law of nature to states, which law is immutable, being founded on the nature of things, and particularly on the nature of man, it follows that the necessary law of nations is immutable. Hence, as this law is immutable, and the obligations that arise from it necessary and indispensable, nations can neither make any change in it by conventions, dispense with it in their own conduct, nor reciprocally release each other from it."

Inasmuch, then, as the rights of the Irish nation are rights under treaty, and thus secured by the law of nations ; and inasmuch as the rights so secured were obtained by the surrender of other existing rights, it follows that the Act of Union is one of those fundamental constitutional laws which the Parliament of the United Kingdom cannot annul, abrogate, or repeal. It is held, and rightfully held, by the most eminent jurists and writers on constitutional law, that Parliament has the power of altering or repealing any law which is enacted by a previous Parliament, and the reason is obvious.

If the present Parliament had not that power, it would admit that the previous Parliament had greater power than itself, and that it could bind and fetter its successors ; and thus each Parliament might curtail the action of its successors until its rights and powers were a mere shadow. But it is also held by eminent jurists that organic, constitutional laws, which lie at the very root and are the basis of the power of the goverment of a country, cannot be annulled by mere enactment ; and, therefore, if such an organic law is founded, and proceeds from treaties made in conformity with the laws of nations, it is placed on even higher grounds, and does not come within the purvey of legislative enactment. My argument is, that the separate acts of Union, one passed in the British and the other in the Irish Parliament, dissolved alike the Parliaments of Great Britain and Ireland—that it was their death-warrant, and that these acts created the Parliament of the United Kingdom—that they are organic, constitutional laws, based upon the law of nations, and therefore they cannot be altered, annulled, or repealed by mere enactment.

Having thus laid down the principles on which I base my case, I shall in a future letter proceed to point out what seems to me the infraction of the treaty, and the injustice which has resulted to Ireland and the Irish people from departing from the obvious conditions of the Act of Union, in the imposition of taxes, not only beyond our power of payment, but contrary to the provisions of the Treaty of Union .

LETTER II.

THE FINANCIAL AND INDUSTRIAL HISTORY OF IRELAND FROM 1788 TO 1800.

HAVING, from the law of nations, laid the groundwork on which I propose to base my argument, I must now recede in point of time, in order to give you some idea of the position which Ireland occupied when the Union was proposed, and the progress which she had made, during the period which elapsed from the time she had become independent, in 1782, until 1799, when the proposition of the Union was submitted to her consideration. Previous to 1782, the British Parliament had looked upon Ireland as a subject province, and interfered with her legislation. She was also very jealous of Ireland becoming a manufacturing nation, particularly of woollen goods. It had been argued by some that the Irish Parliament was only a sort of committee, and was inferior to that of England, on the ground that the latter passed laws prohibiting the trading of the British colonies with Ireland, and refused to the Irish people liberty to export their manufactured goods to England; but this was completely refuted by the fact, that the colonies were the property of England, and that the English Parliament had full authority to make laws and govern them. So early as the reign of Charles I., the English manufacturers became jealous of the woollen manufactures of Ireland, and they made every effort in their power to cripple that branch of industry in this country. It then became a matter of direction from the King of England, to his deputy in Ireland to endeavour to induce the Irish people to give up their woollen manufactures, and to apply themselves altogether to the manufacture of linen. In fact, the export of manufactured woollen goods to England was strictly prohibited, and the export of wool was restricted to certain ports, so that it would be impossible that it could be sent

across channel in its manufactured state; and a fleet was ordered to cruise off the southern coast of Ireland, to intercept
and confiscate such ships as might be found conveying woollen goods to Spain or any other foreign countries; and so
jealous was England with regard to the woollen manufactures that, as late as 1800, there was a duty of ten per
cent. on all wool exported from Great Britain to Ireland.
The result was the total extirpation of this manufacture in
Ireland, and a consequent decadence of industrial resources
of the country; but when the Irish Parliament became independent the woollen manufactures revived.

With such jealousy towards her manufactures, and such
interference with her rights, it is not surprising that Ireland
should have suffered greatly; she was, until the achievement
of her independence, in 1782, depressed and backward, her
resources were undeveloped, and her people ignorant. She
was prostrate and neglected. Her position, when dependent
on Great Britain, is thus described by one who must be admitted to be an impartial witness.

The celebrated William Pitt, when speaking, in 1782, said,
(see Plowden, vol. ii., p. 116)—

"The system had been that of debarring Ireland from
the enjoyment and use of her resources, to make that kingdom completely subservient to the interest and opulence of
this country, without suffering her to share in the bounties
of nature, in the industry of her citizens, or making them
contribute to the general interests and strength of the Empire. This system of cruel and abominable restraint has,
however, been exploded."

Arthur Young writes, (1776-7) :—

"British legislation on all occasions controlled Irish commerce with a very high hand—universally on the principle
of monopoly, as if the poverty of Ireland were her wealth."

Mr. Greville, (afterwards Lord Greville,) said—

"If England were heavily taxed, she had now, and had
had for a whole century past, the benefits of a widely-ex-
tended trade, from which she had excluded Ireland; and the
latter had already given to England all that she could have
made, if, by a barbarous and equally absurd policy, she had
not been debarred from those advantages that God and nature had given her."

William Pitt, in 1799, referred to the subject, and said—

" Ireland had long felt the narrow policy of Great Britain, who, influenced by views of trade and commercial advantage, and stained and perverted with selfish motives, had
treated her with partiality and neglect, and never looked
upon her prosperity as that of the empire at large."

Mr. Huskisson, in March 2, 1825, thus alludes to the
treatment of Ireland :—

" It is not well known, that till 1780 the agriculture ,inter-
nal industry, manufactures, commerce, and navigation of
Ireland were all held in the most rigid subserviency to the
supposed interests of Great Britain. In 1778, there was a
proposal to allow her to import sugar direct, and to export
everything, but woollens, to pay for it; and this proposal was
almost made a question of allegiance by the great towns of
Britain, and so it was lost ! In 1779, a more limited conces-
sion to her was also lost ! But towards the close of that year, the
disasters in North America, and the state of things in Ireland,
produced a different feeling in the British Parliament. State
necessities, acting under a sense of political danger, yielded,
without grace, that which good sense and good feeling had
before recommended in vain; and in 1782, under the like
pressure, those concessions were rendered irrevocable."

Mr. Labouchere, President of the Board of Trade, on
March 12, 1841, said :—

" Ireland was, under an old colonial system, prohibited from
any direct trade with British colonies. This system was
maintained with all its vigour till 1780, when, after the close
of the American war, it became imperatively necessary to
look to the rising spirit of discontent in Ireland, much fo-
mented by the illiberal and unjust policy of this country
(England), in respect to commerce."

There is no lack of evidence, from influential parties, and
at different times, to show that the policy pursued towards
Ireland was, as described by William Pitt, " a system of cruel
and abominable restraint." I might, were I so disposed, furnish
a catalogue of the Acts of the British Parliament which were
passed from time to time, restricting the intercourse between
Ireland and the British colonies; I might shew the measures
which were taken by the British Parliament to destroy the
woollen manufactures of Ireland; but I think the evidence
which I have given above is quite sufficient to establish the fact
that, previously to 1782, the legislation of Great Britain to-

wards Ireland was, to use the language of Lord Greville, "a barbarous and equally absurd policy." Ireland "had been debarred from those advantages that God and nature had given her." It is not surprising that the Irish people should have risen in 1782, and demanded their independence; and that the ministers of Great Britain, standing affrighted in the presence of an armed nation, and having before them the example of revolt in America, should have recognised that independence.

The effects of this foreign legislation, and commercial jealousy were felt by the Irish Nation, and when Ireland was left altogether dependent upon herself—when the British Parliament was unable to furnish troops to defend Ireland from foreign invasion, when her sons rose up voluntarily to protect their homes, their country, and their altars—and when, having removed from the people's mind the dread of an invasion, they demanded their rights, and said—"Our Parliament shall be a a reality, and shall make laws for her own people— you shall give us our independence, or else——" they attained that independence. From north to south, the Volunteers, composed of the most influential men in Ireland, met together, and demanded that Ireland should be legislated for on just, and fair, and equitable grounds. And calmly and moderately did they employ the victory which they had achieved. There were in Ireland, none of those excesses which devastated France, when her people rose armed to enforce their freedom. At the end of the first session of the Irish Parliament, under the constitution of 1782, the then Lord Lieutenant (the Duke of Portland) bore testimony to the efforts it had made in the cause of good government. "You have," said he, "provided for the impartial and unbiased administration of justice, by the act for securing the independency of the judges. You have adopted one of the most effective securities of British freedom, by limiting the Mutiny Act in point of duration. You have secured the most invaluable of human blessings, the personal liberty of the subject, by passing the *Habeas Corpus* Act. You have cherished and enlarged the wise principles of toleration, and made considerable advances in abolishing those distinctions, which have too long impeded the progress of industry, and divided the nation. The diligence and ardour with which you have persevered in the accomplishment of these great objects, must ever bear the most honourable testimony to your zeal and industry in the service of your country, and manifest your knowledge of its interests." What must have been the social condition of Ireland, when her first Independent Parliament had to consider and pass so many vital measures, whose efforts drew from an English Viceroy such encomiums as these?

A few further extracts will shew the feeling of other Lord Lieutenants as to the usefulness of the Irish Parliament.

In 1784, the Duke of Rutland, who was then Lord Lieutenant, thus addressed the Irish Parliament at the close of the session:—

"You will have much satisfaction in reflecting, that the various objects which, in consequence of the acknowledged independence of the legislature, were recommended for your deliberation in the opening of this session, have been diligently pursued and accomplished. You have wisely given your sanction to the extraordinary expedients which it has been necessary to employ, in order to preserve the kingdom from famine, and I feel great satisfaction in the prospect that they will be prevented for the future, by the new and judicious arrangement of the Commons, and the improved extension of your agriculture. I see with pleasure the exertions of a humane and liberal principle, which has prompted you to give encouragement to the national industry, by favourable regulations and well-directed bounties. I have warmly at heart the advancement of your trade and the success of your manufactures, and I shall not fail either to consider or to represent those instances whereof the peculiar circumstances of the empire have hitherto prevented a full investigation, and which shall be found to require a further adjustment. The useful regulations proposed to be introduced into the collection and management of the revenue—the security of private property, and the extension of national credit, by depositing in the Bank of Ireland the money of suitors in the Court of Chancery and Exchequer—the plans for improving the metropolis, calculated not more for ornament and splendour than for health and convenience—your unanimous determination to defend the freedom of the constitution against the attacks of licentiousness, and your attention to the support of charitable institutions, are all unequivocal testimonies to your *wisdom, humanity, and justice.*"

In 1791, the Lord Lieutenant, at the prorogation of Parliament, again bore testimony to the ability and vigour of the Irish Parliament. He said—

"I have seen with great satisfaction the constant attention and uncommon dispatch with which you have gone
through the public business. I am thereby enabled now to
relieve you from further attendance in Parliament. The
harmony of your deliberations has given no less efficacy
than dignity to your proceedings; and I am confident that
you will carry with you the same disposition for promoting
the public welfare to your residences in the country, where
your presence will encourage the industry of the people, and
where your example and your influence will be happily
exerted in establishing general good order and obedience to
the laws."

I have adduced these addresses from different Lord
Lieutenants, to shew that the Irish Parliament turned its attention to the promotion and development of the resources
of Ireland, and to improve the condition of the people of this
country. It is not my purpose to trace the history of the
Irish Parliament, or to recount the struggles which took
place, for securing to a large portion of the Irish people those
social rights and privileges which were enjoyed by others.

The Irish Parliament was re-formed after the demon-
stration of 1782. Under the impetus then given, and owing
to the lighter taxation of Ireland, she put forth her energies
in a career of improvement—every branch of industry shewed
the rebound which took place. Her manufactures increased·—
her trade revived—her commerce spread—her people were
employed—and, if not comfortable, they were gradually becoming so, as is very fully shewn by the returns of revenue
and excise.

The principal manufacture of Ireland, that of LINEN, increased in this period with wonderful strides. In 1783, Ireland exported 16,093,705 yards of linen cloth, valued at
£1,069,313; in 1796, she exported 46,705,319 yards, valued
at £3,113,687. Here was an increase in twelve years of
nearly 300 per cent., or at the rate of 25 per cent. per annum.
Notwithstanding the vast improvement in machinery within
the past sixty years, the value of the exports of linens has only
increased 33 per cent., or at the rate of a half per cent. per
annum. Last year the estimated value of the linen cloth exported to Great Britain and foreign countries was £4,400,000.
Mr. Pitt, in 1799, in reply to Mr. Foster, stated that the
imports into Ireland from Great Britain were only about
£1,000,000 a-year, while Ireland was sending to Great Bri-

tain linens to the value of £3,000,000 per annum, and provisions to the value of about £3,000,000, thus leaving a large balance in favour of Ireland.

The test of revenue is generally considered to indicate the condition of a people; I regard it as a fallacious one, and that a proper comparison can only be made by contrasting the quantities of commodities consumed. I give the quantities of tea, tobacco, foreign spirits, wine, sugar, and coffee, which were consumed in Great Britain and Ireland in the years 1788 and 1800, and also the amount of duty raised thereon. They shew that the increased consumption of these commodities in Ireland was not only considerable, absolutely, but also comparatively, as it was at a larger ratio than that of Great Britain in the same period. This tendency towards habits of greater comfort was partly produced by the general prosperity of this country, and partly by the lighter duties levied on the articles to which I refer. The quantities consumed, and the amount of duties raised, were as follows:—

					Duty.
TEA.					
Ireland,	...	1788	...	1,545000 lbs.,	£ 29,708
,,	...	1800	...	2,926,166 ,,	69,824
Great Britain,		1788	...	13,218,665 ,,	547,176
,,	...	1800	...	20,358,702 ,,	1,176,861
TOBACCO.					
Ireland,	...	1788	...	3,120,048 ,,	128,896
,,	...	1800	...	6,737,275 ,,	327,916
Great Britain,		1788	...	6,858,668 ,,	441,429
,,	...	1800	...	11,796,415 ,,	987,110
SUGAR.					
Ireland,	...	1788	...	196,623 cwt.	125,431
,,	...	1800	...	355,662 ,,	327,028
Great Britain,		1788	...	1,775,681 ,,	1,033,436
,,	...	1800	...	1,506,921 ,,	1,835,112
COFFEE.					
Ireland,	...	1788	...	38,458 lbs.	887
,,	...	1800	...	120,925 ,,	2,792
Great Britain,		1788	...	758,403 ,,	41,333
,,	...	1800	...	822,590 ,,	142,867
WINE.					
Ireland,	...	1788	...	1,219,970 gals.	121,914
,,	...	1797	...	2,558,166 ,,	343,194
Great Britain,		1788	...	6,761,433 ,,	666,134
,,	...	1800	...	7,728,871 ,,	1,967,213
FOREIGN SPIRITS.					
Ireland,	...	1788	...	1,365,523 ,,	221,849
,,	...	1800	...	1,241,961 ,,	331,833
Great Britain,		1788	...	4,050,151 ,,	924,888
,,	...	1800	...	4,815,455 ,,	1,825,276

D

HOME-MADE SPIRITS.

Ireland,	...	1790	...	2,599,576 gals.	...
,,	...	1800	...	4,140,429 ,,	...

Thus we see that in the twelve years the consumption in Ireland of tea, tobacco, sugar, and wine had doubled, that of coffee had trebled, the only article in which there was a falling off was in foreign spirits, while in Great Britain the consumption of none of these articles had doubled in that period, and there is an actual decrease in that of sugar; the British increase in the consumption of tea was about 50 per cent.; in tobacco 80 per cent.; in coffee of 10 per cent.; in wine 16 per cent., and foreign spirits of 20 per cent. Taking into consideration the aggregate of these commodities, the increase in the quantity of these articles consumed in Ireland, in the 12 years, was 65 per cent., in Great Britain it was only 32 per cent. The consumption of these commodities in Ireland, in 1788, was about one-fifth of that of Great Britain, and in 1800 it had increased to one-fourth; thus shewing great absolute progress, when measured by herself, and great relative progress when contrasted with Great Britain. This great progress was one of the consequences arising from the independence of Ireland. Her people (never deficient in energy and enterprise,) put them forth when their country was free, and their commerce unfettered—when the policy, so forcibly described and condemned by William Pitt, that which he denounced as " cruel and abominable restraint," was laid aside, then Ireland made rapid progress. The figures which I have given above shew this. The increase in the consumption of these articles, was the result of judicious economy in the administration of her finances, and under this system the customs duties were less than one-half of those levied in Great Britain ; thus the duty on tea was only 5d. per lb.; on home-made spirits, 1s. 1½b. per gallon ; on tobacco, 9d. per lb; on wine, 2s. 1d. to 3s. 9d. per gallon ; on brandy and rum, 3s. 6d. to 4s 11d. per gallon , on timber, 1s. 10d. per load; on deals 9s. 1d. per hundred. The revenue raised in Ireland in the ten years from 1791 to 1801 was £13,911,834. Under her own Parliament she was not only lightly taxed but she was comparatively free from debt. As to the loyalty of the Irish Parliament, and its efforts to support the crown, I will quote the address of the Lord Lieutenant, the Marquis of Cornwallis, when opening the Irish Parliament, on the 22nd January, 1799; he said :—

" It is with great satisfaction I observe, that, notwithstanding our internal calamities, this kingdom blended, as its interests are in the general prosperity of the empire, has participated in the effects of the immense wealth and commerce of Great Britain, and that our revenues, and our trade have increased. Your agriculture, your manufactures, and particularly the Protestant Charter Schools, and other charitable institutions, will require, and will, I am sure, continue to receive that aid and encouragement, which they have uniformly experienced from the liberality of Parliament."

At the close of the session, this same nobleman had the pleasure of again addressing them as Lord Lieutenant, and he said :—

" I thank you, in his Majesty's name, for the large and extraordinary supply which you have so honourably voted to meet every wish of the government, and every exigency of the state."

Ireland had that year, according to the return No. 447 of the session of 1858, increased her debt by over £2,000,000 to meet these exigencies. Another Parliamentary return makes the increase £6,000,000; but it is quite evident from his Excellency's speech, that Ireland had shewn no unwillingness to meet the exigencies of the state, or reluctance to aid the king in the expenses of the war in which he was embarked.

Earl Fitzwilliam, who had been Lord Lieutenant, in speaking on the proposed Union, on the 8th May, 1800, urged the following argument:—" No satisfactory reason has yet been given for moving the seat of legislation from Dublin to London. During the late unfortunate rebellion in Ireland, the government, backed by the Parliament of Ireland, were able to suppress the rebellion. Why then, after such recent proof of the advantage of a resident Parliament was the kingdom of Ireland to be deprived of reaping again the same advantage, should any such occur?"

There is no lack of proof of the loyalty of the Irish Parliament, and we have ample evidence, that while the Irish Parliament had largely promoted the prosperity of Ireland, they were no less attentive to the wants of the Crown. The addresses of the several chief governors which I have quoted place this subject in a very strong light.

The evidence of the material progress of Ireland during the period to which I have referred is abundant and satisfactory ;

it shews that in the period of her independence, from 1782 to the Union, in 1800, she increased her consumption of those commodities which prove the comfort of her people. I extract a few testimonials to shew what were the opinions of those most competent to form a correct judgment upon this point. I might lengthen these extracts very greatly, but I do not consider it expedient; my object in adducing them is to show the condition of Ireland antecedent to the Union, because it casts a strong and powerful light upon the effort to carry it, and the mode in which we are to interpret the treaty, and to judge of the way in which it operated upon the subsequent progress of that nation.

Amongst those witnesses are the Earl of Clare (Fitzgibbon), Lord Chancellor of Ireland. In 1799 he said:—

" No nation on the habitable globe advanced in cultivation, in commerce, in agriculture, in manufacture, with the same rapidity."

Mr. Plunket, afterwards Lord Chancellor, thus describes her state:—

" Her revenues, her trade, her manufactures, are thriving beyond the hope or example of any other country of her extent, within these few years, with a rapidity astonishing even to herself, not complaining of deficiency in these respects, but enjoying and acknowledging her prosperity."

Mr. Grey, afterwards Earl Grey, and Prime Minister of England, said:—

" Since the abolition of hereditable jurisdiction, the prosperity of Scotland had been considerable, but certainly not so great as that of Ireland had been within the same period."

Mr. Jebb (afterwards Judge Jebb), said, 1798:—

" In the course of 15 years our agriculture, our commerce, our manufactures, have swelled to an amount that the most sanguine friends of Ireland would not have dared to prognosticate."

On the 18th December, 1798, the Bankers of Dublin had a meeting, in which they passed these resolutions:—

" Resolved, that since the renunciation of the power of Great Britain, in 1782, to legislate for Ireland, the commerce and prosperity of this kingdom, have eminently increased.

" Resolved, that we attribute these blessings, under Providence, to the wisdom of the Irish Parliament."

On the 14th January, 1799, the Guild of Merchants resolved:—

" That the commerce of Ireland has increased, and her manufactures have improved beyond example, since the independence of this kingdom was restored by the exertions of our countrymen, in 1782."

21st January, 1800. The Weaver's Hall resolved:—

" That previous to 1782, while the Parliament of Great Britain assumed a control over the Parliament of this country, our manufactures were in a languishing and decayed state. That since that period, having had the benefit of enjoying the paternal care and solicitude of a resident Parliament, the manufactures of Ireland have increased at a rapid rate."

27th January, 1800. The Catholics of Louth resolved:—

"That this country, since 1782, has advanced with firm and progressive steps in the possession of political and commercial advantages, unexampled in the history of any other nation in the same space of time."

1800. The nobility and gentry of the county Cork, at a public meeting, resolved:—

" Since the glorious period of 1782, when the independence of our constitution was finally established, we have seen this kingdom advancing in prosperity in a manner almost unexampled in the history of nations; as its commerce and agriculture, its arts and manufactures have extended and improved, its resources and revenues have increased; and in proportion to its improvement, has this kingdom become a more effectual support to the strength of the Empire at large."

3rd March, 1800 Orange Lodge, 652, resolved:—

" That we consider a Union with Great Britain a measure which would destroy our existence as a nation, and eventually involve the rights, liberties, and even the lives of the people of Ireland."

19th Feb., 1800. Orange Lodge, 651 resolved:—

" That we see with unspeakable sorrow an attempt made to deprive us of that constitution, of our trade, our rising prosperity, our existence as a nation, and to reduce us to the degrading situation of a colony to England."

Mr. Pitt adds his testimony. Speaking in 1799, he thus describes the position which Ireland had attained:—

" In the present time the trade is still more advantageous, as far as relates to the interchange of manufactures; the manufactures received in Ireland amounting to one million, while Great Britain, on the other hand, imported manufactured produce from Ireland to the amount of between £4,000,000 and £5,000,000 sterling."

The evidence of the progress of Ireland is abundant and unimpeachable. She had, in 1800, reached a very high position; she was lightly taxed, and possessed many immunities and privileges which were not enjoyed by Great Britain. The English ministry, in asking her to accept the Union, could not have hoped that their offer would be accepted, if the intended treaty did not contain provisions for continuing to Ireland the same or similar advantages to those she possessed—first, in the comparative freedom from debt, and next, in the enjoyment of a much lighter system of taxation. It will be necessary to consider the relative condition of each nation with regard to DEBT, and the allurements which were held out to the Irish nation, in order to induce it to surrender its nationality. But, before proceeding to do so, it is right we should recall to mind the fact, that the surrender of its nationality was unpalatable to the Irish people. They believed themselves competent to manage their own affairs— they saw that in the period from 1783 to 1799 Ireland had made great progress—they felt that they were, as compared with Great Britain, unincumbered with debt, and that, in point of taxation, they were much better off; the lighter taxes brought commodities more within the reach of the middle classes, and there was, in comparison with Great Britain, a larger increase in the consumption of those articles which are supposed to convey an idea of the comforts of the people. The taxation of Ireland, in 1799, was about 8s. per head of the population, while in Great Britain it was about £3 10s. per head. These circumstances shewed the Irish nation the advantages of self-government; their feelings and interests were alike opposed to the Union, and that measure was only carried by the most lavish use of the most objectionable means. It is with profound surprise we now look back at the payment of £1,237,500 to those who claimed to have the nomination of members of Parliament for the boroughs, which were at the Union deprived of their representatives, and at the very unsparing system of bribery which was resorted to. But the mere fact that it was necessary to do so, places in stronger light the consciousness that the Union could only have been accomplished by offering to the nation, as well as to individuals, inducements to adopt the sacrifice. It is with the inducements offered to the Irish nation, accepted by her, and ratified and confirmed by the Acts of Union, that I have to deal. It is so evident that the Union could not have been carried, had not such blandishments been held out, that I do not think it requisite to argue what is self-evident. But I must remark, that the Irish people believed that the conditions of the Union secured them advantages in exchange for the privileges they surrendered; they looked for a continuance of the freedom from taxes which they so long enjoyed, and for those social and personal privileges which were intended by the sixth article. It is a matter of history that PITT (who carried the Act of Union) resigned office because his Royal master refused to grant those privileges which he had personally promised, and which the sixth article of the Act of Union so fully conferred, and that the rights and privileges so granted by the Union were only obtained after a long struggle—a struggle which existed for nearly thirty years, during which different classes of Irishmen were forced into a conflict of opinion, which has hardly disappeared after a further lapse of thirty years.

We cannot properly consider the language of the Act of Union without glancing at the growth and progress of the National Debt in both countries, and it is very fortunate that we are able to refer to that high authority supplied by parliamentary papers. The tables from which the following information relative to the National Debt is extracted is a House of Commons return on the NATIONAL DEBT, (No 443, session 1858.) It appears from it that the National Debt of England originated in loans, in anticipation of the revenue; the first of which was made in 1691, when the sum of £3,130,000 was temporarily borrowed. The first permanent loan was contracted in 1694, when £1,200,000 was borrowed from the Bank of England. During the following six years the funded debt did not increase, but the unfunded ran up to £13,321,938. The policy of lessening the floating debt was then adopted, and in 1758 the only unfunded debt was £1,371,862 of navy bills, while the funded debt had increased to £81,756,147. This return states that the first Irish debt was in 1717; it was a loan of £46,153 at 7 per cent. interest. No increase took place until 1729. In 1733, it was £276,923; and in 1759, (the last year of the reign of George the II.,) the Irish Parliament had nearly paid off its National Debt, and it was only £4,892. The American war increased it, and in 1783 it was £1,967,262; in 1790, it was

£2,215,695; during the following ten years it had increased six-fold; and in 1800, it stood at £13,704,615. In 1816, when the exchequers were consolidated, it is stated to have been £28,740,246.

This return states the debt of each country, and the interest to which, when the Act of Union passed in 1800, they were respectively liable, to have been as follows:—

		Debt.		Interest.
Great Britain,	...	£457,188,665	...	£17,805,075
Ireland,	...	13,706,615	...	777,875
	Total	£470,894,280		£18,582,950

Thus proving how lightly the interest of the National Debt was felt in Ireland previously to the Union. The lighter taxation of Ireland is shown, by contrasting the taxation of the period under consideration with that of subsequent times. The Irish revenue was:—

In the ten years from	1791 to 1801,	...	£13,911,834
„	„ 1801 to 1811,	...	47,237,560
„	„ 1811 to 1821,	...	55,268,913

In considering the debates on the Act of Union, it is well to have regard, not only to the actual debt due by each country at the time it was passed, but also to the additions which were made to the debt of each country, during the previous fifteen years. We must remember that the Irish Parliament, when discussing the treaty of Union, had before them the manner in which it would effect Irish interests and Irish taxation; the facts which were patent to the world, as the debt-contracting efforts of each nation, were these. During the fifteen years, from 1785 to 1800, the debts of both countries were increased by loans. The amount borrowed in that period, was £231,308,310. Had the Union taken place in 1785, on the principle of making Ireland liable for 2-17ths of this debt, as was proposed by Lord Castlereagh and carried, she would have become chargeable with the sum of £27,212,742; whereas, during the fifteen years, from 1785 to 1800, Ireland had only borrowed £11,467,308; so that in fixing two-seventeenths as the proportion of the annual charge on the joint debt, to which Ireland should become liable during the ensuing twenty years, (from 1801 to 1822,) the Parliament of Ireland assented, or rather the British minister, forced the majority of the Irish members, whom he had purchased or bribed, to agree, that Ireland should bear a proportion of future liabilities, at more than double the rate she had heretofore done. Great Britain saw that in the new partnership she would be able to transfer to Irish shoulders the annual payment of a charge more than double that which Ireland, while separated, had paid.

The British minister and his representative, when urging the Irish Parliament to accept this contract, promised the continuance of that freedom from taxation which Ireland had enjoyed; and even those which were purchased, imagined that this contract was so solemnly secured that it could not be broken. But this relative freedom from taxation has proved quite unattainable, and many attribute to those who framed the Act of Union the intention to disappoint the Irish people, and to use it as a means of taxing them. In looking back to the period of the Union, and in weighing the clauses of the treaty, we can well afford to lay aside all acerbity of feeling; we can endeavour calmly to weigh the intention of the parties, as expressed in the debates previous to the passing of of the act. There is no need of heat or warmth in reviewing the tenor of the clauses, and considering the manner in which the subsequent accounts of each nation were made out. But I think a calm and dispassionate reasoner, looking at the facts, must feel convinced that a great financial injustice has been done to Ireland, and not only have the promises of those who proposed the treaty, but the obvious meaning of the treaty itself, been violated.

I submit that the Parliament of the United Kingdom, which owed its birth to the Act of Union, which was the creation of the act, could not vary, alter, or annul the conditions. There is a reservation in the treaty, that the Parliament of the United Kingdom might take certain steps, if certain previous conditions had been arrived at; but I think it can be proved that those conditions never were arrived at, and therefore, that the assumed legislation is null and void, and that Ireland has a right to those privileges and immunities for which she covenanted at the time of the Union. The facts I have adduced and the authorities I have quoted suffice to show that Ireland made very great progress under her Parliament, and that she was in the enjoyment of many immunities and privileges. It is evident that since the Union her taxation has increased, her manufactures have disappeared, her commerce has declined, and she manifests many indications of the disastrous nature of the bargain forced upon her

LETTER III.

THE next subject for consideration will be this—Ireland was progressing so rapidly in many respects, what gave rise to the idea of an Union? How was it brought forward? What were the ideas thrown out in the debates? and how was it ultimately carried? was it against the wish and will of the Irish Parliament? was it a free and voluntary contract? did the Irish people consider themselves incapable of self-government? did they feel that the burthen of watching over and protecting the interests of their country was so onerous that it could be better performed in London?

Such questions are not only natural but pertinent, and the answer is best given in the simple recital of the history of the debates on the measure. Historians generally consider that the idea of an Union occurred to WILLIAM PITT, at the time of the Regency debates, when the Irish Parliament took a somewhat different course to that of the British Parliament, and that he awaited a favourable moment for carrying it into effect. The Rebellion in Ireland, which was connived at, if not actually promoted by this minister, furnished the pretext for suggesting such an Union, and the idea was first thrown out by Mr. Edward Cooke, the Under-Secretary of the Civil Department, in a pamphlet, published anonymously in 1798, entitled, "Arguments for and against an Union between Great Britain and Ireland," which was understood as speaking the sentiments of the British administration. It was circulated with incredible industry and profusion throughout every part of the nation. It was followed by no less than thirty pamphlets, before the close of the year 1798. In December of that year, meetings against the Union occurred in Dublin and most parts of Ireland. The Bar pronounced their condemnation of the measure by a majority of 166 to 32, and their example was followed by the Corporation of Dublin, by the University, and by an assembly of bankers and merchants, headed by the Lord Mayor. The agitation on the subject was in no small degree increased by the dismissal of Sir John Parnell from the office of Chancellor of the Exchequer, and Mr. James Fitzgerald from that of Prime-Sergeant, on the avowed grounds that they had expressed a decided hostility to a Legislative Union.

The Parliaments of both countries assembled in the January of 1799, and on the 22nd January in that year, the following message on the subject of the Union was laid before the British House of Commons:—

"GEORGE R.,   "January 22nd, 1799.

"His Majesty is persuaded that the unremitting industry with which our enemies persevere in their avowed design of effecting the separation of Ireland from this kingdom cannot fail to engage the particular attention of Parliament; and his Majesty recommends it to this house to consider the most effectual means of finally defeating the design, by disposing the Parliaments of both kingdoms to provide, in the manner which they shall judge most expedient, for settling such a complete and final adjustment as may tend to improve and perpetuate a connection essential for their common security, and consolidate the strength, power, and resources of the British Empire."

Mr. Secretary Dundas moved that this message be taken into consideration the next day.

Mr. Sheridan said he supposed the reply would contain an assurance that the House would proceed to consider the subject, and he gave notice of his intention to oppose a measure replete with so much mischief.

The Chancellor of the Exchequer, Mr. Pitt, replied that he only wished the House to consider the question.

I do not attempt to give the debate on the subject, I merely extract from a few of the speakers those expressions which seem to have a relation to the meaning we should attach to the conditions of the treaty of Union.

On the motion for taking his Majesty's message into consideration, on January 23, 1799, Mr. Sheridan moved, as an amendment, "At the same time, to express the surprise and deep regret with which the House, for the first time, learned from his Majesty, that the final adjustment, which, upon his Majesty's gracious recommendation took place between the two kingdoms, in 1782, had not produced the effects expected by that solemn settlement; and farther, humbly to express to his Majesty, that his faithful Commons had strong reasons to believe that it was in the contemplation of his Majesty's ministers to propose a Union of the legislation of the two kingdoms, notwithstanding that final and solemn adjustment, humbly imploring his Majesty not to listen to the counsels of those who should advise such a measure at the present crisis."

Mr. Sheridan supported his amendment by a powerful speech, in which he contended that the settlement of 1782 could not be disturbed, and in the course of it he said, he was the more strongly impressed with this belief, because a solemn declaration of the Irish Parliament, sanctioned by all Ireland, was now on record, wherein it was stated that the independence of Ireland, would be asserted by the people of Ireland, and that their Parliament was an independent Parliament, and that there was no other power whatever competent to make laws for that country. From this consideration, he said, he must think that the people in that country, who really loved national liberty, would come forward to a second adjustment with a temper, which he was afraid would augur not tranquillity but disquietude.

Mr Pitt, Chancellor of the Exchequer, in replying, said, the honourable gentleman did not scruple to assert, that final adjustment with Ireland, in 1782, had been found competent to settle every difference, and that he wished to perpetuate the connection between Great Britain and Ireland: but, for his part, he did not wish it to be perpetuated, but that Ireland should participate in all the blessings of the British empire.

This motion was withdrawn by Mr. Sheridan, as informal. He said he would move it as a substantial resolution on a future occasion.

I must now relate what occurred in the IRISH Parliament.

On the 22nd of January, 1799, the subject was thus introduced by the Lord Lieutenant. In his speech, great satisfaction was expressed, that, "notwithstanding its internal calamities, the kingdom had participated in the effects of the increasing wealth and commerce of Great Britain, and that the revenue and trade had increased."

The speech concluded in these words:—

"The unremitting industry with which our enemies persevere in their avowed design of endeavouring to effect a separation of this kingdom from Great Britain, must have engaged your particular attention; and his Majesty commands me to express his anxious hope, that this consideration, joined to the sentiment of mutual affection and common interest, may dispose the Parliaments in both kingdoms, to provide the most effectual means of maintaining and improving a connection essential to their common security, and of consolidating, as far as possible, into one firm and lasting fabric, the strength, the power, and the resources of the British empire."

Amendments were moved to the address, on this occasion, in both houses. Lord Powerscourt, in the Upper House, proposed the insertion of the following words:—

" That it is our most earnest desire to strengthen the connection between the two countries by every possible means; but the measure of a Legislative Union, we apprehend, is not within our power; we beg leave, also, to represent to your Majesty, that, although this house were competent to adopt such a measure, we conceive that it would be highly impolitic so to do, as it would tend, in our opinion, more than any other cause, ultimately to a separation of this kingdom from Great Britain."

In the House of Commons, the amendment was, that after the passage which declared the willingness of the house to entertain a consideration of what measures might best tend to confirm the strength of the empire, the following words should be inserted:—

" Maintaining, however, the undoubted birthright of the people of Ireland, to have a resident and independant legislature, such as was recognised by the British Legislature in 1782, and was finally settled, as the adjustment of all differences between the two countries."

In support of this amendment, the dismissed Prime Sergeant quoted the words of Dr. Johnston, who said to an Irishman, " Don't unite with us; we shall only unite with you to rob you; we should have robbed the Scots if they had anything to be robbed of."

Mr. Lea reminded his hearers, that even the nabob had representatives in the virtuous Parliament, to which they were called upon to give up their interests.

Mr. O'Hara said, that the Irish Parliament had been making acquisition for the country, from the time of the octennial bill to that day.

Mr Cruikshank called upon the representatives of the people to preserve that constitution under which the country had prospered beyond example.

Mr. Barrington and Mr. Plunket declared that means had

been taken by the minister to corrupt the Irish Parliament.
The former said that, " treacherous reasons assigned for this
project were their differences and misfortunes—differences
which arose from the duplicity of that same minister who
sought to subdue them, and misfortunes, which were stimu-
lated by him to adapt them for his own conquest."

Mr. Dobbs said, that though he was a friend to British connection, he would meditate separation from the moment the
Legislative Union should be carried by force.

Mr. Knox charged the minister with having long promoted
and kept alive distinctions and divisions among the people
to carry an Union.

Mr. Plunket reiterated the assertion, that base and wicked
as was the object proposed, the means used to effect it had
been more flagitious and abominable.

Col. Maxwell concurred with Mr. George Ponsonby, that
Parliament was totally incompetent to entertain the measure.
He conjured the house, as it valued the British connection, to
support the rights and liberties of Ireland.

Mr. Hans Hamilton would oppose an Union within the
walls of Parliament with his vote, and without them with
his life.

Mr. D. B. Daly, (father of Lord Dunsandle, and of the
present Lord Bishop of Cashel,) said, he would venture his
life and property in resisting an Union.

Col. O'Donnel said, that should the legislative independence of Ireland be voted away, he should hold himself discharged from his allegiance.

Mr. J. C. Beresford said, that no consideration on earth
could induce him to give a vote in Parliament, whereby he
should conceive himself accessory to the annihilation of the
legislative independence of this country.

Mr. Ball pronounced the measure unconstitutional and
profligate, and said that, if carried, it would, at no very remote period, end in a total separation from England.

Lord Corry regarded the measure as pregnant with every
possible mischief to the constitution of the country—its
commerce and manufactures.

Lord Cole pledged himself to oppose it in every shape.

Mr. J. M. O'Donnell pronounced it infamous, wicked, and
degrading.

Mr. Saunderson, as an independent Irish country gentleman, would oppose it in every shape.

Sir Edward O'Brien would resist it whenever proposed.

Mr. W. P. Ponsonby declared the very attempt at an Union an attack on the constitution of Ireland, and argued unpardonable temerity.

Mr. Arthur Moore (at ten o'clock in the morning, after a night's debate) was as willing to perish as to speak in opposition to an Union.

Mr. George Ponsonby closed the longest debate that ever took place within the walls of the Irish Parliament, by declaring that, " never, in the course of his life, did he feel such delightful sentiments as at that moment, when he contemplated the virtue and spirit, the proud integrity displayed by the gentlemen with whom he had the honour of acting, and, he trusted, of closing in honest victory an honest contest." On the house dividing there appeared 106 votes for the minister, and 105 against him, leaving him a majority only of one, on an occasion on which some held that the question was not whether there should be an Union, but whether such a measure should ever be discussed. The debate lasted 22 hours, and " it must," (said Plowden) " be impartially allowed that in the contest, talent, energy, and independence predominated on the side of the minority."

The next struggle was on the motion of Sir Laurence Parsons. On the 24th the address was reported; and on reading it, Sir Laurence objected to the paragraph as pledging the house, under a metaphorical expression, to admit the principle of a legislative Union.

Mr. M. O'Donnell asked what Union could Ireland have with England but a Union of debt and taxation?

Mr. Edgeworth, though at first inclined to regard the measure with some favour, changed his mind on seeing the repugnance of the country to it, and he hoped its opponents would triumph over the minister, or of any cabal of pensioners and placemen.

Sir John Parnell, Dr. Arthur Brown, Mr. Moore, Colonel Vereker, Sir John Freke, and others strongly condemned an Union on various grounds. On a division, the majority was on the side of the anti-Unionists, the numbers being, for Sir Laurence Parson's motion, 111; against, 106, leaving the minister in a minority of *five*.

The result appears to have been quite unexpected by Mr. PITT, who, in his reliance on a different issue, commenced in the British Parliament a discussion of the Union on the same day that it was brought formally under the consideration of the Irish Parliament, and, notwithstanding their decision, on the 31st January, Mr. Pitt rose to propose his resolutions, and, in the course of his speech, he said he was convinced that the Parliament of Ireland possessed the power, the entire competence, to accept or reject a proposition of this nature—a power which he by no means wished to dispute—but, while he admitted the rights of the Parliament of Ireland, he felt that, as a member of Parliament of Great Britain, he had a right to exercise, and a duty to perform, viz., to express the general nature and outline of the plan, which, in his estimation, would tend to insure the safety and the happiness of the two kingdoms. Should Parliament be of opinion that it was calculated to produce mutual advantage to the two kingdoms, he should propose it to be recorded that the Parliament of Great Britain was ready to abide by it, leaving it to the legislature of Ireland to reject or adopt it hereafter, upon a full consideration of the subject. Notwithstanding the opinion expressed by the Irish House of Commons, he was convinced that the measure was founded upon such clear and demonstrable grounds of utility, and attended with so many advantages to Ireland, all that could be said for its ultimate adoption, was, that it should be stated distinctly, temperately, and fully, and then left to the unprejudiced judgment of the Parliament of Ireland. He next made some remarks on the obvious impediments to the prosperity of Ireland; one of the most prominent features was a want of industry and capital, which, he said, were only to be supplied by blending more closely with Ireland the capital and industry of this country. The manufactures exported to Ireland from Great Britain, in 1797, very little exceeded a million sterling (the articles of produce amounted to nearly the same sum,) while Great Britain, on the other hand, imported from Ireland to the amount of near three millions in manufactured articles of linen and linen-yarn, and between two or three millions in provisions and cattle, besides corn and other articles of produce. No man, he said, who held the Parliament of Ireland to be co-equal with that of Great Britain, could deny its competency on this question. He moved eight resolutions, the seventh of which reads as follows:—

"That, for the like purpose, it would be fit to propose that the charge arising from the payment of the interest of sinking fund, for the reduction of the principal of the debt incurred in either kingdom before the Union, shall continue to be paid separately by Great Britain and Ireland respectively. That for a number of years, to be limited, the future ordinary expenses of the United Kingdom, in peace or war should be defrayed by Great Britain and Ireland jointly, according to such proportions as shall be established by the respective Parliaments previous to the Union; and that after, the lapse of the time so limited, the proportions shall not be liable to be varied, except according to such rates and principles as shall be, in like manner, agreed upon previous to the Union."

Mr. Sheridan moved the adoption of the resolution which is given in page 45, but on the motion that the speaker leave the chair being put, the ayes were 140, and the noes 15.

The resolutions were then read in committee, and the house adjourned.

On the 7th February, the debate was resumed, when Mr. Sheridan moved, " that no measures could have a tendency to improve and perpetuate the ties of amity and connection now existing between Great Britain and Ireland, which have not for their basis the manifest, fair, and free consent of the two countries. That whoever shall endeavour to obtain the appearance of such consent, and approbation, in either country, by employing the influence of Government for the purpose of corruption and intimidation, is an enemy to his Majesty and the constitution."

Mr. Pitt, in moving the order of the day, said he should make a few remarks on the motion of the hon. gentleman, as it stood divided into two parts, the first was, that no measure of the Union could be pursued without the unbiassed consent of the Parliaments of both countries. This he said was a truism which was never attacked, but must be assented to as soon as stated.

Mr. Sheridan, in reply, said, the right hon. gentleman well knew that there were 116 placemen in the Irish House of Commons, and that, by dismissing the Chancellor of the Exchequer and the Prime Serjeant, the others would be sure to remain staunch there out of fear. If the Union was desirable as the right hon. gentleman had said, the people of Ireland ought to know upon what principle it was to be carried, and not to be deceived by false appearances, and dazzled by the splendour of the Imperial Parliament. He remarked, that if the measure were carried by threats, this country would

E

have ample cause to repent, as it would give a perpetual pretence to rebellion. He therefore deprecated the idea of a Union on such terms.

Mr. Grey, (afterwards Earl Grey,) said, " look at the history of Ireland, and you will find that if it had not been for the interference of British councils and British intrigue, none, or but few of the evils which were felt, would ever have taken place, evils of which Government was the parent, and which were now made the reason of taking away all semblance of liberty among the Irish people. All the feuds and religious animosities and dissensions which had distracted Ireland, had been caused by Government, and yet Government was making use of these evils, as a pretext for taking away the liberty of the people of Ireland."

General Fitzpatrick closed his speech against the Union by saying, " with respect to the terms of the Union, he did not mean to say anything, nor was it necessary in the view he had of the matter, to consider anything about terms, because he looked upon the whole as a flagrant breach of faith."

In the debate on the resolutions, Mr. Carew inquired what would be the exact taxation.

Mr. Pitt, in reply, said it was impossible, at present, to fix the exact proportion to be paid by the two countries. When he opened the subject, (he said,) he then stated that the proportion *Ireland ought to pay, would not be greater than that which she now paid.*

Mr. Peel, afterwards Sir Robert Peel, urged on the house, that each country was to provide for its own public debt, and that of Great Britain being infinitely larger than the debt of Ireland, heavy taxes were necessarily imposed on almost every article of consumption, which had a strong tendency to reduce the price of labour; that goods manufactured under such a pressure, could not be tendered on equally low terms with the produce of labour in places where similar burthens did not exist.

Lord Sheffield bore testimony to the great manufacturing facilities of Ireland. No country, said he, was better circumstanced for manufactures, than Ireland, for she has plenty of water and fuel, the first requisites in manufactures.

Mr. Canning, who advocated the Union, was desirous that it should not be carried, save in accordance with the wish of the Irish people; he said, " strong as his conviction was of the advantages to be derived to Ireland from the Union, he should be as averse as any man from pressing it upon the Irish Parliament in any manner which would be injurious to its honour and independence."

Lord William Russell thought the settlement of 1782 was the solemn recognition of a right which we could not call upon the Irish people to abandon.

But Mr. Pitt succeeded in carrying his resolutions, and the subject was sent to the House of Lords, when Lord Grenville, on behalf of the government, echoed the opinions of Mr. Pitt in the Lower House. His lordship repeated, "that whatever step they should take on the present occasion, the sole and exclusive rights of the Irish legislature should be duly respected, and considered upon the same footing as that of Great Britain."

Lord Holland, the Earl of Moira, opposed the resolutions on various grounds.

The Bishop of Llandaff, in common with other peers, deprecated the use of any but honourable means; he said, "Though he was a friend to an Union, he was no friend to its being accomplished by any but the most honourable means. Ireland at present seemed not disposed to contract."

The resolutions were carried through the House of Lords that session, but no further steps were taken in either Parliament, to give effect to the resolutions, which owed their existence to Mr. Pitt, the Prime-Minister of Great Britain, who was determined at all cost to carry the Union.

Mr. Godkin, one of the authors of the "Repeal Prize Essays," thus describes the reasons which Mr. Pitt had for deferring the consideration of the Catholic claims.

"There is good reason to believe that Pitt regarded the independence of the Irish Parliament as a measure yielded to intimidation, therefore, unconstitutionally obtained and to be "recaptured" as soon as possible by fair means or foul. To do him justice, we must admit he tried the fair means first. He sent Lord Fitzwilliam as Viceroy, with the understanding that the Catholics should be emancipated. . . . . . The selection of such a Viceroy was an omen for good, which exceeded the liveliest hopes of the Catholic population, and the friends of freedom in general. But no sooner was the cup of joy raised to the lips of Ireland, than the minister of England, like a mocking demon, dashed it to the ground, exposing the nation to the most perilous risk of insurrection. On this occasion the mind of Pitt, certainly his policy, underwent a sudden change. He earnestly urged Lord Fitzwilliam to postpone the question of Emancipation, assigning a reason, of which time has too clearly developed the mystery. He intended, in fact, to make Emancipation the price of the Union; and, therefore, wished that subject kept in abeyance till circumstances should be ripe for the accomplishment of his darling scheme. In urging Lord Fitzwilliam to keep back the question of Emancipation, he said it would be the means of doing a greater service to the British empire, than it had been capable of receiving since the revolution, at least since the Union (with Scotland). But that noble lord disdained to be the instrument of a sinister policy, and so left the stage clear for the tragedies in which Castlereagh and Clare were to be the chief actors."

The Irish Parliament was prorogued the 1st June, 1799, and Lord Cornwallis, the Lord Lieutenant, thus acknowledged that it had done its duty. "I thank you," said he, "in his Majesty's name, for the large and extraordinary supply which you have so honourably voted to meet every wish of the government and every exigency of the state."

Up to this, the legislative rights of Ireland were preserved in the Parliament itself, though out of a House of Commons of 300 members, no less than 116 were placemen. Mr. Fox, when speaking in the British House of Commons, said, that nine years had been spent in a regular system of enslaving Ireland," and he added, " a person of high consideration was known to say that £500,000 had been expended to quell an opposition, and that as much more must be expended to bring the legislature of Ireland to a proper temper." All the bribery and other efforts had, up to this time, failed to produce that subservience so much desired by the British Minister. That Parliament, which, according to GRATTAN, "had done more than the Barons at Runnymede, or the Convention Parliament—which had acquired free trade— the repeal of the 6th of George the First—which restored the appellant jurisdiction—which framed the mutiny bill—in a word, which obtained all that could be desired or demanded, had spurned the allurements of the British Minister, refused to be corrupted by him, and was true to the cause of its country." PLUNKET rejoiced over its virtue and patriotism: he exclaimed, "That accursed measure has been dismissed and defeated by the instinct, and the reason, and the virtue, and the property of the country." But the British minister determined to carry his measure, *per fas et nefas*, and as soon as Parliament was prorogued, all the machinations at the command of Government were put into operation. Though repeated assurances were given, in the British Houses of Parliament, that no attempt would be made to bias the Irish representatives, or coerce the Irish people, yet these promises were flung to the wind. The Lord Lieutenant started on a tour, for the express purpose of making a personal canvass. The number of soldiers in Ireland was largely increased, and directions were given to the generals and commanders to prevent and disperse any public meetings. The army expenditure in Ireland was increased in 1800 beyond precedent. During the six years, from 1799 to 1802, it was as follows:—

1797,	Army Expenditure in Ireland,	...	£2,227,457
1798,	„	„	...	3,216,228
1799,	„	„	...	3,528,800
1800,	„	„	...	4,011,783
1801,	„	„	...	3,305,000
1802,	„	„	...	2,133,000

The appointment of sheriffs was used as a means to stifle public opinion; care was taken that they should be mere minions of the Crown, who should refuse to convene meetings, in their bailiwicks, and when the people assembled, the military—horse, foot, and artillery—were called out to disperse legally convened meetings, to expostulate or petition against the Union.

Lord Plunket thus described the manner in which force was used:—

" I will be bold to say that licentious and impious France, in all the unrestrained excesses that anarchy and atheism have given birth to, has not committed a more insidious act against her enemy, than is now attempted by the professed champion of civilized Europe against Ireland—a friend and ally—in the hour of her calamity and distress. At a moment when our country is filled with British troops—whilst the *Habeas Corpus* Act is suspended—whilst trials by courts-martial are carrying on in many parts of the kingdom—while the people are made to believe that they have no right to meet and deliberate—and whilst the people are palsied by their fears—at the moment when we are distracted by internal dissen-

sions—dissensions kept alive as a pretext of our present
subjugation, and the instrument of our future thraldom!!!
Such is the time in which the Union was proposed."

The Government did not confine themselves to these
means, objectionable as they were; they proceeded to secure a
majority in the Houses of Parliament. At that time the
right of nomination for several of the boroughs in Great
Britain and Ireland was considered property, and was regularly
bought and sold. Government proceeded to purchase a
number of these boroughs, and, in many cases, where those
holding the seats had not the face to turn completely round
and vote for the Union, they succeeded in inducing them to
retire and make way for more supple representatives. I shall
have to treat on this subject more at length when I come to
relate the events of the session of 1800. I am now merely
describing the means which were taken by ministers to carry
their point, which is thus pictured by the late Lord Chief
Justice Bushe.

He stated that " the basest corruption and artifice were exerted to promote it; that all the worst passions of the human
heart were entered into the service, and all the most de-
praved ingenuity of the human intellect was tortured to
devise new contrivances of fraud."

I have necessarily condensed the debates which took place,
and endeavoured to allow the *dramatis personæ* to express
their sentiments in their own language. Thus fell the cur-
tain in 1799 on the scheme of the Union.

LETTER IV.

THE DEBATES ON THE UNION 1800.

WE now approach the last session of the Irish Parliament! Ministers had made sure of their victim, and they hastened to the sacrifice: the Annual Register for 1800, has the following account of the previous preparations.

"The proceedings of the British Parliament, relative to an Union with Ireland, were rendered abortive by the spirit, or the precipitancy of the Irish legislature. They opposed with violence, and dismissed with contempt, a proposition which was a sentence of death upon themselves; and the British Ministry found, too late, that they had been deficient in address, or, perhaps, too parsimonious in their arrangements, to secure a measure which embraced a variety of conflicting interests. With his usual tenacity, however, the British Minister determined to persevere. Though rejected by the Irish Parliament, a series of resolutions were adopted in that of Great Britain, as a basis of the proposed Union; and the Lord Lieutenant of Ireland closed the session with a hope, that the measure would be re-considered and adopted in such a manner as might be most conducive to the happiness and prosperity of both nations."

"Of the means which were employed in the course of the recess to facilitate the intended arrangement, it is scarcely the time as yet to speak with either certainty or safety. The conciliatory spirit, and the popular character of the Lord Lieutenant, in the course of a political tour, might make some proselytes; and some seats in the Irish Parliament were vacated by persons who had pledged themselves to oppose the Union, and filled by others, less hostile to that favourite measure. At the meeting of the Irish Parliament, considerable activity was displayed by the partisans on each side, for the purpose of procuring signatures; and at a very early period, the table of the House of Commons was loaded with petitions."

Ministers were sanguine that they had secured such a majority as would carry their measure, while the Anti-Unionists believed that they had strengthened their hands during the recess, and, having defeated Government the former session, they hoped to succeed in doing so again, and did not shrink from the conflict.

The session opened the 15th January, 1800. The Lord Lieutenant, in the opening speech, studiously avoided introducing the subject, as "the pear was not quite ripe." Arrangements had been made with some members, and on the first day of the session, writs were moved for no less than 20 seats, the occupiers of which had received reasons for retiring, five days after, 12 more vacancies occurred, and before the end of April, 28 more were added, making the entire number of seats thus vacated before the end of April, no less than sixty, or one-fifth of the number of the Irish House of Commons. The speech from the throne made no mention of the Union, though the speech at the close of the preceding session recommended it in the name of the King. Sir Laurence Parsons, (grandfather of the present Earl of Rosse,) regarded it as a stratagem of the Minister, to prevent any expression of opinion on the subject, "until his machinations were completed." It did not succeed, for Sir Laurence moved an amendment to the address, in which he introduced the expression of a desire, for the preservation of a resident and independent Parliament. "It matters not," (he said,) "whether the representatives of that great nation were turned out of that door by the sword of an army, or the gold of the Treasury, by a Cromwell or by a Secretary; in both, the treason against the constitution, was the same. One of the greatest offences of James II. was attempting to pack a Parliament. Of that offence, he (the honourable baronet,) arraigned the Minister of the Crown, by prostituting the prerogative, in order to pack a Parliament. A string of men who were against the Union were to go out, that a string of men who were for it might come in." A long debate followed. While one of the speakers was referring to '82, Mr. Grattan re-entered the house, having accepted a seat for Wicklow, to join in the struggle for the maintenance of the Irish constitution. His appearance at that moment is said to have produced an effect on the house entirely without a parallel. He made one of his longest and most animated speeches, in support of the amendment. The discussion was protracted to ten the next morning, the result exhibited very strikingly the success of the arts of the minister, for, on a division, there ap-

peared for the amendment 96, and against it 138, giving him
a majority of 42.

Several days were allowed to pass, without any decisive
movement on the part of the executive. The 5th, of February
was the day on which a formal message was delivered from
the Lord Lieutenant, and resolutions were proposed by Lord
Castlereagh, which were to form the basis of the act of incor-
poration. Several petitions presented against the project had
been previously presented.

Lord Castlereagh, in introducing the resolutions,
said:—

"In respect to past expenses, Ireland was to have no concern whatever with the debt of Great Britain, but the two
countries were to unite, as to future expenses, on a *strict
measure of relative ability.* He should have considered it a most
valuable circumstance in this arrangement, if the countries
could have been so completely incorporated as not to
have had distinct revenues—a part of the system of the
Scotch Union, which had been felt to be of such importance
that a great effort was made to equalize the circumstances of
the two countries for that purpose. England had a large
debt, Scotland had none charged upon her revenues; an
accurate calculation was made of the sum to be paid to Scotland, to justify her in accepting her share of the debt, and
the sum was paid accordingly by England. The taxation of
the two countries was accordingly fixed at the same scale,
except in the article of land-tax, which was fixed at a
different rate, because the land-tax in England was imposed
so unequally, that had Scotland paid in the same rate as the
nominal land-tax of England, she would really have been
taxed much higher than her just proportion. He mentioned
this to show the pains taken to incorporate the two countries,
and lamented that the circumstances of Great Britain and
Ireland did not at present enable the measure of identity to
be preserved with equal strictness. . . . Such, however,
was the disproportion of the debts of the two kingdoms, that
a common system was then impossible, nor could any system
of equivalent, as in the case of Scotland, be applied for
equalizing their contributions. It was, therefore, necessary
that the debts of the two kingdoms should be kept distinct,
and that, of course, their taxation should be *separate* and
proportionate."

will be diminished a million a-year; and we shall be able to support our peace expenditure with a very slight addition to the present taxes."

Mr. Foster, (speaker of the House of Commons,) when the resolutions were in committee, spoke on them at length, and exposed the fallacy of Lord Castlereagh's assumption, and the inaccuracy of his figures; he said:—

"It is curious to observe the noble lord's arguments, last year and now. Our growing wealth was *then* held out by him as tending to render us too difficult to be governed by our present constitution, and there was the greater hurry for taking away our Parliament. *Now* our poverty is made the pretence—we must take the Union to save us from bankruptcy! we have not the means to go on. We have overpaid our due proportions of the war expenses by a million a-year; and of the peace expense by £500,000 ! we have almost ruined the kingdom by this profusion, and Britain, in proposing the measure, means to give us that million and half a million, and hereafter tax herself to pay it !

" I own we have granted largely—we have not measured our grants by our means, so much as by our zeal to uphold Great Britain; but we are for this to be punished, and our Parliament to be transported like a felon, for its extravagant efforts to maintain British connection, by maintaining the cause of Britain?

" Did the noble lord sit by during the two last sessions—the most expensive we ever saw—and not only see, but urge us to give the supplies we gave, meaning at a future day to make our liberality, and these cordial effusions of our loyalty, so many arguments for taking away our Parliament, and annihilating our constitution? . . . Is there any child so weak as to believe he is in earnest, or that he means to load England to save Ireland? And how is this £1,000,000 to be paid us—in money? are our past advances to be repaid? No! Taxes to be taken off? No! He gives us *calculation*, nothing but calculation! . . . I will go into his detail, and shew you the imposition. He states the relative ability of the two countries to be as $7\frac{1}{2}$ to 1; stating peace expenses at $5\frac{3}{4}$ to 1; and war expenses as 9 to 1; and making the medium $7\frac{1}{2}$ to 1, (considering the proportions of the years of peace and war in this country.) This makes $\frac{2}{7}$ for Ireland to pay to future aggregate expenditure, and $\frac{1}{7}$ for England. I take the statement of last year:

" British expenses as   £32,700,000
    But I find no authority for his state-
ment as to Ireland, so I take them per
last year, although then unusually great.
The report of the committee of accounts
makes them   4,347,000

                            Total   £37,047,00
$\frac{2}{17}$ whereof being   £4,358,470
would have been our share had his Union been in force;
which exceeds by a trifle the sum we did actually pay.
    " But he goes further, for he makes our war
share   £4,492,000
which exceeds what we did pay, namely,   4,347,000

So his arrangement, which is to save us a
    million, would have cost more to us by   £145,000

    " Again, Britain in six years, up to 1799, increased her debt
in the sum of £186,000,000, and Ireland, up to March, in
that year, increased hers nearly £14,000,000; total,
£200,000,000! whereof $\frac{2}{17}$ would have been £23,530,000
But Ireland increased her debt only £14,000,000, so that,
by not having a Union, she has escaped £9,530,000. This
would have caused an increased average annual charge of
£1,134,666 instead of the promised saving of one million per
annum!
    " Again, Great Britain, during those six years, has imposed
permanent taxes of the net amount of $7\frac{1}{2}$ millions a year, of
which $\frac{2}{17}$ must have been raised by Ireland; making annually
£882,352, and this is another way in which the generosity
of the Union would be shewn to us.
    " Further, she has, by temporary taxes on exports, imports,
and income, (or by mortgaging them,) to the amount of
£11,500,000 a year, of which Ireland would have had to pay
$\frac{2}{17}$ or £1,352,940. Thus, had we been united in 1793, we
should now owe £10,000,000 more debt, and pay annually
£4,156,239 more than now!
    " Now for his peace establishment. He states it at £1,500,000,
although he confesses that the last year it was only £1,012,000.
He takes the produce of a year's taxes to 25th March, 1799,
at £1,860,000 omitting the balances in the collectors' hands,
which were £257,822 more at the end than at the beginning

of the year. This was part of the income of the year, and
might have been had, if called for. The whole, then, was
£2,118,000. He estimates the permanent increase of the
revenue, in 1800, as £4,500,000; forgetting the lotteries, which
may be reckoned at a profit of about £70,000, making
altogether an income of £2,638,000, which leaves for the peace
establishment, after paying the charges of the debt, namely,
£1,400,000, at least, £1,238,000, and this after a year of
rebellion!"

Mr. Foster proceeded to urge that, if there were to be an
Union, Ireland's proportion should be $\frac{2}{16}$, instead of $\frac{2}{17}$, as proposed by Lord Castlereagh. His speech was not only unan-
swered but unanswerable.

Mr. Bagwell, one of the representatives of Tipperary, announced his intention of voting against the measure, though
he was at first favourable to it, in consequence of the decided
hostility against it, expressed by the property and independence of his county.

The leading men of both parties again delivered their sentiments at great length.

Amongst the Anti-Unionists was Mr. Saurin, who laid it
down as an incontrovertible principle, that " the trustees of
power have no right, of themselves, to destroy that which they
are delegated to preserve." He said:—

" You may make the Union binding as a law, but you cannot make it obligatory on conscience. It will be obeyed as
long as England is strong, but resistance will in the abstract
be a duty; and the exhibition of that resistance will be a
mere question of prudence."

Mr. Plunket warned the Government not to lay their hands
on the constitution. " I tell you (said he,) that if, circumstanced as you are, you pass this act, it will be a mere nullity,
and no man in Ireland will be bound to obey it."

Mr. Bushe denounced the measure as one by which it was
proposed to surrender the independence of the country to a
nation, by which it was treated for six hundred years with
marked oppression."

Doctor Duignan, who took part in the debate, on the side
of Government, said, " It is objected that the superior number
of British members in the Imperial Parliament will give them
the power of oppressing Ireland, and infringing the conditions, on which an incorporate Union may be concluded."
After stating several reasons to shew that such an event was

possible, Doctor Duignan thus proceeds:—"There still remains a more powerful answer to this objection, and that is, that the conditions of an incorporating Union must be canvassed fully in the two Parliaments of Great Britain and Ireland, before any Union can be effected. And it is morally certain that no conditions will be agreed to, which shall not be deemed by these Parliaments, who are supposed to understand the interests of their country, advantageous as well to the nations respectively, as the empire at large. And when the two nations shall become one, by an incorporating Union, can it be supposed that the Imperial Parliament will ever attempt to infringe the conditions, promotive of the interests of each country in particular, and of the whole body in general? Such a proceeding, with respect to either country, would injure the whole body, and would be, therefore, contray to the interests of the infringers, as it would be destructive to the sanity and strength of the whole human body for all the parts, the leg excepted, to conspire to wither the leg. *Therefore, there can be no apprehension of a breach of the conditions of an incorporating Union by the British Parliament, to the prejudice of Ireland, unless we shall suppose that the British members shall all become blind, as well to justice, as to their own interests.*"

In the division, the minister had only gained one on his former majority, the numbers being, for an Union, 158; against it, 115. Members, voting with the Minister, complained that in returning from the house the populace insulted them; and during the remaining debates, a troop of dragoons remained mounted before the House of Parliament.

In the subsequent debate, 17th February, 1800, Lord Castlereagh spoke as follows:—

"I shall obviate the impression which may be made, that common taxes with Great Britain, will impose upon this kingdom heavier burthens than she would otherwise be called upon to support. Let the house, then, first consider that the charges of the debt of Great Britain amount to £20,000,000 a year, and the charges of the debt of Ireland to £1,300,000 (British) a year. That common taxes are not to take place till either the past and separate debt of both countries shall be liquidated, or until they shall become to each other in the ratio of fifteen to two. Before this can take place, the taxes of Great Britain must be reduced to the amount of £10,000,000 a year, in which case the scale of her remain-

ing taxation would be levied to the scale of taxation in England, and the adoption of British taxation would become a benefit. A similar result, and to a greater degree, would take place, were the past debt of the two countries to be entirely liquidated."

Lord Castlereagh further adds:—

"The enemies of the measure of Union have founded much of their clamour upon the groundless supposition, that it is a mere financial project of the British minister, to put his hands into the pockets of the Irish people. But, sir, I believe it will be found, upon examination of the terms, that if any sacrifice be made, it will be, not on the part of Ireland, but on the part of Great Britain. The settlement which is offered is that of advantage to Ireland, but it is offered not as a bribe—not upon the mercenary principle, that Ireland would sacrifice what is essential to her happiness to any pecuniary consideration—but it is offered on the fair and liberal ground of equal contributions."

On the 24th of February the resolutions were in committee. There was again a vehement debate. Colonel Vereker contended that the majority gained by the minister was practically a defeat, and urged him to abandon his project, or, at all events, to take the sense of the people fairly upon it.

Mr. Knox observed, that if the Parliament had been removed to Madras, it would still be pretended that no violence was done to the constitution. He deemed it an essential part of the system that there should be " a free, constant, and immediate communication between the legislature and the nation for which it acted." On a motion for adjournment, to procure additional information, the ministerial majority was increased to 47, notwithstanding which, however, an adjournment was assented to by Lord Castlereagh.

When the house again assembled, that altercation occurred between Mr. Grattan and Mr. Corry, which led to their celebrated duel. The house remained sitting while the combatants retired, and exchanged two shots each. Mr. Corry was wounded in the arm. The proceedings terminated by a division, in which the majority was 42.

The next discussion was on a motion that the committee do assent to the article of the Union. On this occasion

Mr. Saurin directed the attention of the house to the means employed to carry the measure. He affirmed that the Minister availed himself of the services of " indigent adventurers from the bar and British army. If the nation should view the majority as composed of such persons, he asked on what ground the Union would stand?" There were continued divisions until the 21st of March, when the last resolution passed the committee. On this occasion the numbers were 150 to 104.

Sir John Freke remarked, that the terms which it was the duty of the committee to scrutinise, were so disadvantageous, that they had not made a convert of a single member who had censured the principle of the measure.

Mr. afterwards Lord Plunket thus challenged the competency of the Irish Parliament to agree to the Union :—

"I, in the most express terms, deny the competency of Parliament to do this act. I warn you not to dare to lay your hands upon the constitution. I tell you, if, circumstanced as you are, you pass this Act, it will be a nullity, and that no man in Ireland will be bound to obey it. I make this assertion deliberately. I repeat it, and call on any man who hears me to take down my words. You have not been elected for this purpose—you have been appointed to make laws, not legislatures. You are appointed to act under the constitution—not to destroy it. You are appointed to exercise the functions of legislators, and not to transfer them; and if you do so, your act is a dissolution of the Government ; you resolve society into its original elements, and no man in the land is bound to obey you. Yourselves you may extinguish, but Parliament you cannot extinguish ! It is enthroned in the hearts of the people—it is enshrined in the sanctuary of the constitution—it is immortal as the island it protects. As well might the frantic maniac hope that the act which destroys his miserable body should extinguish his eternal soul ! Again, I therefore warn you, do not dare to lay your hands on the constitution—it is above your power."

The language of Lord Chief Justice Bushe was even more impressive—he said :—

"I see nothing in it (the Union) but one question—will you give up the country? I forget, for a moment, the unprincipled means by which the Union has been promoted, and I look on it simply as England reclaiming, in a moment of our weakness, that dominion which we extorted from her in a moment of our virtue ; a dominion which she uniformly abused, which invariably oppressed and impoverished us, and from the abolition of which we date all our prosperity."

He adds :—

F

"The Union is a measure which goes to degrade the
country, by saying it is unworthy to govern itself. It is the
revival of the odious and absurd title of conquest. It is a
renewal of the abominable distinction between mother
country and colony, which lost America. It is the denial of
the rights of nature to a great nation, from an intolerance of
its prosperity."

The Right Hon. William Saurin, who was afterwards
Attorney-General for twenty years, said:—

"You may make the Union binding as a law, but you cannot make it obligatory on the conscience. It will be obeyed
as long as England is strong. But resistance to it will be in
the abstract be a duty, and the exhibition of that resistance
will be a mere question of prudence."

History tells us that a sum of £1,275,000 was paid for
the purchase of Irish boroughs, they were paid for at the rate
of £15,000 for each seat abolished, and more than £1,000,000
additional was expended in mere bribes. "Bribery was un-
concealed," said O'Connell, speaking on the authority of
Bushe and Plunket. "The terms of the purchase were quite
familiar in those days. The price of a single vote was
£8,000 in money, or an appointment to an office of £2,000
a-year, if the parties did not choose to take ready money.
Some got both by their votes; and no less than twenty peer-
ages, ten bishoprics, one chief-justiceship, and six puisne
judgeships were the price of votes for the Union." It is
foreign to my purpose to relate the names of those who were
bought, or the sums paid to them. Those who are curious
on the subject will find them in Sir Jonah Barrington's
"Personal History of his Own Times." My object has been to
give, in a condensed shape, the debates on the Union, in order
to discover the intention of the legislature.

I now pass to the proceedings in the HOUSE of LORDS.

1800, February 7. The Lord Lieutenant, the Marquis
Cornwallis, sent a message to the House of Lords, which was
read by the Lord Chancellor. It laid before the House the
resolutions of the British Parliament of 1799.

February 10.—The House proceeded to consider the message and resolutions. "A motion was made to resolve that, in
in order to promote and secure the essential interests of Great
Britain and Ireland, and to consolidate the strength, power,
and resources of the British Empire, it will be advisable to
concur in such measures as may best tend to unite the two

kingdoms of Great Britain and Ireland into one kingdom, in such manner, and on such terms and conditions, as may be established by acts of the respective Parliaments of Great Britain and Ireland." A long debate ensued, and the question being put, the house divided. The contents below the bar were 53, the non-contents, 19. Proxies being called for and read over, the contents were 75, the non-contents, 26. Total for the resolution 128, against 45.

A protest was immediately put on the journals. Amongst the reasons assigned were, " Because it does not proffer to this country any benefits of which she is not already in possession, or offer any remedy, for any of the evils, which it at present has reason to apprehend. Because, next to the protection of Divine Providence, we hold this country indebted for its preservation to the vigilance of its resident Parliament, and the loyalty of its resident gentry, the former of whom the proposed measure necessarily removes from the country, and the latter of whom it must powerfully operate to withdraw; and, above all, because we conceive that no scheme of national adjustment, can be honourable, satisfactory, or permanent, which is not considered with mature deliberation, presented by fair and temperate means, and founded on the uninfluenced sense of Parliament, no one of which essential requisites can we find in the present project."

It was signed by—

Leinster.	Charlemont.	Dillon.	Richard, Waterford
Downshire.	Kingston.	Strangford.	and Lismore.
Percy	Mountcashel.	Powerscourt.	Louth.
Meath.	Farnham.	De Vesci.	Lismore.
Granard.	Massey.	William, Down	Sunderlin.
Ludlow.	Enniskillen.	and Connor.	
Arran.	Kilmore.		

Lords Bellamont and Blayney also put the following pro-test upon the books of the House of Lords:—

" Dissentient,   Monday, February 10.

" Because we consider the measure of an Incorporate Legislative Union unadvisable: that it exceeds the lines of modification or innovation, leaving in existence no principle of our Imperial Constitution, as originally and fundamentally established, save only that of unity of executive of both kingdoms: that any compact, founded upon unity of executive alone, divested of the protection and control of a distinct inde-

pendent, internal legislature, would be *ipse facto* a radical
change, from a free-balanced constitution, to an absolute
Government of Ireland by the British Parliament; as the
relative situation of the respective kingdoms, in whatsoever
point of view considered, renders it impossible for Ireland
to derive any benefit from that species of representation, on
any scale of proportion which the objects and nature of the
Imperial Constitution of the United Kingdoms can admit of.
It is unnecessary to state that the Parliaments of the respective
kingdoms as they have stood, and as they do stand, are not
only fully competent to, but are the only constitutional
organ of any explanation or adjustment which may be found
necessary for ever effectually to remedy, or to prevent
misconceptions or misconstructions as to any point whatever.

" We therefore find ourselves called upon by our attach-
ment, duty, and allegiance to our most gracious Sovereign, by
the preservation and maintenance of the just rights and
liberties of our country, and by our affection and regard to
our sister kingdom in Union, by every loyal means to
oppose the destruction of a constitution, which, during the
period of more than 600 years, has withstood the shock of
every event, or the adoption of a system which, as it does in
no sort apply to the relative situation of either kingdom,
could not on its bearings, tendencies, operations, and consequences fail of destroying the inseparable joint interests of
both.

" BELLAMONT.
" BLAYNEY, (by Proxy.)"

On the 22nd March, the resolutions for the Union were
read, the first of which states " that in order *to promote and
secure the essential interests* of Great Britain and *Ireland*, and
to consolidate the strength, power, and resources of the British Empire, it will be advisable to concur in such measures
as may best tend to unite the two kingdoms of Great Britain
and Ireland into one kingdom," etc., etc. Then follow the
several resolutions, which were twenty-five in number.

On the 24th March, a petition was presented by the cotton
manufacturers, in which they say that they had thirteen
spinning mills and twenty-three printing grounds, on which
they had expended a large sum; that these manufactures
give support to not less than 50,000 persons. The petitioners state that the terms of the intended Union would be

fatal to the cotton manufactures of Ireland, and pray for relief.

On the 26th March, the resolutions were considered and amendments made. On the motion that the amended resolutions should pass, another division took place, but it was carried by 48 to 16.

A protest was again put upon the journals of the House, it says, (see Journals vol. viii. p. 385.)

1. " Because in the present awful state of affairs when the most unremitting industry is made use of to unhinge every established government in Europe when revolutionary principles have produced the overthrow of several ancient established governments, we think every loyal subject who regards the liberties of his country, called upon to rally round the constitution and to preserve its stability, and therefore we cannot help protesting against the rashness of the Minister, who, in such times hazards the experiment of annihilating that constitution which has for so many ages maintained the connection between Great Britain and Ireland, and of substituting in its stead in opposition to the general voice of the nation, a new system, totally subversive of every fundamental principle of that constitution, which we consider, as the best security for those liberties which the subjects of Ireland now enjoy."

2. " Because, however willing we now are, and always have been, to contribute in proportion to our means, to the support and defence of the empire, we hold it our bounden duty, before, that we shall irrevocably enter into any engagement, to take upon ourselves any particular proportion of the expences of the empire, to ascertain the probable amount of that proportion, and to enquire into the ability of Ireland, to discharge the same, and to examine whether such part be proportionate to the relative ability of the two nations, upon such inquiry we find :—

The expense of Great Britain in 1799 was		...	£32,000,000	
... Ireland	...	...	6,000,000	...
2-17ths of the proportion for Ireland	...	£4,400,000		
Present interest	...	...	1,400,000	
Interest on loan of this year	...	250,000		
	Total	£6,050,000		
Revenue	...	...	2,800,000	
Deficiency	...	..	£3,250,000	

As to the relative Ability.

Balance of Trade of Great Britain	...	...	...	£14,800,000
... Ireland	...	...	...	509,312

Proportion, 29 to 1.

Current Cash, Great Britain	...	...	...	43,000,950
Ireland	...	...	...	...	3,350,000

Proportion 12 to 1.

Cash remittances from the East and West Indies

to Great Britain	...	...	...	...	£4,000,000
To Ireland	...	...	...	...	509,312

Ireland remits to England.

To pay interest of Debt, etc.	...	...	£720,000
To pay 3,284 men for service in Great Britain	...	...	...	...	101,575

" Under these circumstances, it appears to us, that, if this kingdom should take upon herself irrevocably, the payment of 2-17ths of such expenses, she will not have the means to perform her engagement, unless by charging her landed property with 12s. to 13s. in the pound. It must end in drawing from her her last guinea, in totally annihilating her trade for want of capital, in rendering the taxes unproductive, and consequently in finally putting her into a state of bankruptcy. We think ourselves called upon to protest against a measure so ruinous to this country, and to place the responsibility for its consequences, upon such persons as have brought it forward and supported it."

" For these reasons, and believing the above statement to accurate, we thus record our dissent."

3. " For these and many other reasons, too tedious and too obvious to be here dwelt upon, we have deemed it our bounden duty, both to ourselves and to our descendants, thus publicly to declare our dissent from those resolutions, approving of the measure of a legislative Union, which have passed this house. Calling upon our latest posterity, to entreat that, in virtue of this our solemn declaration, they will acquit us of having been in any wise instrumental to their degradation and to the ruin of that country which they may hereafter inhabit.".

Leinster.	Arran.	Powerscourt.	Louth.
Downshire.	Charlemont.	De Vesci.	Massey.
Meath.	Mount Cashel.	William Down	Riversdale.
Granard.	Farnham.	& Connor.	Sunderlin.
Ludlow.	Dillon,	Richard Water-	
Moira.	Strangford.	ford & Lismore.	

May 10. The resolutions of the British House of Commons respecting the Union, were submitted to the House.

June 13. The motion was made that the bill be read the third time, and a division took place.

Present	for	41	against	14
Proxies		73		21
		———		——
		114		35

No less than three protests appear on the Journals, one is signed by the twenty noblemen whose names are given above; another by Lord Bellamont, and another by Lord Glandore,

The former complained that it degraded the Irish Peers and Commons. That the proposed Union was only nominal. That the adjustment of the number of representations was unfair and unequal. That the precedent set by Lord Somers in the Union with Scotland was not followed. That the purchase of Irish boroughs by ministers, was corrupt and unconstitutional. That the proportion of contribution to the taxation was unfair and inequitable, and would produce a gradual destruction of her capital, the decline of her trade, and the probable failure of her taxes. That it would increase the remittances to absentees, and the discontent of the people That it was a gross breach of trust, and a departure from the settlement of 1782. That it was carried by the most unconstitutional means it concludes .

" We enter our protest against the project of Union, against the Yoke it imposes, the Dishonour it inflicts, the disqualification passed upon the Peerage, the Stigma thereby branded on the realm, the disproportionate principle of Expense it introduces, the means employed to effect it, the Discontents it has excited, and must continue to excite : against all these and the fatal consequences they may produce, we have endeavoured to interpose our votes; and failing, we transmit to after times, our names, in solemn protest, on behalf of the Parliamentary constitution of this realm, the liberty which it secured, the trade which it protected, the connexion which it preserved, and the constitution which it supplied and fortified—this we feel ourselves called upon to do in support of our characters, our honour, and whatever is left to us, worthy to be transmitted to posterity."—*Journal of Lords*, vol. viii, p. 467.

I now turn to the BRITISH PARLIAMENT.

On the 2nd of April, the Duke of Portland delivered the following message from his Majesty to the House of Lords:—

"GEORGE, R.—It is with the most sincere satisfaction that his Majesty finds himself enabled to communicate to this house the joint address of his Lords and Commons of Ireland, laying before his Majesty certain resolutions, which contain the terms proposed by them for an entire Union between the two kingdoms. His Majesty therefore earnestly recommends to this House to take all such further steps as may best tend to the speedy and complete execution of a work so happily begun, and so interesting to the security of his Majesty's subjects, and to the general strength and prosperity of the British empire."

A debate ensued, in the course of which Lord Holland opposed the Union, he urged that the Union was not the remedy adequate to the occasion, nor were the good effects that might probably result from it forty or fifty years hence, (as the Parliament of Ireland were taught to expect a proportionate price,) to satisfy that country for the considerable advantages she was called upon to surrender at the present moment. To render the remedy applicable, as a compensation for the purpose in so great a bargain, present benefits, equal in value, ought to be immediately made over to Ireland. He therefore maintained that speculative ideas of distant advantages, were but visionary and delusive, when set in competition with invaluable rights, and the glory of independence. His lordship next adverted to the solemn assurance which his Majesty's Ministers had given in both houses, that, although, in their judgments, an Union of both countries was most desirable, yet, that it should not be accepted, unless it were the pure and spontaneous offer of the Parliament of Ireland, uninfluenced by corruption or menace. He would, however, appeal to the feelings of any individual, whether it was doubted that corruption and intimidation had been practised, to obtain a majority in support of a measure, in both Houses of the Irish Parliament. The prejudices of the Irish Protestants and the Catholics of Ireland had been played upon, and both one and the other had been taught to expect a full gratification of all their wishes, provided an Union took place.

Lord Caernarvon said, that in the present moment, Great Britain had a debt of four hundred and sixty millions, paying seventeen millions interest, and Ireland a debt of twenty-five millions; from which he contended that it was impossible to expect, under such circumstances, a complete Union of advantages and burthens should take place.

Earl Fitzwilliam said, nothing but a sense of duty could have induced him to oppose the measure, at the same time, that no man was more ready to admit, that a perfect and complete Union, was of all things most desirable to his mind; yet he felt himself bound to look at, and examine whether the articles proposed as the grounds of that Union, carried in them sentiments of unison, or whether they did not contain principles and seeds of disunion and separation. To form a real Union with Ireland, there ought to be a free and open participation of advantages of every description between the two countries. His lordship contended that this was not the case in the present instance. In the commercial article, there were innumerable clogs and shackles put upon the commerce of Ireland. In the financial article, the taxes and contributions of the people of Great Britain and Ireland are distinct and different in an essential degree. In the article of a legislative nature, a direct and violent infringement was made on the constitution of this country—an infringement attended with the greatest danger. His lordship said, there had been no satisfactory reason given as yet, why it was necessary to move the seat of legislature from Dublin to London. During the late unfortunate rebellion in Ireland, the Government, backed by the Parliament of Ireland, were able to suppress the rebellion; " why, then," said his lordship, " after such a recent proof of the advantages of a resident Parliament, was the kingdom of Ireland to be deprived of reaping again the same advantages, should any such occur?" After some observations of the same nature, his lordship concluded by signifying his dissent from the measure.

The Earl of Hillsborough reprobated the measure as fraught with every possible mischief to Ireland. In 1782, indeed, up to the year 1785, an Union would have been very desirable, but, from that time down to the present, her commerce and prosperity had increased so rapidly, that an Union was no longer necessary. Another objection to the measure was, it was directly against the sense of the Irish people; and no Union, if it really deserved that name, ought to be forced on any country against its will. He should, therefore, give it his decided negative.

In the House of Commons, on the 21st April, 1800, Mr. Pitt, in introducing the measure, said, that the great object was to communicate to Ireland a fair participation of the resources and prosperity of Great Britain, by transferring to it a share and just proportion of that capital and industry which, he said, had raised this nation to its present power and opulence. He said, it was a circumstance much to be wished, that the finances of both countries were so nearly alike that the system of both could be identified; but, as, from the different proportions of debt, and the different stages of civilization and commerce, and the different wealth of the countries, that desirable object was rendered impracticable, at least for some time to come, it therefore became an important question—would they defer the advantage of the Union, because they could not at once carry it to the extent they would wish? Or would they defer it until, by *the decrease of the debt of England*, through the means of the sinking fund, the two countries had so far approximated each other, that an identity of finance could be established in the first instance?

Mr. Sheridan said, that it appeared now to be fairly understood that, the Chancellor of the Exchequer had brought the question to this issue, that the measure of the Union should be persisted in, because it was courted and sanctioned by the general and independent assent of the Irish people; and that as this point was ascertained or disproved, the measure should be persevered in or abandoned. But where was the proof that the Union had that general approbation—that independent assent of the Irish nation? A number of addresses and declarations were mentioned as a proof; but where were those addresses? The addresses against were easy to be found. If the measure was to be carried thus, he had no hesitation in saying, that it was an act of tyranny and oppression, and must become the fatal source of new discontents and future rebellions.

Mr. Secretary Dundas said a few words in answer to what had been asserted, viz., that the measure was contrary to the consent of the Irish people; he urged:—

"If it be true," as insisted on by Mr. O'Connor, in his evidence, "that the people of England, according to their present form of government, have no cause of complaint, when compared with the state and suffering of the people of Ireland, then it consequently follows that a Union between the two nations, formed on principles of *common freedom and common interest*, will at once remove every cause of grievance on the part of the people of Ireland. *By the participation of the freedom of Britons—by the full enjoyment of all the privileges* attached to a member of such an honourable community, the Government of this country endeavours to destroy the hopes of the enemy, and to strengthen and consolidate the interests of the empire. If it be true, as generally acknowledged, that the poor of Ireland experience all the miseries concomitant to a state of want and wretchedness, then it follows that their participation of the privileges of Britons will rouse and animate to laudable exertion that useful description of our fellow-subjects in the sister kingdom—that liberty which awakened the commercial enterprise of Scotland—that liberty which expanded its genius in the most laudable pursuits—that liberty which confirmed every sentiment that can dignify human nature, will, sir, I am sure, have the same happy influence on the people of Ireland, connected with us by the dearest reciprocal obligations."

Mr. Tierney had no objection to the measure, if it could be proved that it was the choice of the Irish people. But, from the information he had received, he had not the smallest doubt but the sense of the Irish people was against the Union. But it was alleged, that the sense of the Irish Commons was in favour of the Union. Now, what was the fact? Why, the last year there were but 105 against the project of Union, whereas the minority this year amounted to 120 members. Was this a proof of the policy and justice of an Union?

Doctor Laurence moved, that after the words "twenty years," there should be inserted, "contributions to be payed by each nation, shall be imposed by its own representatives."

To remove the fears of those who urged that the Parliament of the United Kingdom might set aside the conditions of the Act of Union; and Legislate for Ireland, in a different spirit, the strongest arguments were used. Mr. Pitt, when urging these arguments, styled the treaty of Union, "a solemn and irrevocable compact."

Mr. Douglas, afterwards Lord Glenbervie, so well known to lawyers as the able writer of Douglass's Reports, and who was also a most distinguished statesman, was the lawyer principally put forward by the Government of Mr. Pitt to explain, in the British House of Commons, the legal import and consequences of the Union with Ireland. Upon the subject of

the limitation of the powers of the United Parliament, Mr.
Douglas is reported, in the 34th volume of the Parliamentary
History, p. 834, to have thus expressed himself in the House
of Commons:—

"In short, it appears to me that a common Parliament
such as was formed on the Scottish Union, and such as must
be in contemplation now, must have power of altering or repealing any of the former acts of either local legislature, i. e.
either English or Scotch, British or Irish; a power daily exercised in regard to English and Scotch, acts made previous to
1707; but that such common Parliament cannot legitimately
repeal or alter any of the fundamental and essential clauses,
articles, or conditions of that treaty, by which the Union shall
be constituted; since the treaty, authorised by each legislature, concluded by commissioners, and then again ratified
by each legislature, when carried into effect, will render it
impossible, upon any breach, for either party to resume its
former situation, and avail itself of the nullity thereby occa-
sioned, and, of course, impossible; consistently with moral
right and duty, for the united Parliament, i. e. beyond its
legitimate power to commit such a breach."

The manner in which the British Ministry carried the resolutions for the Union through the Irish Parliament, in defiance
of the known wishes of the Irish people, is thus described by
Mr. Grey, who was afterwards Earl Grey, and Prime Minister
of the United Kingdom ; speaking in 1800, he said :—

"Twenty-seven counties have petitioned against the measure (the Union). The petition from the county of Down is
signed by upwards of 17,000 respectable, independent men,
and all the others are in a similar proportion. Dublin petitioned under the Great Seal of the city, and each of the cor-
porations followed the example. Drogheda petitioned against
the Union, and almost every other town in the Kingdom, in
like manner, testified its disapprobation. Those in favour of
the measure possessing great influence in the country, obtained a few counter petitions ; yet, though the petition
from the county Down was signed by 17,000, the counter
petition was signed by only 415. Though there were 707,000
who had signed petitions against the measure, the total
number of those who declared themselves in favour of it, did
not exceed 3,000, and many of these only prayed that the
measure might be discussed. If the facts I state be true,
and I challenge any man to falsify them—could a nation in

more direct terms, express its disapprobation of a political measure, than Ireland has of the Legislative Union with Great Britain ? In fact, the nation is nearly unanimous, and this great majority is composed, not of fanatics, bigots, or Jacobins, but of the most respectable of every class in the country."

Mr. Grey further added :—

"If the Parliament of Ireland was left to itself—untempted, unawed, unintimidated—it would, without hesitation, have rejected the resolutions.   There are 300 members, in all, and 120 of these strenuously opposed the measure, amongst whom were two-thirds of the county members, the representatives of the city of Dublin, and almost all the towns which it is proposed shall send members to the Imperial Parliament. 162 voted in favour of the Union ; of those 116 were placemen, some of them were English generals on the staff, without a foot of ground in Ireland, and completely dependant upon Government. . . . . Let us reflect upon the arts which have been used since last sessions of the Irish Parliament to pack a majority in the House of Commons.   All persons holding offices under Government, even the most intimate friends of the Minister, if they hesitated to vote as directed, were stripped of their employments.   Even this step was found ineffectual, and other acts were had recourse to, which, though I cannot name in this place, all will easily conjecture. A bill framed for preserving the purity of Parliament was likewise abused ; and no less than 65 seats were vacated by their holders having received nominal offices."

On the 6th June, an address to the King was moved in the Irish House of Commons; it contained the following paragraph :—

" Finding the sense of the people, as well as the Parliament, to be against the Union, your Majesty's Ministers, (to quote the words of the document referred to,) attempted to change the Parliament itself; and refusing to take the sense of the nation by a general election, they procured a partial dissolution, and did so publicly abuse the disqualifying clause of the Place Bill, which was enacted for the express purpose of preserving the freedom and independence of Parliament, that by vacating seats under its authority, very many new returns were made to this house for the purpose of carrying it—and thus did they change the Parliament, without resorting to the people; that before the ministry had perverted the Place Bill, the sense of Parliament was against the Union, and if that bill had not been so perverted, that sense would have remained unaltered. That, of those who voted for the Union, we beg leave to inform your Majesty that 76 had places or pensions under the Crown; and others were under the immediate influence of constituents who held great offices under the Crown, that the practices of influence above mentioned were accompanied with the removal from office of various servants of the Crown, who had seats in Parliament, particularly, the Chancellor of the Exchequer, and the Prime Sergeant, three Commissioners of the Revenue, a Commissioner of Accounts, a Commissioner of Barracks, and the Cursitor of the Court of Chancery, because they would not vote away Parliament; also, by the withdrawing their confidence from others of your Majesty's faithful and able councellors for the same reason; that they procured or encouraged the purchase of seats in this house, to return members to vote for the Union; also the introduction of persons unconnected with the country to vote away her Parliament: that they have also attempted to prostitute the peerage, by promising to persons, not even commoners in Parliament, her sacred honours if they would come into the House and vote for the Union; and that finally they have annexed to their plan an artful device, whereby a million and a half of money is to be given to persons possessing returns, who are to receive said sum in the event of the Union, for the carrying of which to such an amount said persons are to be paid; and this nation is to make good the sale by which she is disinherited of her Parliament."

This address was voted for by 77 members, but the majority against it was 135.

Thus the Union was carried. I have not sought to describe it, by any quotations from those who related the facts, but have given the *ipsissima verba* of those who framed, and brought forward the resolutions of the Union, as well as the language of those who opposed it. It is quite evident that the Union was forced upon the Irish people against its wish, and had it not been for the unsparing use which was made of the means and influence of the British Government, it never would have been carried, but having been so carried, there is the greater reason why it should be observed in its integrity.

Mr. John Claudius Beresford, a man of prominent station, who had occupied a high post as financial minister, moved in the Irish House of Commons, that the proportion for Ireland

shewed 2-20ths or 1-10th, but this resolution was lost. A letter from the Marquis Cornwallis to the Duke of Portland, (see
correspondence, p. 199), says "Mr. Plunket, entered into a
detail of the reasons which led him and his friends to object
to amending the resolutions, (on which the Act of Union was
to be founded,) and confine their opposition to the principle."

Even its conditions were hardly discussed. The majority
which voted for the principle of the measure was so great,
that it carried the details, without alteration. There seemed
no use in remonstrating, as to the proportion which was to be
paid by Ireland, when the Minister had his purchased sup-
porters to carry his conditions. This is the more striking
when we find that Mr. Pitt, with the knowledge, that
the Irish Parliament, had refused even to consider the Union,
determined on hurrying forward his resolutions, and placing
them upon the records of the British Houses of Parliament,
and having done so, he used all the influences at his command to carry them through the Irish Parliament; the arrangement loses all the semblance of a bargain, or even of a
contract, the terms of the British Minister were forced upon
the Irish people, but this forms, the stronger ground for
requiring a strict and literal fulfilment, of the offer so made
and forced upon Ireland.

The lawyers in the British Parliament, and the advisers
of the Crown, must have known the decisions in the British
courts of law, with reference to such an act as that which they
were promoting. The British act, was as much the death-
warrant of the British Parliament, as the Irish act was that
of the Irish Parliament. The Parliament of the United Kingdom was the offspring of these acts. The English lawyers
must have known that the treaty of Union would be governed
by the decisions of the English courts of law, which are defined in the work from which I have previously quoted in the
following language:—

"The law of nations, which declares the legislature incompetent to repeal a fundamental law, is a portion of the
common law of England. This was decided in the case of
Triguet a. Bath, Burrow's Reports, 1478. "In that case Lord
Mansfield recognised and confirmed the decision of Lord
Talbot, in the case, of Buvot a. Barbut, ' that the law of nations
in its fullest extent, was part of the law of England,' and
declared that the law of nations was to be collected from the
practice of different nations, and the works of writers of estab-

lished reputation, such as Grotius, Barbeyrac, &c. Lord Mansfield, in this case, also cited the authority of Lords Hardwicke and Chief Justice Holt, in confirmation of this decision."

" Lord Mansfield's decision, in the case of Triquet a. Bath, has been sustained by every decision made since it. The Court of Queen's Bench, in the case of Viveach a. Beecher, 3 Maule and Selwyn's Reports, p. 289, seems to have even extended the rule. In that last case, Lord Ellenborough, expressing the unanimous decision of the court, used the following words: " If we clearly saw that the law of nations was in favour of the privilege sought, it would be afforded to the defendant ; *and it would be our duty rather to extend than to narrow it.*"

" The rules for the construction of statutes laid down by the Barons of the Exchequer, in Heydon's case, 3 Coke's Reports, p. 7, aid powerfully in detecting the falsehood of the limited exposition attempted to be given to the covenant securing the rights of the Irish people."

" For the sure and true interpretation (say the Barons in this case,) of all statutes in general, be they penal or beneficial, restrictive or enlarging of the common law, four things are to be discerned and considered. First, what was the common law before the making of the act ? Second, what was the mischief and defect against which the common law did not provide ? Third, what remedy the Parliament hath resolved and appointed to cure the disease of the commonwealth ? And, Fourth, the true reason of the remedy."

" It was then held to be the duty of the judges at all times to make such construction as should suppress the mischief and advance the remedy, putting down all subtle inventions and evasions for continuance of the mischief, *et pro privato commodo*, and adding force and life to the cure and remedy, according to the true intent of the makers of the act *pro bono publico.*"

I have briefly related the history of the debates in the Houses of Parliament in both kingdoms, on the resolutions which preceded the adoption of the articles which were embodied in the treaty of Union, I shall next proceed to examine the treaty, as recited in the act of the Irish Parliament, and try to explain the obvious import of its several clauses.

The advantage of its Parliament to Ireland was thus stated by Henry Grattan, in one of his speeches:—

" I do not mean to approve all the Parliaments that have

sat in Ireland. I left the former because I condemned its proceedings. But I argue not, like the Minister, from the misconduct of one Parliament against the being of Parliament itself. I value the parliamentary constitution, by the average of its benefits; and I affirm that the blessings procured by the Irish Parliament in the last twenty years, are greater than all the blessings afforded by the British Parliament in Ireland for the last century; greater even than the mischiefs inflicted upon Ireland, by the British Parliament; greater than all the blessings procured by those Parliaments, for their own country within that period. Within that time the legislature of England lost an empire, and the legislature of Ireland recovered a constitution.

LETTER V.

THE TREATY OF UNION.

HAVING described the condition of Ireland previous to the Union, and stated the manner in which that measure was carried, I am naturally led to consider the expressions of the treaty itself. I am forced to look at them, as far as possible, in the light in which they appeared to those who framed, and those who assented to them, but we now have a further light, in the manner in which they were acted upon. I cannot bring myself to charge those who framed and brought forward the Treaty, with an intention to defraud Ireland, because I see that they admitted the stipulation, that if Ireland would lay down her sovereign rights, as an independent state, she should be secured, and guaranteed *for ever*, in the enjoyment of certain privileges and immunities. I see that these privileges and immunities are not now in existence; that they have been filched away from us; that this land, which was comparatively free from debt, when it joined Great Britain, is now stated to be overwhelmed with it; that Ireland, which, previously to the Union, was much more lightly taxed than Great Britain, is now more heavily taxed. I see that this is done contrary to, and in defiance of the Act of Union; and I am, therefore, compelled to examine that act for a solution of this anomaly.

G

The Treaty of Union consists of eight articles. The preamble, which I have given in the first letter, page 25, recites the object which Parliament had in view at the Union, and we ought, in order to ascertain how that object was carried out, to have this object constantly before us ; it was " to promote and secure the *essential interests* of Great Britain and *Ireland*."

The 1st article relates to the perpetual Union of Great Britain and Ireland.

The 2nd to the succession of the Crown.

The 3rd to the title of the new Parliament

The 4th the number of representatives in the Houses of Peers and of Commons.

The 5th to the Church.

The 6th to the privileges of the Subjects of each country.

The 7th to the Financial arrangements.

The 8th to the courts of Justice.

My argument relates mainly to the financial arrangements, which are defined in the seventh article of the Treaty. I extract it in full. It consists of ten paragraphs, and as it will be convenient to refer to each of them, I shall number them, but the numbers do not appear in the Act of Union; they are used for convenience in reference.

" I. That it be the seventh article of Union ; that the charge, arising from the payment of the interest and the sinking fund for the reduction of the principal of the debt incurred in either kingdom before the Union, shall continue to be separately defrayed by Great Britain and Ireland respectively, except as in hereinafter provided."

It is to be noticed that it was only the interest and sinking fund of the debt incurred *before the Union*, which was to be separately defrayed—not the debt contracted after the Union. Indeed, the whole tenor of this article of the treaty shews that the intention of the two Parliaments was, that Ireland should not, under any circumstances, be called upon to contribute towards the interest of the British debt contracted before the Union. When Mr. Pitt, brought forward the resolutions, January 31st, 1799, one of them was, " that the interest or sinking fund for the reduction of the principal of the debt, incurred in either kingdom before the Union, shall continue to be separately defrayed by Great Britain and Ireland respectively;" and to this he induced the British House of Commons to pledge itself, though, at the time, he knew the Irish Houses of Parliament refused even to consider

the question of an Union. When Lord Castlereagh brought
the subject on in the Irish House of Commons, February 5th,
1800, he said:—

" In respect to *past expenses,* Ireland was to have no concern
whatever with the debt of Great Britain; but the two countries were to unite as to future expenses on a *strict measure
of relative ability.*"

Nothing could be more explicit than this language, which
explains the paragraph under consideration. On the 17th
February, 1800, Lord Castlereagh returned to the subject, and
endeavoured to clear away any doubts about it; he then said:

" The enemies of the measure of Union have founded much
of their clamour upon the groundless supposition, that it is a
mere financial project of the British Minister to put his hands
into the pockets of the Irish people. But, sir, I believe it
will be found, upon examination of the terms, that if any
sacrifice be made, it will not be on the part of Ireland, but
on the part of Great Britain. The settlement which is
offered is that of advantage to Ireland, but it is offered not
as a bribe, not upon the mercenary principle, that Ireland
would sacrifice what is essential to her happiness, to any
pecuniary consideration, but it is offered on the fair and
liberal ground of equal contributions."

I think it is evident that the just construction to be put
upon this article is this :—The separate debts of each kingdom, previous to the Union, were to close on the 31st
December, 1800; that no additions were, under any circumstances, to be made to these separate debts; and that the
interest and charges arising out of them was to be borne
exclusively by each country.

" II. That for the space of twenty years, after the Union shall take place,
the contribution of Great Britain and Ireland respectively, towards the
expenditure of the United Kingdom, in each year, shall be defrayed in
the proportion of fifteen parts for Great Britain and two for Ireland ; that
at the expiration of the said twenty years, the future expenditure of the
United Kingdom (other than the interest and charges of the debt to
which either country shall be separately liable) shall be defrayed in such
proportion as the Parliament of the United Kingdom shall deem just and
reasonable, upon a comparison of the real value of the exports and imports
of the respective countries, upon an average of the three years next preceding the period of revision, or on a comparison of the value of the
quantities of the following articles consumed, within the respective countries, on a similar average, viz.—beer, spirits, sugar, wine, tea, tobacco, and
malt ; or according to the aggregate proportion resulting from both these
considerations combined, or on a comparison of the amount of income in

each country, estimated from the produce of the same period of a general tax, if such shall have been imposed on the same descriptions of income in both countries. And that the Parliament of the United Kingdom shall afterwards proceed in like manner to raise and fix the said proportions, according to the same rules or any of them at periods not more distant than twenty years, nor less than seven years from each other, unless previous to any such period the Parliament of the United Kingdom shall have declared, as hereinafter provided, that the expenditure of the United Kingdom shall be defrayed indiscriminately by equal taxes imposed on the like in both countries."

When Mr. PITT was questioned, on the 12th February, 1799, as to the exact taxation of each country, he replied, " that the proportion which Ireland ought to pay would not be greater than that which she now paid." This was before the propositions were submitted to the Irish Parliament. On the 21st May, when he moved that the house should go into committee on the resolutions, he urged that, " the great object was to communicate to Ireland a fair participation in the resources and prosperity of Great Britain, by transferring to it a share and just proportion of that capital and industry which had raised England to its present power and opulence;" and, with reference to the seventh article, " which," he said " related to apportioning the shares of the revenue of each country respectively. It was a circumstance much to be wished that the finances of both countries were so nearly alike that the system of both could be identified ; but, from the different proportions of debt, and the different stages of civilization and commerce, and the different wealth of the countries, that desirable object was rendered impracticable, at least for some time to come."

The data which was furnished to the Irish House of Commons, by Lord Castlereagh, for arriving at this proportion of 2-17ths was as follows. I quote from his speech of 5th February, 1800 :—

" Taking the exports and imports for the last three years, those of Ireland would be found to be £10,925,000 and of Great Britain £73,961,000; that is, the proportion of 7 to 1. The next proportion was to be found in the excised articles of consumption, such as malt, beer, spirits, wine, tea, and tobacco. The average of these for the last three years has been, Ireland, £5,954,000; Great Britain, £46,891,000, being in the proportion of $7\frac{7}{8}$ to 1. These two proportions come so close, he would take $7\frac{1}{2}$ to 1, as the just ratio of the ability of Great Britain to that of Ireland."

Mr. Foster, who spoke after Lord Castlereagh, furnished different data, and urged that, the proportion should have been 10 to 1. Extracts from his speech are given in pp. 62, 63.

The protest of the House of Lords adopts a still lower scale, and makes the proportion 18 to 1, it adopts as data a comparison of the balance of Trade of Great Britain and Ireland, which was as 29 to 1, the current Cash of both countries which was as 12 to 1, and the permanent Taxes, which were as 12 to 1, and adopts the mean 18 to 1, as the proportion which Ireland should pay; experience has shewn that the proportion adopted by Lord Castlereagh, and forced upon the Irish Parliament was excessive in the extreme.

Lord Castlereagh, in his speech introducing the Union, made the statement given in p. 59.

It was admitted, previously to the Union, that Ireland was entitled to a payment similar to that given to Scotland, if Ireland became liable to the British debt of £457,000,000 due before the Union. She has never received any such compensation, though, from the system of accounts adopted, she has been made liable to that debt. It was estimated by Mr. Pitt and Lord Castlereagh that the amount which Ireland should have received would have been so great that Great Britain could not have paid it; and it will be shewn that the mode by which the Irish debt was nominally run up, was by increasing it at compound interest, under which the capital sum doubles in fourteen years. Were the amount which Ireland should have received in 1800 only £11,000,000, (which would have been about the sum she should have been paid in comparison with to Scotland,) it would have been of vast service to her, indeed it is difficult to estimate the advantage which it would have been to Ireland, to have had the interest on such a sum as £11,000,000, devoted year by year to local improvements. Had it accumulated at compound interest, it would have grown at the following rate :

1800, Value of compensation to Ireland for taking her share of the British debt			...	£11,000,000
1814 At compound interest would be			...	22,000,000
1828	,,	,,	,,	... 44,000,000
1842	,,	,,	,,	... 88,000,000
1856	,,	,,	,,	... 176,000,000
1870	,,	,,	,,	... 352,000,000

It was by the accumulations at compound interest, that the

Irish debt was made to appear so great in 1817; but of that I shall treat farther on.

It will be observed that the fixed proportion 2-17ths, was, as I have stated, strongly objected to, and formed the subject of protest in the Irish House of Lords, this proportion was only fixed for twenty years. The relative amount would in due course have been altered in 1821; but in 1816, under the pretence " of further carrying into effect the provisions and purposes of the two several acts for the Union of Great Britain and Ireland," an act—the 56 Geo. III., cap. 98— was passed, nominally for the object of relieving Ireland, but really for the purpose of doing away with the protection given in the above condition. I shall hereafter have to speak of this act, but I think there can be no doubt as to the con- struction of this paragraph of the treaty.

If there was any doubt, it should have been removed by the speech of Mr. Pitt, who, on proposing, the first Budget brought forward after the Union, in 1801, when the provi- sions were fresh in every one's mind, stated, (see the Annual Register, 1801, page 33,) that the total supplies were £35,587,462; of this sum, said he, " the part to be borne by Great Britain was fifteen-seventeenths, which amounted to a sum of £31,400,702 and 2-17ths by Ireland, or £4,186,760. The permanent charges of the civil list, and other charges of the consolidated fund, not relating to the public debt, was to be allotted in its due proportion. This sum amounted to £1,170,000. Of course, the sum which would fall upon Ire- land, being 2-17ths of that sum, would be £137,000. *What- ever else remained, with the exception of the National Debt of Ireland, was to be provided for by Great Britain.*"

This statement from the author of the Act of Union re- moves any doubt as to the construction of the treaty.

I now pass to the consideration of the next paragraph.

" III. That for defraying the said expenditure, according to the rules laid down, the revenues of Ireland shall hereafter constitute a consolidated fund, which shall be charged in the first instance with the interest of the debt of Ireland, and with the sinking fund applicable to the reduction of the said debt, and the remainder shall be applied towards defraying the proportion to the United Kingdom to which Ireland may be liable in each year."

The position in which Great Britain and Ireland stood at the time the treaty was under consideration was this,—Great Britain owed, £457,188,655, which was charged solely on the land and property of Great Britain; Ireland owed, in 1800, (according to the return of 1858,) £13,703,615, (or according to the return of 1819,) £23,100,785, charged solely on the property of Ireland. The public creditor was secured, by having his rights preserved as the primary charge on the property mortgaged to him. The interest and sinking fund for the *debt due previous to the Union* was made the first charge upon the revenue of each country. The balance of the revenue of Ireland was to be applied towards defraying the proportion to which Ireland should become liable each year.

" IV. That the proportion of contribution to which Great Britain and Ireland will be liable, shall be raised by such taxes in each country respectively, as the Parliament of the United Kingdom shall from time to time deem fit, provided always that in regulating the taxes in each country, by which their respective proportions shall be levied, no article in Ireland shall be made liable to any new or additional duty by which the whole amount of duty payable thereon would exceed the amount which will hereafter be payable in England on the like article."

This paragraph was framed to protect Ireland from undue taxation. No article to be taxed higher in Ireland than it paid in England, and if the Irish revenue fell short of the proportion, the balance would be supplied by England, except (as provided in the next paragraph,) there was a surplus in the Irish revenue, when it might be applied to clear off the deficiency. The previous paragraph says, the balance, after paying the interest on the debt of Ireland, should be applied towards defraying the Irish proportion of the expenditure of the United Kingdom. This paragraph was designed to prevent excessive taxation in Ireland. It must be borne in mind that the separate debt-account of each country closed at the Union, and the public creditor got a well-defined position. This paragraph does not make any deficiency in the Irish proportion, *a debt*, nor does it say that the interest on any such debt was a separate charge, but it protects Ireland from undue taxation.

" V. That if at the end of any year any surplus shall accrue from the revenues of Ireland, after defraying the interest, sinking fund, and proportional contribution, and separate charges to which the said country shall then be liable, taxes shall be taken off to the amount of such surplus, or the surplus shall be applied by the Parliament of the United Kingdom to local purposes in Ireland, or to make good any deficiency which may arise in the revenues of Ireland in time of peace, or shall be invested by the Commissioners of the National Debt of Ireland in the funds, to accumulate for the benefit of Ireland at compound interest, in case of the contribution of Ireland in time of war; provided that the surplus so to accumulate shall at no future time be suffered to exceed the sum of five millions."

With reference to this paragraph, Lord Castlereagh thus spoke—"The next provision would be, that any surplus which should remain of this Consolidated Fund might be applied to local purposes of improvement, or to accumulate to form a fund for war contributions." But the British Parliament took good care there should be no surplus, by arbitrarily violating the first paragraph, and charging the separate debt of Ireland with an undue and excessive proportion of the joint debt of both countries.

"VI. That all moneys to be raised after the Union, by loan, in peace or war, for the service of the United Kingdom, by the Parliament thereof, shall be considered to be a joint debt, and the charges thereof shall be borne by the respective countries in the proportions of their respective contributions; provided, that if at any time, in raising their respective contributions, hereby fixed for each country, the Parliament of the United Kingdom shall judge it fit to raise a greater proportion of such respective contributions in one country, within the year, than in the other, or to set apart a greater proportion of sinking fund for the liquidation of the whole, or any part of the loan raised on account of the one country than of that raised on account of the other country, then such part of the said loan, for the liquidation of which provisions shall have been made for the respective countries, shall be kept distinct, and shall be borne by each separately; and only that part of the said loan be deemed joint and common, for the reduction of which the respective countries shall have made provision in the proportion of their respective contributions."

This paragraph raises very important considerations; the previous ones treat of the separate debts—that is, the debts due by each country previous to the Union, as things in existence. This treats of a new debt, which might be brought into being. The debts in existence were: 1st. That of Great Britain, for which the property of Great Britain was security; and 2nd. The debt of Ireland, for which the property of Ireland was the security. This section deals with a new debt, i. e., the debt of the United Kingdom, which was to be a joint debt, and for it the property of *both* countries (though subject to the former mortgages) was liable. This joint debt was not capable of division; the interest or charge for it was a joint charge, to be defrayed like the other expenses of the United Kingdom out of the common purse. In other words, it was " to be borne by the respective countries in the propor tion of their respective contributions." There is a provision for either country increasing its annual contribution to meet special loans for its own special purposes—or for liquidating its separate debt. The statesmen of that time had an idea that the national debt could be paid off; and Lord Castlereagh appears to have expected that Great Britain would have gone on for years, raising by special taxes about £10,000,000 a year, and applying it to the reduction of the separate debt. Thus, in his speech in 1799—

His lordship stated the " difference between the situation of Great Britain and Ireland, which required some consideration. Great Britain raised a great proportion of her war expenses within the year. This island had not the ability to do so, the consequence of which was that Ireland must, if she continued separate, get into debt much faster than Great Britain." The obvious inference is, that if the Union took place, all future debt would be a joint debt, the separate debt of Ireland would not increase at all, though she would be liable to a portion of the charge on the joint debt.

When discussing the question, in 1800, Lord Castlereagh made the following statement :—

> " The expenses of Great Britain for 1799 £32,700,000
>   "   Ireland   ...   5,439,000
> Had this been borne in the proportion of $7\frac{1}{2}$ to 1,
> the expenditure would have been, Great Britain, 33,695,100
>   "   Ireland, 4,492,686
> Ireland would consequently have saved   947,314"

When this is compared with the first post-Union budget, the difference is apparent. Mr. Pitt, in his budget, states the case very fairly, but Mr. Corry, the Chancellor of the Irish Exchequer, abandoned Mr. Pitt's principles, and placed the Irish charges on a very unfavourable basis. In March, 1801, Mr. Pitt submitted his budget; he stated (see annual Register 1801, page 33) that the total supplies were £35,587,462; of this sum, said he, " the part to be borne by Great Britain was $\frac{15}{17}$, which amounted to a sum of £31,400,702 and $\frac{2}{17}$ by Ireland, or £4,186,760. The permanent charges of the civil list, and other charges of the consolidated fund, not relating to the public debt, were to be allotted in its due proportion. This sum amounted to £1,170,000. Of course, the sum which would fall upon Ireland, being $\frac{2}{17}$ of that sum, would be £137,000. *Whatever*

*else remained, with the exception of the National Debt of
Ireland, was to be provided for by Great Britain."* When
the Irish budget was brought forward by Mr. Corry, on the
31st March, he stated (see Annual Register, page 41,) that the
debt of Ireland was £36,000,000, though, on the 1st January,
it was only £27,792,975. It seems to have wonderfully increased in the interval—two months! Mr. Corry* then states
the interest at £1,696,000, whereas the return quoted makes
it £1,157,064, the increase being more than £500,000. He
adds—" The proportion of the sinking fund for Ireland, to
the debt of that country, was 1 in 70, whereas in England it
was 1 in 230," thus increasing the charge on Ireland for this
item three-fold. He then goes on to say—" The next charge
of Ireland was the sum of £622,000 for the compensation of
the boroughs, which was all that was thought desirable to
raise in one year. These sums made together something
more than £2,400,000, which formed the separate charge
which was to be provided for by Ireland. The other part of
the joint charge, which was for civil purposes, amounted to
above £600,000, making together something more than
£4,700,000, exclusive of £300,000 for the vote of credit.
This, added to the sum which he stated as necessary for the
separate charge of Ireland, would make the supplies necessary
for that country £7,100,000" (though Lord Castlereagh had
estimated them at £4,492,680). He then states in detail
the probable funds to meet it; they make £5,247,000, and he
deducts from it two sums—" one £230,000 for the loyalists,

---

* The account is so very differently given by Mr. Pitt and Mr. Corry
that I give each :—

MR. PITT.		MR. CORRY.	
2-17ths. Army, Navy, &c.,	£4,186,760	2-17ths. Army, Navy, &c.,	£4,186,760
2-17ths. Civil Expenses,	137,000	2-17ths. Civil Expenses,	600,000
		Compensation Boroughs,	622,000
		Inland Navigation,	100,000
		Loyalists,	230,000
		Army in England,	70,000
	4,323,760	Total	5,808,760
Interest on National Debt,	1,157,064	Interest on National Debt,	1,696,000
	£5,470,834		£7,504,760

in order to enable them to rebuild their houses, &c., and £70,000 to pay the Irish garrisons in England;" but he adds—"the ways and means being therefore unequal to the supply of the year, it became necessary to borrow the sum of £2,500,000." The return of 1849, shews that the debt of Ireland was increased that year by £4,433,337, that is, nearly £2,000,000 more than Mr. Corry stated was necessary.

Mr. Pitt's statement does not exceed Lord Castlereagh's estimate of the Irish proportion, but Mr. Corry makes an enormous debt against Ireland.

The Ways and Means acknowledged by Mr. Corry were £5,247,000, and in this he only estimates the revenue at £2,600,000, though it yielded £2,931,680. Mr. Pitt distinctly said that the charge on Ireland was confined to the three items which I have given above, and which amount to £5,470,834, while the income, including balances, was stated to be £5,247,000, so that, according to Mr. Pitt's statement, the income of Ireland that year was nearly equal to the charge. Mr. Corry persuaded Parliament that it was necessary to borrow £2,500,000 on Irish account! but the sum raised and charged to her was £4,433,337!! These errors run through the whole accounts after the Union; thus, in 1802, the portion of the general expenditure for Great Britain (see page 101 of Annual Register,) was £24,184,237, and for Ireland £3,815,763, adding the interest on the debt due before the Union by Ireland—£1,157,064—the total charge would be £5,009,769. The revenue of Ireland in 1802 was £4,337,269, so that the deficiency was only £644,458, and yet £4,273,311 was raised on Irish account in that year. I have introduced this history of the earlier Budgets, to illustrate the section under consideration. There can, however, be no doubt as to the intention of the Irish Parliament, it was stated in Lord Castlereagh's speech of 5th February, 1800, his lordship said:

" By the salutary operation of the sinking fund, it was not impossible that at some period not very remote, Great Britain should liquidate so much of her debt as to descend in point of debt to nearly her proportion with respect to Ireland. And if this should ever occur, it would be right to leave to the United Parliament a power of fixing the same scale of reduced taxation for the United Kingdom."

As far as is shewn by the accounts, which were presented by the Chancellors of the Exchequer to Parliament, there never

was such a thing (until after the consolidation of the Exchequers, which took place in 1816, under the next paragraph
of this article) as a *joint* debt. The Parliament of the United
Kingdom, contrary to the letter and spirit of these articles,
kept the separate debt accounts open—whereas they should
have been closed—and charged to each country such amounts
as it chose, and even after Parliament authorized sums to be
raised for the Irish account, the amount raised and charged
to Ireland, was far in excess of these sums.*

I shall hereafter point out, not only the amount which should
have been charged, but also shew the sums which were improperly charged. I am at present dealing with the true tenor
of the paragraph under consideration, and I think the plain
and obvious meaning of it is, that all moneys raised after the
Union, by loan, in peace or war, were to be considered a *joint
debt*, the contributions for the charges of which, were to be
borne by the respective countries in the proportion of their respective contributions. Therefore, to treat any debt contracted
after the Union, as a separate debt, was a violation of this condition and a breach of the treaty; and as the next paragraph
was founded upon this, and a sequence from it, we must give
due weight to the important provisions it contains.

"VII. That, if at any future day, the separate debt of each country
respectively shall have been liquidated, or if the values of their respective
debts (estimated according to the amount of the interest and annuities
attending the same, and of the sinking fund applicable to the reduction
thereof, and to the period within which the whole capital of such debt shall

* The loans required by the Budget, and the amount raised was as
follows :—

Loan required as per Budgets.				Irish Debt Created per Return of 1849.
1801	£2,500,000	„	„	„	£4,433,337
1802	1,660,000	„	„	„	4,273,311
1803	3,160,000	„	„	„	3,210,524
1804	1,404,000	„	„	„	9,486,490
1805	3,708,000	„	„	„	4,660,000
1806	2,000,000	„	„	„	5,886,153
1807	not stated				5,470,548
1808	not stated				5,042,837
1809	4,500,000	„	„	„	4,984,615
1810	5,849,000	„	„	„	7,585,971
1811	not stated				2,770,154
1812	6,250,000	„	„	„	9,329,538
1813	8,500,000	„	„	„	12,415,385
1814	8,958,338	„	„	„	10,687,454
1815	9,000,000	„	„	„	16,517,385

appear to be redeemable by such sinking fund,) shall be to each other in the same proportion with the respective contributions of each country respectively ; or, if the amount by which the value of the larger of such debts shall vary from such proportion shall not exceed one-hundredth part of the said value, and if it shall appear to the Parliament of the United Kingdom that the respective circumstances of the two countries will thenceforth admit of their contributing indiscriminately, by equal taxes imposed on the same articles in each, to the future expenditure of the entire kingdom, it shall be competent to the Parliament of the United Kingdom to declare that all future expenses thenceforth to be incurred, together with the interest and charges of all joint debts contracted previous to such declaration, shall be defrayed indiscriminately by equal taxes imposed on the same articles in each country, and thenceforth from time to time, as circumstances may require, to impose and apply such taxes accordingly, subject only to such particular exemptions or abatements in Ireland, and in that part of Great Britain called Scotland, as circumstances may appear from time to time to demand."

In this paragraph a new element is introduced—that is, the right or power, or, as it was defined in the report of the Finance Committee of 1815, " the competence" which was given to the Parliament of the United Kingdom, under a certain contingency to adopt a system of uniform taxation for each country—in considering it, we must bear in mind the solemn and oft-repeated promise, that Ireland should in no event, be called upon to bear any portion of the charge for the debt contracted by Great Britain previously to the Union. This was the language of Pitt and Castlereagh ; this was the condition stated in the preamble to the Bill ; this is the true intent and tenor of the previous paragraphs. In reference to this paragraph, I find that on the 17th February, 1800, Lord Castlereagh spoke as follows :—

" I shall obviate the impression which may be made, that common taxes with Great Britain, will impose upon this kingdom heavier burdens than she would otherwise be called upon to support. Let the house, then, first consider that the charges of the debt of Great Britain amount to £20,000,000 a year, and the charges of the debt of Ireland to £1,300,000 British a year. That common taxes are not to take place till either the past and separate debt, of both countries shall be liquidated, or until they shall become to each other in the ratio of fifteen to two. Before this can take place, the taxes of Great Britain must be reduced by the amount of £10,000,000 a year, in which case the scale of her remaining taxation would be levelled to the scale of taxation in England, and the adoption of British taxation would become a benefit. A similar result, and to a greater degree, would take place were the past debt of the two countries, to be entirely liquidated."

The section deals with two contingencies. The first was that if, by the liquidation by Great Britain of such a portion, of the debt, which she owed previously to the Union, as would have brought it to bear the same proportion to the Irish debt as the respective contributions, then a consolidation might take place. The debt of Great Britain in 1800 was £457,000,000, and the debt of Ireland £13,000,000, (according to the returns of 1858,) and £23,100,785, (according to that of 1819,) consequently they were in the proportion of 35 to 1. The contributions of the respective countries were in the proportion of 7½ to 1, so that it would, in order to have availed of this section of the treaty, have been necessary for Great Britain to have raised by taxation a sum of £350,000,000, and thus, have reduced her separate debt by one account; or £200,000,000 by the other account; it would have borne to the separate debt of Ireland the proportion of 7½ to 1, and then it would have been legal to have availed of this clause of the treaty ; but Ireland would have the advantage of joining Great Britain upon equal terms. It is almost needless to say that Great Britain never tried to liquidate her debt, wholly or in part, so as to enable her fairly and legitimately to take advantage of this section.

There is a second condition in this paragraph ; it is to this effect, " that if the British debt was not so fully liquidated as we have stated, but that it was reduced so much that it did not vary from said proportion, by the one-hundredth part, and that it shall appear to the Parliament of the United Kingdom that the respective circumstances of the two countries will thenceforth admit of their contributing indiscriminately, by equal taxes imposed on the same articles in each, to the future expenditure of the entire kingdom, it shall be competent to the Parliament of the United Kingdom to declare that all future expenses, thenceforth to be incurred, together with the interest and charges of all *joint debts* contracted previous to such declaration, shall be defrayed indiscriminately by equal taxes imposed on the same articles in each country."

It will be seen that the second contingency only deals with the *joint debt* of both countries, it leaves the separate debts to be dealt with separately ; and the only condition upon which the *separate debts* could have been consolidated was, the payment by Great Britain of the portion which was in excess of the contribution of each country ; but it is more curious to note, that the declaration required by this section, never was made.

The Parliament of the United Kingdom have not, even to the present time, levied the same taxes indiscriminately in both kingdoms. It is very true, that since 1853, Parliament has, by piece-meal legislation, sought to annul and abrogate the Treaty of Union, under which Great Britain should raise £17,800,000 per annum to pay the interest of her own debt contracted previously to the Union ; whereas, since Mr. Gladstone come into office, she has avoided this, and only pays about £3,140,000 towards this sum. Thus acting most unfairly towards Ireland, and asking her to bear a portion of the charge of that debt, to which she was not, and is not liable, in the most wanton disregard of this solemn treaty, which the Parliament of the United Kingdom is bound faithfully to " observe, perform, fulfil, and keep ;" and which every candid and impartial person must see, has been shamefully disregarded and broken. I am aware that additions have been made, since the Union, to the separate debt of Ireland, but I say, it was contrary to the Act of Union. I am aware that in making these additions to the separate debt, Ireland was wrongfully charged with more than the portion which she was bound to contribute; and having thus, by error and wrong, brought up the nominal debt of Ireland to the desired scale, an act was passed, nominally for the purpose of giving further effect to the Treaty of Union, but really to defeat its provisions. The obvious answer to both these arguments is this :—The Parliament of the United Kingdom had no legal power to make any addition to the separate debt either of Great Britain or Ireland. These debts closed with the Union, and all future debts were *joint debts*. It may be further alleged, that as Ireland was unfairly charged with a greater portion of the joint debt, than she was liable to, any legislation on that miscalculation must be null and void. The state could not first do a wrong, and then justify legislation founded upon that wrong; because, if the calculation was in error, and if the preceding condition was not arrived at, then the legislation based on it must be vicious, and as such, altogether invalid.

" VIII. That, from the period of such declaration, it shall no longer be necessary to regulate the contributions of the two countries towards the future expenditure of the United Kingdom, according to any specific

proportion, or according to any of the rules hereinbefore prescribed, provided, nevertheless, that the interest or charges which may remain on
account of any part of the separate debt with which either country sh all
be chargeable, and which shall not be liquidated or consolidated proportionably as above, shall, until extinguished, continue to be defrayed by
separate taxes in each country."

This section bears out the view which I have so fully tried
to elucidate in my remarks on the previous one, and shews that
nothing could absolve Great Britain from the liability to pay in
perpetuity, the interest on the ante-Union debt, but the payment of such a portion of the capital, as would have reduced
the debt due previous to the Union, so as to bear to that of Ireland the proportion of $7\frac{1}{2}$ to 1, or by paying to Ireland, as was
done with Scotland, such a sum as would compensate her for
becoming liable to the debt of Great Britain, contracted
before the Union; and even after "such declaration that
country should contribute, by equal taxes," Great Britain
must, under this paragraph, have continued to pay the interest
on her separate debt. This is so obvious that I shall not
add any further argument to enforce it.

The remaining paragraphs are as follows, but they do not
require any comment :—

"IX. That a sum, not less than the sum which has been granted by the
Parliament of Ireland, on the average of six years immediately preceding
the first day of January, in the year 1800, in premiums for the internal
encouragement of agriculture or manufactures, or for the maintaining institutions for pious and charitable purposes, shall be applied for the period
of twenty years after the Union to such local purposes in Ireland, in such
manner as the Parliament of the United Kingdom shall direct."

"X. That, from and after the first day of January, 1801, all public
revenue arising to the United Kingdom from the territorial dependencies
thereof, and applied to the general expenditure of the United Kingdom,
shall be so applied in the proportions of the respective contributions of the
two countries."

The condition in the last paragraph was never performed.

I have endeavoured, fairly and impartially, to state what
seems to me to be the true intent and tenor of each of the
above paragraphs, and to explain them in the very words of
those who introduced them into the Irish Parliament. In
construing the treaty, we must bear in mind that it was
meant "to promote the essential interest of Ireland as well
as Great Britain" ; and, therefore, the proper construction to
be put upon the above conditions cannot be, that which
would consult alone the essential interests of Great Britain,

by sacrificing those of Ireland.   We must explain those conditions, so as to comport and agree with the leading idea, that
is, " to promote and secure the essential interests of Ireland,"
that object cannot be accomplished by unduly and unfairly increasing her taxation, until the very CAPITAL stock
of the country is swept into the Imperial treasury, to meet
the annual expenditure of the United Kingdom which has
taken place during the past five years, when, in consequence
of the excessive taxation, the value of the live stock of Ireland has been reduced about £4,000,000.   The amount of
investments on Irish account in the funds have been reduced
nearly *four millions,* and the deposits in the joint-stock banks
have lessened by over two millions, and, at the same time,
the taxation of Ireland has been increased enormously.

I have now cleared the ground for considering the manner
in which, after the Union, Ireland was dealt with by the
Parliament of the United Kingdom; and how, contrary to
the Act of Union, the taxation of Ireland has been so greatly
and unfairly increased.   But I must reserve these considerations for a future letter

LETTER VI.

IRELAND AFTER THE UNION.

THE MANNER IN WHICH THE TREATY WAS CARRIED OUT.

In the preceding letters I have tried to elucidate the principles of the law of nations, which govern such a treaty as that which preceded the Act of Union between Great Britain and Ireland; to shew the ideas which were present in the mind of Mr. Pitt who proposed the treaty, and forced it upon those who ought to have represented the Irish people in the Houses of Parliament, I have briefly sketched the progress of the Irish nation, during the twenty years antecedent to the Union. I have given the text of the 7th article of the treaty, and explained its construction, and it now remains to examine how was that treaty carried into effect?—Were its conditions faithfully performed? Was due effect given to them? Was the promise of Lord Castlereagh to the Irish Parliament realized? Were the professions of Pitt and Lord Glenbervie, in the British House of Commons, acted upon? In short, did the Union between Great Britain and Ireland prove a benefit to Ireland? Did it promote and secure the " essential interests of Ireland," or did it fail in those conditions? And, if it failed, was its failure was the result of imperfection in the arrangements, or did it arise from want of faithfulness in giving effect to those conditions which were agreed upon? To estimate these results and to reply to these queries will require an examination into the mode of ascertaining the revenue of Ireland, as well that which was acknowledged, as that which was uncredited. To explain the difference, I may state, that previously to the Union all the revenue of Ireland was raised in that kingdom, but after the Union, part of the revenue of Ireland was raised in Great Britain. The Irish revenue raised in Great Britain was not placed to the credit of Ireland, but was credited to that of Great Britain; an examination into this will form an important branch of my inquiry.

. It will be seen, that the treaty of Union recognised, in general terms, the whole revenue of Ireland, and that it included the duties paid in England, on articles consumed in Ireland, as well as the duties paid in Ireland on similar articles. Previously to the Union *all* the Irish duties were collected in Ireland ; subsequently to the Union, a portion of the Irish duties was collected in Great Britain ; thus, at one time all the Irish tea duties were collected in London—at present, a large portion of the duty on sugar consumed in Ireland, and therefore paid by the Irish people, is collected in England and Scotland. The Act of Union made no provision for ascertaining the amount so collected, and, therefore, there is some difficulty in ascertaining what were the " contributions of Ireland," as described in the 2nd, 3rd, 4th, 5th, 6th, and 7th paragraphs of the 7th article of the treaty. Ireland is not only paying revenue in England in the customs' department, but also in the excise and stamps, while a portion of her revenue, that from Crown lands, though collected in Ireland, is put to the credit of the British revenue ; and, even under the head " miscellaneous revenue," we find large sums placed, year after year, to the credit of the revenue, which consist mainly of moneys arising from the sale of old materials, or repayments to the Exchequer of moneys previously levied by taxation. These miscellaneous receipts ought either to be excluded from the calculation, or they should be credited to each country, in proportion to the amount which each contributed thereto. In 1862 these miscellaneous receipts were £1,743,533 14s. 11d.—Ireland contributed over one-tenth to the revenue, and should have got credit for one-tenth of this sum, or £174.553, but was only credited with £32,118 7s. 6d—shewing the want of some definite construction being put upon the expression, " contributions of Ireland," in the Act of Union.

The principal articles of consumption in Ireland, which pay Customs' duties in England, are chicory, coffee, corks, currants, figs, spices, plums, prunes, raisins, sago, brandy, rum, sugar, &c. ; and it is calculated that at the present time the amount of Irish contributions received in Great Britain on these articles is fully £2,000,000 a year.

Under the head of excise, Ireland " contributed" in Great Britain, on home-grown chicory, hops, malt, and paper.

Under the head of stamps, Ireland also paid contributions

in Great Britain, on marine insurances, on newspapers, on gold and silver plate, on cards, &c.

Immediately after the Union, there were duties on printed calicoes, and other similar articles, which were collected in Great Britain. Some writers on the subject claim credit for £3,000,000 per annum, as the Irish duties received in Great Britain on these different articles, and I do not think their claim is excessive; some of them also claim, and not without justice, credit in the " contributions from Ireland" of all duties paid by absentee landlords on those goods which are purchased with Irish rents, even though they were consumed in Great Britain. They say that the rents drawn from Ireland are about £4,000,000 per annum, and as the contributions to the Imperial Exchequer average about five shillings in the pound, of the Income, one-fourth of these rents, must have found their way into the Exchequer, and these payments ought to be considered part of the contributions of Ireland, as it is evident, they were part of the property included by Lord Castlereagh, when he made his estimate of the relative contributions of Ireland and Great Britain. Any calculation of the relative contributions of each country, would be materially imperfect, if it did not embrace the value of these contributions.

It is somewhat curious to trace the efforts, not of the Irish Parliament alone, but also that of England, to compel Irish landed proprietors to reside upon and improve their estates; in 1357 an act was passed, which Sir J. Davis, Attorney-General to James I. termed:—" The first statute made against absentees, commanding all such as had lands in Ireland to return and reside therein, on pain of forfeiting two-third parts of the profit thereof." " This ordinance (says he) was put in execution for many years after, as appears by sundry seizures made thereupon, in the time of Richard II., Henry IV., Henry V., and Henry VI., whereof there remain records in the Remembrancer's office.—Here among the rest, the Duke of Norfolk was impleaded on this ordinance for two parts of the profits of his lands in the County of Wexford, in the time of Henry VI., and afterwards, for the same reason of state, all the lands of the House of Norfolk, of the Earl of Shrewsbury, Lord Berkeley and others, (who, having lands in Ireland, yet resided continually in England,) were entirely resumed, and vested in the Crown by the Act of Absentees made 28th of

Henry VIII. The Act 10 Charles I., cap .21, declares that "The King and his progenitors, out of their princely wisdom, had thought proper to confer upon several able, worthy, and well deserving persons, inhabiting or dwelling in England, and elsewhere out of the kingdom of Ireland, titles of honour, whereby they do enjoy places of precedency according to their titles respectively; so that it cannot be denied, but that, in a just way of retribution, they ought to contribute to all public charges and payments taxed by Parliament in that kingdom from whence the titles of their honours are derived, and whereunto others of their rank there resident are liable. And that therefore it is enacted that all and every person or persons now being or which shall hereafter be an Earl, Viscount, or Baron, of that kingdom, and have place and voice in the Parliament of the realm, though resident or dwelling in England or elsewhere, shall be liable to all public payments or charges which shall be taxed or assessed in this or any other Parliament, and shall from time to time contribute thereunto, and pay their rateable parts thereof, in such manner and form as others of their rank are liable unto or shall pay."

A later act of the same reign recites—"That as divers persons advanced to benefices within Ireland do absent themselves out of the said land, in other lands, whereby the issues and profits of the said benefices are yearly taken forth of the said land of Ireland, to the great impoverishment and weakening of the same, diminishing of God's service, and withdrawing of hospitality; it enacts that if they do not keep residence in Ireland, their income is to be forfeited, and one half to go to the support of the Divine service, and the other to assist the King in his wars; and this act deprived the King of any power to grant writs of absency. In 1715, an act was passed, whereby all persons who had any salaries, profits of employment, or pensions in Ireland, should pay unto his Majesty four shillings out of every twenty shillings yearly which they were entitled to, unless they should reside within the kingdom six months in every year. In 1773, Mr. Flood tried to introduce an absentee tax of 2s. in the pound, but it was defeated owing to the influence of five great lords, the Duke of Devonshire, the Marquis of Rockingham, Lord Bessborough, Lord Milton, and Lord Upper Ossory. In reference to the partisans of these great personages, Mr. Flood said—"I am amazed that gentlemen can be so inconsiderate as to agree to tax three millions of the useful and industrious natives of Ireland, rather

than five great men who are its bane." In 1783, Mr. Molyneux
again raised the question in the Irish Parliament; and in 1797,
Government wanted £150,000, and Mr. Vandeleur recommended that it should be raised on absentee estates. The
principle was not denied, but as the money was wanted
directly, and that the absentee tax would not be available
until the end of the year, the proposition was rejected.

I think I have said sufficient to establish my point, which
is this—that in a matter of account between Great Britain
and Ireland, the Irish revenue is fairy entitled to credit for
all the taxes paid in Great Britain in consequence of the
expenditure in that country of the Irish absentee rents, and
that this contribution should not be estimated at less than 5s.
in the pound on the Irish absentee rents, which are estimated
at £4,000,000, per annum. Thus, Ireland would be entitled
to credit for £1,000,000, a year under this head. If that is
not done, then the amount of the property liable to income
tax in Ireland ought to be reduced by £4,000,000 a year,
remitted to and spent in Great Britain. If it be considered
Irish income, and as Irish, used in contrast in order to ascertain our proportion of the taxation, we ought to get credit
for the taxes paid in its expenditure. If we are denied credit
for the expenditure, it ought not be considered property in
Ireland in the adjustment of the accounts. I shall have to
refer to this hereafter, and I only call attention to it here in
connection with the absentee rents of Ireland.

The fact, that there were large payments made out of the
income of Ireland, which were not credited to the revenue of
Ireland, was very clearly admitted, in the course of a debate
which took place on April 25, 1815, on the motion of Mr.
Bankes, for the extension of the property tax to Ireland. Mr.
Vesey Fitzgerald, the Irish Chancellor of the Exchequer, opposed the motion. In the course of his speech, having
shewn the increase in the Irish taxes, he proceeds, with reference to the proposed property tax, to shew the amount which
was paid by Irish income. He says—" It would not be too
much to estimate the remittances to absentees at the annual
sum of £3,000,000. He was sure that he was warranted in
estimating it at that sum. The tax received upon Irish incomes in the Exchequer of England was £300,000. The
interest payable in Great Britain on the funded debt of Ireland
was upwards of £4,000,000, but allowing the portion which

might be reduced, he might state the amount of the property tax thus received from Ireland at £300,000."

Sir H. Montgomery very pertinently added, " The right hon. the Chancellor of the Exchequer of Ireland had estimated the annual amount of absentee income, which was spent in Great Britain, at £3,000,000 annually, and the amount of the interest of debt payable to English creditors at £4,000,000, the income tax on which, amounting to £700,000 a year, ought, in justice, be carried to the credit of Ireland, which would make good the present deficiency in the revenue, and provide for the loan of the year.

Of course, not only this sum, but also the amount paid as Customs and Excise out of Irish income spent in Great Britain, and all duties received in Great Britain for goods consumed in Ireland, should be also put to the credit of the Irish revenue, and had this been done, it would have been found that she largely overpaid her quota.

There is yet another point connected with the Treaty which deserves consideration, before proceeding to consider its influence, and the way in which it was carried into effect, and that is :—The treaty did not constitute any court or tribunal, in which the value of the contributions of each country, was to be ascertained, and which would arrange between the conflicting claims of each, and, consequently, the legal effect of the Acts of Union was left for the consideration of the courts of law, which would put a construction upon the treaty of Union, and also decide whether the subsequent legislation was in accordance with the Acts of Union, and whether, if it was not, such laws were not, therefore, null and void. In America, the Supreme Court of Judicature, decides whether the acts of Congress are in conformity with the Constitution; and, as the treaty of Union has not provided any court of that character, it appears to have left the question of any breach or violation of the Union, to be dealt with in our ordinary courts of Law, which would thus be called upon to pronounce, whether an act of Parliament which violated the Treaty of Union, was not, therefore, absolutely null and void.

There are three recognised classes of law, one rising above the other; the lowest is common law, the *lex non scripta*, which may be set aside by statute law. The *statute law* (acts of Parliament) comes next, but they are of inferior force, and subject to the control of *treaty law*. The relative force of these laws was explained in the judgment in Heydon's case, see ante p. 82. If Parliament enters into a treaty with another kingdom it cannot annul that treaty by its own act, *i. e.* by an act of Parliament. I claim that the act of Union is one of those fundamental, organic treaty laws, which cannot be dispensed with or annulled by any legislation ; and *I hold the opinion that the imposition of any law in Ireland, contrary to the treaty of Union, is illegal, and that our courts of justice would, on the facts being proved, decide that any law contrary to the treaty of Union, is null and void, and of no effect whatever.*

This state of facts is striking and illustrates the necessity which exists of applying, very rigidly, the principles of the Act of Union, and requiring a full and plain statement of the accounts between both nations. Such a statement as will satisfy the Irish taxpayer, that he is only contributing his fair quota, and the English ratepayer, that he is not saving his own pocket at the expense of his Irish brother. I must confess, that a close examination of the accounts, convinces me the Act of Union has been grossly violated, and that Ireland has been called on to pay far more than her contribution, and I think I can satisfy any impartial person, from the accounts of the Exchequer of the United Kingdom, that great injustice has been done to Ireland.

It is the more necessary to consider this subject, because an act was passed on the 1st July, 1816 (the 56th Geo. III., cap. 98,) " To Unite and consolidate into one fund all the public revenues of Great Britain and Ireland, and to provide for the application thereof to the general service of the United Kingdom." This act recognises the full force of the observations I have made as to the binding nature of the treaty of Union ; for the preamble states—" Whereas, it hath become expedient, for further carrying into effect the provisions and purposes of two several acts for the Union of Great Britain and Ireland (the one made in the Parliament of Great Britain, in the 39th and 40th years of his present Majesty's reign, and the other made in the Parliament of Ireland, in the 40th year of his said Majesty's reign,) that all the public revenues of Great Britain and Ireland should be consolidated and applied to the service of the United Kingdom." And it proceeds to enact the manner in which this was to be carried into effect. This act, while thus recognising the full force of the Acts of Union, does not contain any declaration that

the debts of the two countries had reached the proportion to
each other required by that act ; nor does it state that " the
respective circumstances of the two countries will thenceforth
admit of their contributing indiscriminately by equal taxes
imposed on each ;" nor does it make provision for the payment,
by each country, of the interest on their separate debt,
as required by the Act of Union; nor has the revenue been
yet raised by equal taxes, levied indiscriminately in each
country.

The competency of Parliament to alter the conditions of the
Act of Union, was frequently discussed in the Houses of
Commons, and it was invariably admitted, that Paliament
did not possess that power; in support of this assertion, I will
quote an instance, as it affords me the opportunity of bringing forward a speech which was delivered by Ireland's great
patriot, Henry Grattan. Similar opinions were held by Lord
Eldon and the Duke of Wellington. The occasion was a debate on June 24, 1814, on the " Spirits Intercourse Bill." A
committee had been appointed in 1809, and it recommended
the house, to adopt a course in opposition to the spirit of the
Act of Union, and that had been persevered in for some
years.

Mr. Weston urged that, it was a disadvantage to the
English distiller to allow the Irish distiller the privileges of
free intercourse, to which he was entitled by the Act of
Union.

Lord Castlereagh urged, " that it would be a breach of
faith of Parliament to deny to Ireland permission to export
spirits." Though this right had been denied from 1809 to
1814. His Lordship added, " The trade in spirits was intended to be free at the Union, and he hoped the House
would give effect to the principle established at that time.
That was a debt of duty to the whole United Kingdom."

Mr. Brand concurred that the operation of the bill before
the House would be to give to the Irish distillerst he monopoly
of the English markets, to the obvious prejudice of the
English distillers.

Sir J. Newport observed that, by the undue advantage
derived from the drawback, the Scotch distiller was enabled
not only to reduce the revenue, but to import his spirits into
the Irish market at a bounty injurious to the due interest of
the Irish distillers.

Mr. Hawthorn said, the report of the committee of 1809

was not acted on, because it contained principles at variance
with the articles of Union; and which, if carried into effect,
would render useless those advantages possessed by Ireland,
which gentlemen professed themselves so anxious to improve.

Mr. Grattan supported the bill. " the operation of which
would merely be, to carry the Act of Union more completely
into effect. Parliament, he contended, had no right to alter
that act, every clause was binding on the country and on
the legislature   It was similar to a covenant between
two parties, one of whom was dead.   And on every principle
of justice and honour, the living party ought to adhere
scrupulously to that engagement, which the other was not
in existence to defend. Parliament could not break any
article of that sacred covenant without committing a breach
of faith; and if they committed an infraction of the commercial part, they violated the whole. If they selected any
particular article, (that, for instance relative to the spirits
intercourse,) as a subject for revision, they would establish a
precedent, which they might hereafter deplore, for though
the Parliament of Ireland did not exist, the people of Ireland
were in being, and thousands of petitioners might then come
to the bar of that House, demanding a revision of other
articles, which appeared to affect their interests. The Act
of Union constituted the marriage articles between the two
countries, and none of its provisions could be broken without
annulling the contract. If the Parliament of England set
up a court of equity in its own cause, and dealt out what
it was pleased to denominate justice, but which was, in reality,
no more than what its discretion prompted, nothing could
be imagined more unfair, more impolitic—nothing could be
conceived more calculated to destroy the confidence which
ought to have existed between the two countries."

The force and validity of the Union being thus recognised
and admitted on all hands, I shall proceed to enquire whether
Ireland fulfilled her portion of the contract which was forced
upon her. No one can argue, that the Union was a voluntary compact on the part of Ireland, or that she was bound
to pay two-seventeenths, because in the strict sense of the
terms, she never agreed to pay it. The measure was carried
by the British Minister becoming a great borough-monger,
and purchasing such a number of seats, as to influence the deliberations of the House of Commons. But the Union cannot be
considered as representing the will of the Irish people. Had

it been the expression of their will, Government need not have feared to dissolve the House, and to allow new elections, if the majority was then in favour of the Union, its opinion would fairly represent that of the nation, but it refused to do so; the seats of one-fifth of the members of the House were vacated by arrangement, and new members were introduced in an unconstitutional manner.

I might also, in order to shew how very distasteful the Union was to the Irish people and Irish Parliament, adduce the protests which were recorded among the votes of the Houses of Lords and Commons, and which are on record in the proceedings of the Irish Parliament; or bring forward in evidence the large amount (£1,237,500,) paid directly to those who were believed to have the right of nomination in those towns, which were deprived of their representatives by the Act of Union. I have sufficient evidence to sustain my argument, which is this, *the Union was a bad bargain for Ireland, it was a contract forced upon the Irish people against their wish;* but these very circumstances furnish a reason—a most powerful and cogent reason—that Great Britain should see that Ireland obtained the full benefit of a contract so forced upon her. Previously to entering upon the consideration of the manner in which the treaty was carried into effect, I must consider two subjects connected with the treaty of Union—one is, the manner of ascertaining the amount of Ireland's contribution, and the other mode of obtaining redress, if the treaty were not fully carried out.

In explaining the conditions of the treaty, I have already given, pp. 91 to 93, Mr. Pitt's speech on opening the budget, in 1801, and Mr. Corry's on the Irish budget, in the same year, and shall not repeat them here, but I must repeat the figures of the budgets, because they illustrate the manner in which the conditions of the Act of Union were carried out, and shew that the system of account-keeping between the two nations, which eventually blossomed into such a tremendous debt against Ireland, was commenced in 1801. How it happened that the Irish debt, which, on the 5th April, 1801, was £26,841,219, should, on the 31st March, have increased to the amount stated by Mr. Corry, £36,000,000, I am utterly at a loss to conceive.

Indeed, I must say that it is difficult to state anything authoritatively respecting Irish accounts, as the system pursued

in the keeping of the accounts appears to be so very confused.
There are three or four Parliamentary returns in existence,
none of which correspond in any of the items of receipt, expenditure, or debt. I have examined them all to ascertain
what authority Mr. Corry had for stating that the debt of
Ireland, on the 31st March, 1801, was £36,000,000, and the
interest £1,696,000, and I quote from each of them.

1st. The earliest return from which I quote is the report of
the Finance Committee. (No. 214 of the session of 1815,)
at page 4, it states that the debt of Ireland, on the
1st January, 1891, was (Irish currency) . . £29,077,987
1st January, 1802.   do.   do. . 33,347,202
2nd. The return of 15th April, 1824 (No. 256) in page 8,
states the debt of Ireland, 5th January, 1801, at. . 26,841,219
    do.   do. 5th January, 1802, . 32,217,811
3rd. The return of 26th June, 1849, (No. 443) page 2, states
the debt of Ireland, 5th January, and 1st Feb., 1801, at 27,792,975
And that the increase of debt, in 1802 was, £3,940,812,
thus making the debt, 1802, . . . 31,733,787
4th. The return of 19th July, 1858, (No. 423) page 39,
states the whole national debt, of Ireland, in 1801, at 13,295,471
          ,,   ,,   1802, . 14,378,951

None of them supports Mr. Corry's statement that the debt
of Ireland was, on 31st March, 1801, £36,000,000, and his
statement as to the interest for that year being £1,696,000 is
equally incorrect. Mr. Pitt confines the amount which Ireland should pay to three items: 1st, her proportion of the army
and navy expenses; 2nd, her proportion of civil expenses;
and 3rd, the interest on the national debt; he adds:—" Whatever else remained was to be provided for by Great Britain.
The budgets of Mr. Pitt and Mr. Corry present the following
contrasts.*

* These Budgets were as follows :—

MR. PITT.		MR. CORRY.	
Two-seventeenths. Army,		Two-seventeenths. Army,	
Navy, &c.	£4.186,760	Navy, &c.	£4,186,760
Civil Expenses.	137,000	Civil Expenses.	600,000
		Compensation for Boroughs.	
	£4.323,760	1st Instalment	622,000
		Inland Navigation	100,000
		Compensation for Loyalists	230,000
		Army in England	70,000
			5,808,760
Interest on National Debt	1,157,064	Interest on National Debt	1,696,000
Total	£5,470,834		£7,504,760

There is a difference between them of nearly two millions in
one year; any one can see, that Mr. Corry introduced several items into the Irish account belonging to the imperial expenditure; the boroughs were purchased to carry the Union,
in opposition to the wish of the Irish people. The amount
ought, therefore, to be charged to the British account. The
compensation for loyalists and payment of army in England
both belonged to the expenditure of the United Kingdom.
There is an evident mistake of £500,000 in the interest
account, and a similar error of nearly the same amount in
the Civil expenses. Mr. Corry stated the available funds for
the year were £5,247,000, and proposed to borrow £2,500,000,
yet the return, (No. 443,) of 1849, states that he debt created
was £4,433,269. This was extraordinary book-keeping. Return, (No. 456,) of 1824, states the expenditure for the year
ending 5th January, 1802, as follows:—

Charge on unredeemed debt	£1,265,660		
Interest on Treasury bills	89,229		
		£1,354,889	
Supplies voted		4,747,316	
Other payments for National objects		96,489	

This is in excess of Mr. Pitt's statement by
£670,000, principally in supplies voted, but
it falls nearly £1,500,000 short of Mr.
Corry's statement. It makes the increase
of the debt for that year   3,385,735
It says there was *no debt* due from Ireland to Great Britain.

With reference to the accounts of 1801, the Annual
Register informs us that, on 16th March, 1802, Mr. Foster
remonstrated with regard to the Irish revenue accounts, he
said, " that this, the second session since the Union, was far
advanced, yet no committee, no inquiry, nothing as to Irish
business; nay, ever since the Union, scarce more than one
paper of the state of revenue or treasury was printed. He
reprobated the system of paying money on Irish account
without being previously voted, and called attention to the
provisions of the Union. He pointed out the disastrous effects
on Irish trade, which even then were shewing themselves;
he pointed out the decreased trade and commerce of Ireland,
and queried. Did a country so situated in its finances, its
revenues, its trade, and its exchanges admit of dilatory

counsels? He was satisfied the situation was capable of remedy, and could only become desperate by neglect. He had zealously opposed the Union, but from the day it became irrevocable, no man had been or would be more forward in supporting it, and if Ministers would seriously apply themselves to the concerns of Ireland, there was no assistance in his power which he would not cheerfully give, in public or in private, though he had no communication or connection with them."

On May 10th, in the same year, Mr. Foster moved for various papers relative to Irish finance, and an account for a vote of credit, on which Exchequer Bills to the amount of £334,000 had been issued by the Irish Exchequer.

Mr. Corry said there was a material distinction between Great Britain and Ireland; in the former he understood that votes of credit were applicable to the services of the army and navy. In Ireland, they were voted for contingent civil services. When he opened the budget last year, he stated the ways and means to cover the £300,000 granted as a vote of credit for Ireland.

Mr. Tierney maintained that there had been no vote of credit, and £334,000 had been expended without the authority of Parliament. He had always understood the £2,000,000 voted to be destined solely to the service of England. *The issue of £334,000 for Ireland, was totally unauthorized.*

Mr. Robson said he had discovered this sum to be disposed of among the army extraordinaries of England, where surely it had no right to be.

After more converstion, the motion was changed into an account by what authority this money had been issued, and in this shape it passed.

On Wednesday, the 9th June, Mr. Foster complained that the papers ordered had not been produced, and moved that the proper officers should be called upon to make immediate returns to the orders of the House, respecting those accounts which had not yet been presented. This was seconded by Mr. Corry, and agreed to.

Mr. Foster then called the attention of the House, to the order respecting the authority under which the sum of £334,000 had been raised and paid into the Irish treasury, and how it had been raised and applied. To this order, a return had been made, referring for authority to the 25th sec. of 41st Geo. III., upon referring to this, however, it would be found that no more than two millions was authorized to be raised for the service of Great Britain and Ireland; this, therefore could give no authority for raising the additional £300,000 for the service of Ireland. With respect to the manner in which it had been raised, the return referred, to an aid for the service of Ireland which never existed, and as to the application of it, not a syllable was said. He therefore moved, " That the proper officer should be called upon to make a further return to the order of the 10th May, relative to the above account."

Mr. Corry said he was really concerned and ashamed of this puny warfare of accounts relating to Ireland. The right hon. gentleman knew, (if he knew anything about the matter,) that the money that was raised for covering that part of the vote of credit was raised with the other supplies of the year—he should oppose the motion.

Mr. Foster denied that it was a puny war of accounts, but a subject of great importance. Parliament should take care that no Minister raised money contrary to the constitution.

The house divided,—for the motion, 21; against it, 63; thus proving, that Irish members had no chance of being able to secure a proper revision of the Irish Exchequer payments, in the British Parliament. The complaints which were made, whether on principle or detail, seemed to fall unheeded on the ears of the majority.

1802, on the 14th June, Mr. Corry stated the Irish budget; he represented that there were some small sums for the service of last year, which must be provided, in this there was, for the first instalment of compensations, £327,275, treasury bills £25,700, loyalists' fund, £49,767, lottery prizes, £2,192, Prizage, £2,000; amounting altogether to £406,964. The charges defrayed solely by Ireland, were interest on national debt, £1,880,205. Two instalments of compensations, £555,200, inland navigation, £150,000, prizes in the lottery, £300,000, two sums of £200,000 each, Treasury Bills, making the separate charges of Ireland, £3,298,555, the joint contribution 2-17ths was £4,129,000, making in all, £7,428,425, Irish money. The ways and means were balances in the Exchequer, £393,668, part of the English loan for the service of Ireland, £2,166,666, Irish loan, £1,625,000, lotteries, £500,000; the lottery this year was a joint concern between the two countries, and of the £500,000 which was to be remitted on the part of this country, £300,000 would serve to pay the amount of prices of last year. The next item was £400,000, which ought to have been remitted on the part of Great Britain, but which had been reduced to £300,000; the next item was, £300,000 arising from the revenues of Ireland, making £7,592,000. and leaving a balance of £163,657.

Here we have in the payment two charges for compensation for the boroughs, £882,475, an overcharge of interest of £600,000, while the revenues, which yielded £4,337,267, are put down in the budget at only £3,000,000; such blunders are inexplicable, and they run through the accounts.

Mr. Foster, who rose after Mr. Corry, expressed in strong terms his disapprobation of the length of time which had elapsed since the Union, without any accounts being settled, and of the inaccuracies of many of the accounts returned, some of which he had called for, had not been delivered. He called attention to the falling off in the trade and commerce of Ireland.

Lord Castlereagh made some observations respecting the relative state of the debts of Great Britain and Ireland, and stated several calculations relative to the sinking fund of both countries, to prove that the honourable gentleman's assertion, that England would advance, but that Ireland would retrograde, was not founded on probable circumstances.

The errors that prevail through the whole accounts require minute and careful examination; thus, in 1802, Ireland's proportion of the national expenditure was stated at £3,815,763; (the supplies voted, per Parliamentary Paper of 1824, were £3,116,368,) adding interest on separate debt at the Union, the budget would be £4,972,827. The Irish revenue, in 1802, was £4,337,269, and the deficiency would have been £635,558, yet the debt created on Irish account was £4,273,331; in these two years the deficiency would be—

```
1801, according to Mr. Pitt's Budget,  £270,760
1802, deficiency as stated above,        635,558
      Total deficiency in the 2 years  ————————  £906.218
1801, Irish debt created,             £4,433,337
1802,        ,,                        4,273,211
             Total                     ———————— 8,706,548

      Overcharge against Ireland                  £7,800,330
```

This sum went on accumulating at compound interest, and a sinking fund was added which was at four times as great a ratio as that of Great Britain, and in 1815, the Irish debt

was swelled to such vast proportions, that the interest of her
debt was then stated at £3,821,082, and the sinking fund
£2,087,809, making a total of £5,908.801. A very slight
scrutiny must satisfy any one that the debt so created is a mere
fiction. It was increased, first by making charges to the Irish
account, contrary to the Act of Union—then by borrowing
money to meet these charges, and swelling both at compound
interest. I have shewn that the compensation which Ireland
was entitled to, at the Union, for taking her share of the
British debt, would have been £11,000,000, and at compound
interest this sum would have reached the enormous figure
of £352,000,000 in 1870.* This explains how the Irish debt
was run up ; the charging of compound interest is forbidden
by the state in dealings between private individuals, because
it is held that no debtor could pay it, and what the state
forbids between private individuals cannot be lawful between
the two nations, nor can Great Britain, to use the words of
Grattan, " set up a court of equity in its own cause, and deal
out what it may be pleased to denominate justice, but which
is, in reality, no more than what its discretion prompted."

I shall endeavour to simplify the accounts between the two
nations, and will deal with them in the aggregate, shewing
the total amount with which Ireland might have been charged,
and also the extent of her contributions towards the expenditure of the United Kingdom. I would recall attention to
the great and striking difference which exists between the
amounts which the Chancellor of the Exchequer stated he
would require to borrow, and the amount of debt created,
as given ante page 94. In the accounts which this official laid annually before Parliament, Ireland was charged,
(I think improperly charged,) with interest on an amount
of debt which she did not owe, and with sinking fund
upon that debt, but even when charged with all these
amounts, the budget was made to balance, and loans for the
deficiency sanctioned, yet the debt created was far in excess

* At compound interest the capital doubles in 14 years ; consequently, if
Ireland were to have received £11,000,000 in 1800 as the equivalent for
adopting the British debt it would have grown at the following rate :—

1800	Equivalent for Ireland taking the liability of the British debt	£11,000,000
1814	It would have been	22,000,000
1828	do. do.	44,000,000
1842	do. do.	88,000,000
1856	do. do.	176,000,000
1870	do. do.	352,000 000

of the sum so authorised. This subject possesses so much of significance and importance, that I must try and elucidate it fully, and I think it displays so much very unfair dealing as must convince the meanest mind and persuade the most partial person, that a very great amount of injustice has been done to Ireland, inasmuch as a debt was created which she did not owe; this was done without even the sanction of Parliament; the assumed existence of this debt was made the reason for depriving her of the protection guaranteed to her under the Act of Union, and this very protection was the condition or equivalent which was offered to the Irish people, as compensation for surrendering their sovereign rights. If I can shew that Ireland did not, in 1816, owe the sum with which she was debited, then it would be apparent—

1st. That Ireland was induced to lay down her sovereign rights in exchange for the guarantee which was given, that she should be exempt from paying at any time the interest on the British debt, contracted before the Union, and that her contribution to the revenue should be according to her relative ability, when compared with Great Britain.

2nd. That she never received any compensation for taking upon her a share of the British debt due before the Union, though Scotland received it for adopting her share of the liability to the English debt due before her Union with England.

3rd. That the officials of the British Treasury, without the authority of Parliament, charged Ireland with a large amount of debt, and that all such charges require to be fully investigated and proved before they are allowed to stand as debts against Ireland.

4th. That the Parliament of the United Kingdom constituted itself a court of equity in its own behalf, and charged Ireland at its discretion, with an undue and unfair proportion of the *joint* debt of the two countries, and having thus and by a fallacious system of bookkeeping, increased the nominal debt of Ireland, she used it as the means of depriving this country of the rights, privileges, and immunities, offered to her as compensation for the surrender of her national legislature, and has thus increased the taxation of Ireland, and also forced this country to pay the interest on the debt due by Great Britain before the Union.

This aspect of the question is very interesting and important, and I shall therefore proceed to examine what was the amount placed to the debit of Ireland? and also what were the actual revenue receipts? The amount with which Ireland was debited, as stated in the annual Budgets, from 1801 to 1816, was in the whole £96,021,281*. The actual revenue receipts paid into the Exchequer in the same period as given in Parliamentary paper, 256 of 1824, was £83,994,943†. It is a marvel how Ireland could by any possibility, have contracted a debt of £106,807,794, as stated in another Parliamentary paper, when the debits and credits approached so near each other. The amount of the chargeability of Ireland was ninety-six millions, and the amount of her payment eighty-four millions.

Thus, at the first blush, without giving Ireland any credit for the Irish revenue collected in Great Britain, the total deficiency would, on this account, have been about *twelve millions*, the interest on the Irish national debt for sixteen years, from 1801 to 1816, would have been *eighteen millions*, Ireland's share of the interest on the joint debt £12,340,000, so that the utmost Ireland could be charged in the 16 years, would have been about £43,000,000. The revenues of Great Britain were also deficient, she did not raise a sufficient sum to pay her expenses, and the joint debt of the United Kingdom would be composed of the united deficiencies, the dif-

	* Irish proportion 2-17ths of that of the United Kingdom.		† Revenue Receipts.
1801	...	4,186,761	...	3,341,892
1802	...	3,815,763	...	4,357,267
1803	...	3,187,101	...	3.717,943
1804	...	4,711,650	...	4,383,487
1805	...	5,403,102	...	4,600,953
1806	...	5,137,528	..	5,187,908
1807	...	5,314,275	...	5,718,967
1808	...	5,713,566	...	5,658,753
1809	...	6,273,266	..	5,414,328
1810	...	6,106,000	...	4,881,031
1811	...	7,116,000	...	5,291,381
1812	...	7,611,000	...	5,942,151
1813	...	7,750,000	...	6,225,391
1814	...	8,107,094	...	6,646,766
1815	...	9,760,814	...	6,805,513
1816	...	6,026,731	...	5,803,200
		£96,021,281		£83,994,943

ference between the annual expenditure and the annual
income.

If the Irish revenue was credited with £750,000 per annum,
for duties paid in England on the Irish account, it would
make the revenue receipts £95,994,943, or within £26,338
of the amount with which she was charged, and the only
deficiency would be the interest on the national debt. The
account between the two nations would have stood thus:—

Irish debt in 1801,	£26,841,219	Irish revenue 1801, to 1816,	£83,994,943
16 years' interest on same ...	18,422,024	Do. do. received in Great Britain	12,000,000
2-17ths of general expenditure for 16 years ...	96,021,281		£95,994,943
2-17ths of the interest on debt contracted after the Union	12,340,000	Balance	57,629,681
Total charge against Ireland	£154,624,524		£154,624,524

Thus, the debt of Ireland, including that due at the
Union, if fairly stated, would not in 1816 have exceeded
£57,629,681, whereas the Finance Committee of 1815 and
the subsequent report of 1817 make it £130,000,000, but this
is a monstrous fabrication!

I shall go more at length into this branch of the subject
hereafter, now I only wish to indicate the principle which I
mean to illustrate, but before I pass from the matter in hand,
I must quote the language of some of the most active Irish
members, as it shews the dissatisfaction which prevailed at
the time.

I have already given some of the debates which occurred
in 1802. (ante page 113.)

1805. The Right Hon. James Fitzgerald, on bringing up
the report of the Irish Budget, on March 15th, said:—

"The loan is made to a larger amount than necessary, and
that, if it even were necessary, the interest of it might be
defrayed without having recourse to new taxes. The
revenue of Ireland was only taken at £4,000,000,* though
every one knew it would be much more. The right hon

---

* The revenue receipts of Ireland in 1805 were £4,600,953.

gentleman (Mr. Foster) imposed last year additional taxes of £1,150,000 by way of regulation, and £76,000 to defray expenses of a direct loan; and he now stated that there was, out of last year's revenue, a surplus of £843,000; but that it must remain locked up in the Irish Treasury until the proportion of Ireland to the joint expenditure should be paid. Upon this practice of retaining the supplies of the consolidation fund since the Union, it would follow that there must be now a total surplus of about four millions applicable to the expenses of the year. This was a mode of proceeding very disadvantageous to Ireland. The sums returned of duties due, but not immediately payable, were to the amount £633,346, which either were or ought to be in the Treasury of Ireland."

In this year Sir John Newport said he could not conceive why no account had been given of the £2,000,000 due from Great Britain to Ireland ever since the Union.

Mr. J. Fitzgerald complained that there was a large amount of revenue locked up in the Irish Treasury until Ireland made good her contribution to the joint expenditure. There must, he said, be a total surplus of about £4,000,000 applicable to the expenses of the year.

Mr. Pitt stated, that in order to satisfy the House and the public, he should move next day for a committee to inquire into the state of the accounts between Great Britain and Ireland.

In 1807 Mr. Parnell remarked, in a debate on the Irish Budget, that Ireland was expending £9,000,000 a-year with a revenue of £3,000,000. The new taxes since 1802 were expected to produce £1,888,000, but only yielded an additional revenue of £50,000.

1810. Sir J. Newport, in the debate on the Irish Budget, said:—

" It is lamentable to look at the funded debt of Ireland. This debt had increased in the proportion of 15 to 4, while the revenue increased only in the proportion of 15 to 8½. If the debt of Ireland was raised—like the debt of England—within the country, he (Sir John Newport) really thought that a great part of the debt would be done away."

Mr. Parnell said he " could not help thinking, that the great principle of the revenue in Ireland was overlooked in the desire of extensive patronage of offices, so as to deprive the Irish Treasury Board of its power."

Sir John Newport called attention to the increase of the debt, and the inaccurate manner in which the rate of contribution was arranged at the time of the Union. Ireland had improved since the Union, but it did not follow that she would not have improved with greater rapidity if the Union had never taken place. There was a portion of the property tax which most unjustly, as he thought, was diverted from the Irish Exchequer in England. This ought to belong to Ireland alone, and if it had been allotted to her, and appropriated to the discharge of her necessities, she would not now be obliged to call for relief. The revenues of Ireland had made no progress adequate to the debt. No instance had occurred for the last three years in which the separate charge of Ireland amounted to within £1,000,000 of the joint charge. This was one effect of the rate of contribution fixed at the Union, which, so long as it was acted upon, would render the payment of the debt impossible.

In 1814, on the bringing up of the budget,

Sir Henry Parnell complained of the abuses in the management of the Irish revenue, and asserted that, " If the taxes of Ireland were well managed, they would not only meet the general charge on that kingdom, but leave a surplus to be applied to the assistance of the English revenue."

Sir John Newport, in referring to the abuses in collecting the taxes, said—" That it was well known that the late Chancellor of the Exchequer (Mr. Percival) expressed his astonishment that any public board should so far have neglected its duty, and urged instances in which the collection of the Irish revenue was neglected."

Mr. W. Pole observed that when the Union propositions were settled the expenses of the Empire were but £25,000,000, whereas they were now £72,000,000. It never could have been expected that Ireland would have been able to pay 2-17th of so large a sum as this.

Mr. Vesey Fitzgerald observed that the assertion of the hon. gentleman (Mr. Bankes) as to the inadequate contribution of Ireland was rather unreasonable, at a period when the Irish nation was about to contribute £16,000,000 to the common stock of the year, and to pay in additional taxes £610,000, which amounted to one-half of the addition to which rich and happy England was subjected.

On the 1st of July, 1814, the sum required for the service

of the year was stated to be £18,795,455, with a revenue of £5,350,000. The borrowing in this year was £8,958,338.

New taxes were proposed for Ireland, amongst which were equalization of duties on all foreign articles, including tea, sugar, coffee, wine, tobacco, and foreign spirits, and an increase of duty on several articles used in the manufactories of Ireland. On the 23rd of November, 1814, Sir John Newport animadverted on the new system of imposts adopted with regard to Ireland, and contended that the proposed assimilation of Irish and English duties must have the effect of crushing Ireland.—He particularly applied his observations to the Timber Act, which would have a serious effect on the provision trade.

On the 25th April, 1815, Mr. Bankes proposed the extension of the property tax to Ireland. It was opposed by Mr. Peel, on the ground that the collection of such a tax was not feasible. Sir J. Newport remarked, that in 14 years since the Union, Ireland had brought into the Exchequer in taxes about £60,000,000, exclusive of what she had been called upon to produce in the way of loan.

On the 16th of June, 1815, the new Budget was introduced. The total sum required to be raised was £16,972,364, with a revenue of £6,100,000. The new loan was £9,750,000, all being raised in England. Additional taxes were proposed amounting to £760,000. On this occasion the Irish Chancellor of the Exchequer announced that it was decided that in the next year there should be a consolidation of the Exchequers.

Sir J. Newport observed that in the last 14 years Scotland had raised a gross revenue of £55,722,000, and Ireland £70,240,000, being an excess of taxation in Ireland beyond Scotland of £14,000,000, or £1,000,000 in the average every year.

On the 25th April, 1815, Mr. Vesey Fitzgerald, the Irish Chancellor of the Exchequer, stated "that produce of malt, in 1802, was £116,004 ; in 1811, £348,000 ; and in 1814, £566,000. He would not trouble the house going through all the small articles contained in the paper, but merely touch on the leading ones. Spirits, in 1802, produced £270,000 ; in 1811, £685,000 ; and in 1814, £1,575,000. Tobacco, in 1802, gave £140,000 ; in 1811, £311,000 ; and in 1814, £504,000. Hearth money had increased from £32,000, in 1802, to £64,000, in 1814. The assessed taxes had been doubled, quadrupled, and quintupled. The servants' duty had been increased four fold. Windows, in the last three years, had increased £100,000.

In 1816, the Marquis of Buckinghamshire, in his speech on the state of Ireland, said—"Almost every tax had been doubled. The assessed taxes had been trebled. In short, every effort had been made to screw up the taxes of Ireland to the utmost. What could this be called but a state of national bankruptcy in that country?"

In 1824, Lord Althorp urged the repeal of taxes in Ireland as a measure mainly tending to "Revive the manufactures of that country, and bring it into a prosperous condition."— Hansard, vol. ii., p. 659.

These were the sentiments of the most influential and intelligent Irish members as to the manner in which the accounts between the two countries were kept, and I think they furnish very ample grounds, for our asking to have the partnership accounts of this period re-opened, in order that we may obtain such an equitable settlement, as would satisfy intelligent and reasonable persons in both countries, that the principle of the articles of the Union had been fairly and honestly carried out.

I do not wish to aggravate the weight of these very heavy charges, by any declamatory language. I feel in its full force their serious import, but I am persuaded that good sense, innate honesty, and desire to avoid any mean-ness or subterfuge, are so strong in the mind of the British people, that if they can be satisfied that injury and injustice have been done to Ireland, they will arise to our aid, they will cast from them a policy, which saves their pockets, at the expense of their honour, they will scorn a system which imposes an unfair burthen upon Ireland, to relieve the British ratepayer; and they will see that Ireland shall receive the full meed of justice, which would arise to her from an honest fulfilment of the Treaty of Union, which WILLIAM PITT, in order to promote, as he thought, the security and welfare of the British empire, forced against her inclination, upon the Irish nation, with a rather high hand, but this very fact gives Ireland a greater claim upon the sister country for full and ample justice, and for a complete and literal performance of the treaty of Union.

LETTER VII.

THE IRISH ACCOUNTS AFTER THE UNION.

REVENUE AND EXPENDITURE.

THE examination upon which I am about to enter is one which, I fear, will not be interesting to my readers; long columns of figures are, I am aware, distasteful to the majority of readers; but it is necessary that I should do so, in order to ascertain whether the condition, as to the relative proportions between the debts of Ireland and Great Britain, attained the scale upon which they could have been consolidated. The issues which hang upon the result of these calculations are most important, because they affect the welfare of the whole Irish nation. The issues that are raised are these.

1st. *Was Ireland rightfully deprived of the protection which was guaranteed to her under the treaty of Union?*

2nd. *Is it right and just that Ireland should pay any portion of the interest of the debt contracted by Great Britain previously to the Union?*

These are the issues which are dependent upon the statement of the partnership accounts of Great Britain and Ireland, in the period between the passing of the Act of Union, in 1801, and the passing of the Act for the consolidation of the Exchequers, in 1816. If the debt of Ireland was unduly and unfairly increased, and that she did not, in 1816, honestly and rightfully owe the amount which is stated against her, then the act of 1816 is a nullity. But if she did honestly and fairly owe the amount stated against her, then we have to consider whether even the amalgamation of Exchequers absolved Great Britain from her portion of the bargain, which was to continue to provide, by special taxes, for the interest of the debt due before the Union.

The course I shall pursue will be to examine the accounts

from 1801 to 1816, and then to take up the report of the Finance Committee of 1815; it is quite clear to my mind that Ireland did not owe the amount alleged in 1815, because I hold that, according to the true construction of the Treaty of Union, the separate debt of both countries closed the 31st December, 1800, and that all the subsequent loans were *joint* loans, and were not divisible between the two countries.

The simple statement of the relative position of both countries must shew the simplest mind, without going into figures at all, that Ireland could not have increased her ratio of indebtedness. I may state the problem in this way—

The separate debts of Great Britain and Ireland, at the Union, bore to each other the proportion of 17 to 1.

The debt after the Union was a joint debt.

How, then, could Ireland, so long as she paid her stipulated share, increase her indebtedness? Of course, every one will see that it was impossible. Then, it may be asked, how could the consolidation of the Exchequers take place? and to that I can give the answer which Lord Castlereagh gave before the Union—only by Great Britain paying off such a portion of her debt as would bring it to bear to that of Ireland the proportion of $7\frac{1}{2}$ to 1 ; until this is done I hold the amalgamation of the Exchequers is contrary to the Act of Union, and, therefore, illegal—because the Parliament of the United Kingdom cannot legally pass any act which is contrary to the Act of Union. This is admitted on all hands, and it was especially in the debate on the Spirits Intercourse Bill, from which I made extracts in a previous letter (page) .

I now proceed to the examination of the accounts, and at the outset a difficulty arises, from the vague expressions in the Treaty of Union. The second paragraph of the 7th article says, " That for the space of twenty years after the Union shall take place, the *contributions* of Great Britain and Ireland respectively towards the expenditure of the United Kingdom, in each year, shall be defrayed in the proportion of fifteen parts for Great Britain, and two for Ireland." A difficulty arises as to the meaning of the word " contributions." This expression, seems to me to mean, the entire " contributions" of Ireland to the Imperial Exchequer, as well those paid in Ireland; as those paid in Great Britain upon articles consumed in Ireland, and it also includes the revenue or duty paid in England upon articles consumed there, and paid for by absentee rents.

In 1802, the bonding system, which previously was confined to tobacco, was extended to sugar and port wine. All the Irish duties on tea, were for many years collected in London. In 1801, a general duty bill passed, including 1,500 articles; on its renewal, in 1802, its provisions and effects were debated. Cotton, which before the Union was free, became liable to a duty over 2d. per pound, consequently all cotton goods imported into Ireland, paid duty in Great Britain. There was at this time, and still is, a tendency to consider all revenue received in Great Britain, British revenue, and to regard as Irish revenue, only the amount collected in this country, but this system is manifestly unfair towards Ireland. She has a claim to get credit for all " contributions," which are paid either in Great Britain, on goods consumed in Ireland, or on commodities bought by Irish rents spent there. This principle was admitted by Mr. Vesey Fitzgerald, when Chancellor of the Irish Exchequer, in 1814, he shewed the Irish revenue paid in Great Britain, under the head of property tax, he then said :—

" It would not be too much to estimate the remittances to absentees at the annual sum of £3,000,000. He was sure that he was warranted in estimating it at that sum. The tax received upon Irish incomes in the Exchequer of England was £300,000. The interest payable in Great Britain on the funded debt of Ireland was upwards of £4,000,000, but allowing the portion which might be redeemed, he might state the amount of the property tax thus received from Ireland at £300,000.

Sir H. Montgomery very pertinently added, " The right hon. the Chancellor of the Exchequer for Ireland had estimated the annual amount of absentee income, which was spent in Great Britain at £3,000,000 annually, and the amount of the interest of debt payable to English creditors at £4,000,000, the income tax on which amounting to £700,000 a year, ought in justice be carried to the credit of Ireland, which would make good the present deficiency in the revenue, and provide for the loan of the year."

Ireland never got credit for these payments, nor for the customs, or excise, paid in Great Britain, on goods consumed in Ireland, though they are rightfully included in the term " contributions" which is used in the Act of Union.

It is somewhat difficult to estimate the exact amount of revenue paid by Ireland in Great Britain, but we may arrive at an approximation by contrasting the revenue realised by those articles which, from their nature, are imported direct into Ireland, (the duty on which is therefore paid principally in this country,) with those which are previously imported into Great Britain, and pay their duties in that country. Amongst the former class of commodities are Corn, Tea, Tobacco and Snuff, and Timber; while the latter include Spices, Sugar, Fruit, Wines, and Spirits, &c. The finance accounts of last year (Parliamentary paper, No. 303,) afford the following information as to the duties paid in Great Britain and Ireland on each of these classes of goods. It is as follows:—

	Great Britain.	Ireland.
Corn ...	£658,603 6 5	£142,292 7 7
Tea ...	4,744,051 2 3	772,532 10 6
Tobacco and Snuff	4,626,860 10 4	969,350 13 4
Timber ...	220,456 8 8	20,847 8 11
Total	£10,247,971 7 8	£1,905,023 0 4

On these articles Ireland paid nearly one-fifth of the Customs' duties. The other articles I shall not enumerate in detail, but the amount received on them, among which are spruce beer, books, chicory, cocoa, coffee, corks, currants, figs, hops, mahogany, paper, spices, plums, prunes, raisins, sago, foreign spirits, sugar, &c., were as follows,—as customs duties were—Great Britain, £11,163,114 17s. 11d.; Ireland, £376,835 16s. 2d. The proportion paid in Ireland is only one-twenty-fifth, thus showing that a large portion of the Irish revenue on these articles is paid in England. If the Irish contribution on the latter articles was in the same ratio as the former, the uncredited Irish revenue would be at least £1,500,000 more than is shewn in this return. The Irish uncredited contributions have, since the Union, been very large, but I shall, in my computations, claim credit for so small a sum, that I think no one can take exception thereto. I only ask credit for £750,000 per annum on account of payments made by Ireland in Great Britain, which is far below the actual receipts. It will be necessary to deduct from the amount of revenue collected in Great Britain, a sum equal to the payments which have been made on account of Ireland in that country, and to add that sum to the revenue collected in Ireland.

I shall proceed to a comparison of the revenue raised in

Great Britain and Ireland, in order to ascertain whether Ireland contributed the 2-17ths imposed on her by the act of Union or not? The actual payments in the 16 years, from 1801 to 1816, were—Great Britain, £900,265,464; Ireland, £83,994,942; if we deduct from the former, and add to the latter £12,000,000, being at the rate of £750,000 a year, for 16 years, for payments made in Great Britain, on Irish account, the receipts will thus be, Great Britain, £888,265,464, and Ireland, £95,994,942. I give the details for each year at foot.*

The annual average contributions of Ireland for the 16 years were about £6,000,000, being more than £1,500,000 in excess of what Lord Castlereagh led her to expect; he estimated the Irish expenditure, after the Union, at £4,492,000. This taxation was beyond her "relative ability," as is shewn by the report of the Finance Committee, from which I shall presently quote. In order to discover whether Ireland paid her share

---

* The net amount of the British and Irish credited revenue are given in a paper laid before the House of Commons, and bearing date the 15th April, 1824, No. 236. It is signed by J. C. Herries, who was subsequently Chancellor of the Exchequer.

The revenue of each country for the year ending the 5th January in each year is as follows :—

	Great Britain,	Ireland,
1802—Net Revenue	34,611,296	3,341,892
1803,	36,349,932	4,397,269
1804,	37,875,099	3,717,943
1805,	45,303,386	4,383,487
1806,	49,746,475	4,600,953
1807,	53,230,372	5,187,908
1808,	58,231,737	5,718,967
1809,	60,971,440	5,653,753
1810,	62,966,838	5,414,328
1811,	66,630,571	4,881,021
1812,	64,220,412	5,291,381
1813,	63,650,795	5,942,151
1814,	66,872,587	6,225,391
1815,	69,019,729	6,649,766
1816,	69,858,901	6,805,513
1817,	60,836,853	5,803,220
Total,	£900,265,464	£83,994,942
Deduct from the British Revenue and add to the Irish 16 years' payments of Irish revenue in England at £750,000	£ 12,000,000	£12,000,000
	£888,265,463	£95,994,942

of the " contributions," I must ascertain what was the annual
interest of the separate debt of each country before the
Union; as this was the first claim on the revenue of each
Some difficulty arises from the discrepancy in the several
statements, not only as to the amount of the separate debts,
but also of the principal sum due by each country at the
Union, they are differently stated in Parliamentary papers.
I give the interest due in 1801, as stated in each.

		No. 256, 1824, makes it	No. 445, 1858, makes it
Great Britain,	...	£16,263,088	£17,845,675
Ireland,	...	1,157,284	777,875
		£17,420,372	£18,623,950*

I shall assume the latter figures to be the more correct, and
proceed to ascertain if Ireland raised her proportion. The
revenue in the sixteen years, appears, from the returns I have
quoted, to have been—

	Great Britain.	Ireland.
In the 16 years from 1801 to 1816	£888,265,464	£95,994,942
Deduct 16 years' interest on the debt due in 1800 as above * ...	285,527,000	12,445,000
This will leave the net amount to defray the ordinary current expenditure of each country ...	602,738,464	83,549,942

The Act of Union imposed upon Ireland two-seventeenths of the whole net expenditure, after paying interest on the separate debt it amounts to   ...   80,609,708

So that Ireland overpaid her contribution, (excessive as
it was) by   2,940,234
If the interest on the Irish National debt at the Union
is not correctly given in the return of 1858, and that
we calculate it at the amount stated in the return
of 1824, it would be £18,516,544, instead of
£12,445,000, making a difference of   ...   6,071,544

Or leaving the Irish revenue deficient by   ...   3,131,310

Therefore, according to the above statement of the revenue receipts, Ireland, (taking her interest from the return of
1858,) paid more than the two-seventeenths she was bound to
pay, (or taking her interest from the return of 1824,) she had
a deficiency of only £3,131,310.

This revenue was in excess of her means of payment.   The

finance committee which was appointed in 1815, for the purpose of finding a pretext, to deprive Ireland of the protection which she enjoyed under the act of Union, was forced to say : " Your committee cannot but remark that for several years Ireland has advanced in permanent taxation, more rapidly than Great Britain herself, notwithstanding the immense exertions of the latter country. Including the extraordinary and war taxes, the permanent revenue of Great Britain increased from 1801, when both countries were first made to correspond in the proportion of 16½ to 10, the whole revenue of Britain (including war taxes), is 21 to 10, and the revenue of Ireland as 23 to 10. But in the 24 years referred to your committee, the increase in the Irish revenue has been in the proportion of 46½ to 10."

On the introduction of the report, Mr. Vesey Fitzgerald the Chancellor of the Exchequer said :—

"I hope it will not be said that Ireland throws a great burthen on the empire to save herself. Oh, no. The necessity for revising the act of Union has been caused by the sacrifices she has made, doing her best to keep pace with you, you contracted with her for an expenditure which she could not meet. She had been led to hope that her expenditure would be less, when united to you than before. She has absolutely paid more in taxes since the Union than £78,000,000, being £47,000,000 more than her revenue in the fifteen years on which her contribution was calculated."

The obvious remedy would have been, to have re-adjusted her contribution, and reduced it in amount, according to the provisions of the 2nd paragraph of the 7th article. This must have been done in 1821, according to the Act of Union; and justice would have dictated that it should have been done in 1816.

Mr. Leslie Forster (the late Baron Forster,) who followed Mr. Fitzgerald, thus describes the increase which had taken place in the taxation of Ireland :—

" The taxation of Ireland, at the Union, was £2,440,000, and in 1810, it had risen to £4,280,000. In 1816, it was £5,760,000. *In fact, taxation in that country had been carried almost to its ne plus ultra.*"

As I shall have hereafter to refer to the facts herein stated, I shall not stay here to dwell upon them. I am merely adducing evidence that Ireland endeavoured to raise her quota.

A few years after, in 1822, on a motion of Sir John New-port's, Mr. Goulburn, Chancellor of the Exchequer, referring to the taxation of Ireland, said :—

" The Union contribution of 2-17ths for Ireland is now *allowed on all hands* to have been more than she was able to bear."

He might have added, that at the time the consolidation of te exchequers took place, only four years of the agreement had to run, and that in 1821, the proportion would have to be re-adjusted according to the scale laid down.

Later still, in the year 1830, the Marquis of Landsdowne referred to Ireland, to illustrate the manner in which she was taxed. He said :—

" A case is established in the instance of Ireland, which is written in characters too legible not to serve as a guide to future financiers—one which ought to bring shame on the memory of its authors. The revenue of Ireland, in 1807, was £4,887,000 ; between that year and the conclusion of the war-taxes were successively imposed which, according to the cal-culations of the Chancellor of the Exchequer, were to pro-duce £3,400,000. The result was, that in 1821, when that sum (less about £400,000, for taxes repealed) ought to have been paid into the exchequer, the whole revenue of Ireland amounted to only £3,844,000, being £533,000, less than in 1807, previous to one farthing of these additional taxes having been imposed."

The evidence of these statesmen fully corroborates the state-ment in the report of the committee, that Ireland had increased her taxation at a greater rate than even Great Britain ; and the efforts of the United Parliament, in 1816, ought to have sought to relieve her of the excessive burdens. The act which it passed shews that it tried to do away wih the existing protection, and to acquire, by the previous overcharge of the Irish account, a power of increasing her taxation, which right, could not, according to the treaty of Union, have been exercised, until Great Britain had reduced her separate debt.

I hardly know, whether I feel the greatest surprise, at the manner in which the conditions of the Act of Union between Great Britain and Ireland have been violated, or astonishment at the quietude with which the people of Ireland have sub-mitted to this violation ; but my surprise at the one, and astonishment at the other, are both surpassed by wonder at the flagrant dishonesty of the accounts, which have from time to time been presented to Parliament and to you, (a specimc of which I give at foot*) in order to satisfy you and Parliament, that the ruin which was brought upon Ireland was a portion of her own doing—that it was the natural sequence of the Act of Union which, bad as it was, and prejudicial to Irish interests as it proved to be, has, nevertheless, been set aside to make room for a policy infinitely worse and far more detrimental to the improvement of Ireland.

The note shows a systematic exaggeration in the Revenue of Great Britain, and an equally systematic depression in the Revenue of Ireland; and, as logicians say that two opposites can neither be both true nor both false, I am forced to conclude that one of these returns has been falsified, and no one can blame those who think it has been done for a purpose ; either of them presents a very remarkable increase in taxation when contrasted with the ten years antecedent to the Union. I place the figures in contrast, as they shew very vividly the great disadvantage which the Union was to Ireland—

REVENUE OF IRELAND 1791 to 1801...10 years...£13,912,824
      „   1801 to 1811...10 years... 47,237,360
      „   1811 to 1821...10 years... 55,268,912

* I have above extracted from Parliamentary papers a statement of the revenue of Great Britain and Ireland, from 1801 to 1816, and would now direct attention to the discrepancy between the accounts furnished in 1824 and 1841, and as I wish to remove any doubts which may be entertained as to returns I shall give the respective sums from each return, for the year ending the 5th January.

	Great Britain.		Ireland.	
	Per return of 1824.	per return of 1841.	per return of 1824.	per return of 1841.
1802	£34,611,296,		£3,341,892	£
1803	36,349,932	£36,924,627	4,337,269	3,545,631
1804	37,875,099	38,231,619	3,717,942	3,158,237
1805	45,303,286	45,867,417	4,385,487	3,822,960
1806	49,746,475	50,500,144	4,600,953	3,624,781
1807	53,230,372	54,167,615	5,187,908	4,087,561
1808	58,221,737	58,720,880	5,718,967	4,862,960
1809	60,971,440	62,697,886	5,653,753	4,907,561
1810	62,966,838	63,831,453	5,414,328	4,804,803
1811	66,639,571	67,417,777	4,881,021	4,262,279
1812	66,220,412	65,300,063	5,291,381	4,893,150
1813	63,650,795	68,705,323	5,942,151	5,561,533
1814	66,872,587	67,600,314	6,225,391	5,775,640
1815	69,019,729	70,320,617	6,649,766	6,219,169
1816	69,858,901	70,953,122	6,805,513	6,504,820
1817	60,836,853	61,973,894	5,803,220	6,529,150

K

This increase is startling and appalling, and it illustrates most strikingly the disadvantage, which (in a financial point of view,) the Union was to Ireland. The mode in which it was carried, and its effect upon the social system I shall dwell upon hereafter. I quote it here to shew, the almost unparalleled efforts Ireland made to realize the amount which, by the Act of Union, she was forced to contribute, and I have shewn that she paid proportionately with Great Britain. The empire was engaged in a terrific war, involving a heavy expenditure; and the revenue of either Great Britain or Ireland was not sufficient for its expenditure, hence the necessity of borrowing; and in the debt accounts great injustice was done to Ireland.

The accounts which the Act of Union required were very simple. The Irish Exchequer would, in the first instance, for the period from 1801 to 1821, have to provide the interest on her debt previously to the Union, and then a sum equal to two-seventeenths of the expenditure of the United Kingdom ; but, instead of this, a most complicated system of book-keeping was instituted, which was evidently intended to delude, mistify, and mislead the people of both countries, and, under the guise of that system, Ireland has been most grievously wronged—she has been juggled, or defrauded out of the rights guaranteed to her, as a sort of compensation for surrendering her separate national existence by the Act of Union. Thus, in the first instance, the Union was forced upon her, and then, at the end of 16 years, she was deprived of the rights it guaranteed to her.

It may be said, by those who take but a superficial view of the subject, that Ireland was bound to contribute 2-17ths of the Revenue, and even on the figures which have been given, she did not raise that amount, as her taxation for the sixteen years was only one-ninth of that of Great Britain, but the condition of the treaty was, not that Ireland was to contribute 2-17ths of the whole revenue, but that, after paying the separate interest on the debt due previous to the Union, she should contribute 2-17ths towards the general expenditure, it appears from the returns which I have quoted, that Ireland strained every nerve to comply with the requirements of the treaty, that she advanced her taxation at a more rapid rate than Great Britain, and that the disproportion even on the most exaggerated statement of the interest was so very trivial as hardly to deserve notice. This proportion disappears altogether on the proper appreciation of the fact, that in 1816 the British Chancellor of the Exchequer laid hands on the sinking fund to relieve the taxation of Great Britain.

I shall now proceed to examine how far Ireland contributed as to Expenditure. The budgets of each year state the Irish proportion, as given in page 117. In the sixteen years it amounted to £96,021,291. The revenue receipts in the same period were £83,994,493, adding to them £12,000,000, being the revenue received in Great Britain on Irish account ; it makes the revenue of Ireland in the sixteen years £95,994,943, and there would be a deficit of about one million, but this would not include any provision for the interest on the Irish national debt.

The report of the Finance Committee of 1815 adopts another method of ascertaining the proportion of each country, it takes the amount paid by Great Britain on the general account, and the amount paid by Ireland on the general account, and brings them into one fund, as the total expenditure of the Empire; it then divides them into the proportion of 15-17ths and 2-17ths. The total expenditure for the 16 years was £887,495,670. The proportion of Great Britain is £806,281,497, and Ireland £81,214,171,* which is £16,000,000 less than the sum stated in the budgets, as the amount to which she is liable. This is the expenditure of the United Kingdom, exclusive of interest.

* Expenditure of the United Kingdom from 1801 to 1817, shewing the sums paid by Great Britain and Ireland on account of the present charge :—

Years ending 5 Jan.,	Great Britain.	Ireland.
1802	27,244,649	4,249,157
1803	27,228,897	3,535,651
1804	25,094,264	4,176,133
1805	26,462,371	5,360,744
1806	42,389,260	5,019,070
1807	41,611,232	4,944,670
1808	42,111,252	5,144,389
1809	47,777,220	5,631,241
1810	49,781,846	5,719,057
1811	51,589,475	5,324,105
1812	57,149,935	5,595,483
1813	61,992,253	5,306,218
1814	75,124,728	5,319,457
1815	77,589,312	5,283,628
1816	71,568,763	5,303,162
1817	71,568,763	5,302,062

The annual interest of the national debt is given in the return of 1858. I give the particulars in a note at foot.* This account consists of three items, the interest on the debt due by Great Britain at the Union—the interest on the debt due by Ireland at the Union, and the interest due by the United Kingdom on the debt contracted after the Union, that is, the *joint* debt, which was to be borne by each country, according to the rate at which it was to contribute to the general expenditure of the empire; see paragraph of the 7th article as quoted in page 84.

The interest was divided as follows: Separate interest of Great Britain £285,534,000; Ireland, £12,445,000; Interest of debt of the United Kingdom £105,015,705; Total £403,029,705.

Thus we have the separate items of chargeability the general Expenditure, and the Interest account, and I shall bring them together, and see how they represent the separate liability of each country.

Expenditure, from 1801 to 1816, exclusive of interest				£887,495,670
Interest of debt of United Kingdom, 1800 to 1816				105,351,705
Total to be apportioned	...	...	...	992,547,375
Great Britain, 15-17ths,		£874,600,631		
Ireland, 2-17ths,		117,946,744		
				992,547,374

To ascertain the total indebtedness of each country, we must add to the proportion of the general expenditure and interest

	Total Interest.	Great Britain	Ireland.	United Kingdom.
		* Separate Interest.		
1800	£18,582,950	£17,805,075	£777,865	£
1801	19,819,835	do.	do.	1,236,885
1802	20,268,551	do.	do.	1,675,601
1803	20,812,962	do.	do.	2,230,012
1804	21,608,990	do.	do.	3,076,040
1805	22,568,379	do.	do.	3,976,429
1806	23,196,582	do.	do.	4,613,630
1807	23,373,092	do.	do.	4,790,142
1808	23,696,013	do.	do.	5,112,063
1809	24,292,376	do.	do.	5,709,426
1810	24,553,162	do.	do.	5,970,212
1811	25,484,769	do.	do.	6,901,819
1812	26,854,848	do.	do.	8,271,898
1813	29,898,737	do.	do	11,310,787
1814	31,105,644	do.	do.	12,512,694
1815	32,655,017	do.	do.	14,072,667
1816	32,155,350	do.	do.	13,527,404
	£403,029,705	285,533,000	12,445,000	105,051,705

on the *joint* loan, the separate interest which each country should pay for the debt due before the Union, and then deduct the amount of Revenue the balance will shew the deficiency for the entire period.

Great Britain, proportion as above	£874,605,631	
Interest on separate debt ...	285,533,000	
Total to be provided by Great Britain		£1,160,138,631
Revenue for 16 years, 1801 to 1817,		888,265,463
Deficiency of Great Britain		271,873,168
Ireland's proportion as above ...	£117,946,744	
Interest on separate debt ...	12,445,800	
Total to be provided by Ireland		130,392,544
Revenue of Ireland, 16 years, 1801 1817 ...		95,994,942
Deficiency of Ireland		34,397,302

Thus we see that in both countries the expenditure was in excess of the income, and the deficiency had to be made good by borrowing.

The deficiency in Great Britain was	£271,868,147
Do. Ireland	34,296,802

Making the total deficiency for the United Kingdom   £306,264,949

The utmost with which Ireland could, according to the Act of Union, have been charged with would be 2-17ths of the total loan, it would have been £42,000,000, and as as Ireland's deficit was only 34¼ millions, it is evident that, so far from there being a shortness in Ireland's contributions, there was an over payment of nearly 8 millions, and therefore it is most strange that she should be made to appear to have been so deeply in debt in 1816.

_____

LETTER VIII.

THE IRISH ACCOUNTS AFTER THE UNION.

DEBT CHARGED TO IRELAND.

The fourth and fifth paragraphs of the seventh article of the Act of Union seem to me to preclude Ireland from increasing the separate debt which she owed, nor does this appear to have been contemplated either by those who proposed, or those who opposed the Union. Mr. Pitt, in 1799, informed the British House of Commons, that Ireland was not to be called on to contribute a larger proportion than she had done; and in 1801, in laying his budget before the House of Parliament, he took care to announce very clearly the principle on which Ireland should be charged. He said that "Ireland should contribute 2-17ths of the general expenditure and civil charges, and that all the other expenditure, save the interest of the national debt, should be borne by Great Britain." The fourth and fifth paragraphs of the seventh article of the treaty enact, that Ireland should not pay more than her *quota*, and that Parliament might, in order to raise the quota, levy the same taxes on each article consumed in Ireland, as was raised from similar articles in Great Britain. If there was a larger sum raised in any year than Ireland's quota, taxes were to be taken off to that extent, and the balance might be used to pay off any previous deficiency; the evident meaning is, that Great Britain took the risk of the deficiency in the Irish revenue, and it could not become a debt bearing interest. I can see no other construction which can be put upon these paragraphs. Had a state of peace supervened after the Union, then, the two countries would have apportioned the expenditure each year, and raised the amount, but Great Britain was involved in an expensive war. She had for years been unable to raise sufficient to meet her engagements, and was, year after year, obliged to borrow. In the debates preceding the Union, Mr. Foster called attention to this state of things. He stated the amount which had been borrowed in the previous six years, and showed that, if that debt were governed by the principle of the Act of Union, Ireland would have been charged with a very large sum beyond that which she had borrowed, and he argued that this injustice would be perpetrated towards Ireland after the Union. What he predicted took place. The debt of the United Kingdom advanced at a much more rapid rate after the Union than it had done before. The debt due by both countries at the Union was £470,894,250; in 1816, it was £846,978,483. The capital raised in the sixteen years was £376,074,233. Were this divided in the proportion of 15-17ths and 2-17ths, the amount charged to Great Britain would have been £331,830,205, and to Ireland, £42,492,798. This would have been a most enormous addition to the Irish debt—in fact, in the sixteen years, from 1801 to 1816, a sum would have been added to the Irish debt greater by 150 per cent. than the amount which she owed at the Union. If the Irish debt at the Union were, as stated in the return of 1849, £26,841,219, the addition to it of £42,942,798 in sixteen years would have brought it up to £69,794,017—that is, it would have added 150 per cent. to it. If the capital sum were not divided, but that Ireland paid 2-17ths of the annual charge, which is all that is contemplated in the sixth paragraph of the seventh article of the Act of Union, the result would be the same—the taxation to raise the interest would have been increased. The debt of Great Britain at the Union was £457,188,657, adding to it her 15-17ths of the amount borrowed, or £331,830,205, she would, in 1816, have owed £788,018,970, or an addition of about 70 per cent. on the debt in 1801. This comparison shows, how greatly the proportion which was fixed upon, for Ireland, was in excess of the rate at which she ought to contribute. It is certainly very unfair that the debt of one country should have increased at double the ratio of the other; and had Ireland been chargeable with 1-18th (the proportion stated in the notice of the Lords) of the debt contracted after the Union, she would have been liable to £21,000,000. This would have added about 80 per cent. to her debt, and it would have left £355,000,000 as the addition to the debt of Great Britain, or less than 80 per cent. But the proportion fixed upon by Pitt and Castlereagh, while professing to equalize the contributions, really over-burthened Ireland with taxation, and put upon her an undue proportion of the debt—thus realizing what Dr. Johnson said to the Irishman: " Don't join us; if you do we'll rob you. We would have robbed the Scotch if they had anything to be robbed of."

In the previous letter I shewed that the revenue of Ireland had increased at a very rapid rate, and that it more than kept pace with that of Great Britain; indeed, the increase in the Irish revenue was a marvel to the statesmen of that day; in proof of which I may re-quote the speech of

Mr. Vesey Fitzgerald, Chancellor of the Irish Exchequer, who, in February, 1815, referred to this circumstance in the following language:—

He said "that produce of malt in 1802 was £116,604; in 1811, £348,000; and in 1814, £566,000. He would not trouble the house going through all the small articles contained in the paper, but merely touch on the leading ones. Spirits, in 1802, produced £270,000; in 1811, £685,000; and in 1814, £1,575,000. Tobacco, in 1802, gave £140,000; in 1811, £311,000; and in 1814, £504,000. Hearth-money had increased from £32,000, in 1802, to £64,000 in 1814. The assessed taxes had been *doubled*, *quadrupled*, and *quintupled*. The servants' duty had been increased *fourfold*. Windows, in the last three years, had increased £100,000."

There can be no doubt that, had the Irish contribution been fixed at a lower rate—say one-twelfth—she would every year have paid her *quota*, and had a balance. This would have made her annual contributions greater than the amount estimated by Lord Castlereagh in his speech of February, 1800, in which he stated the probable expenditure of Ireland after the Union would be (even with the continuance of the war) £4,492,686. I have, when explaining the construction to be put on the Act of Union, (ante pp. 65 to 69,) stated the mode in which the conditions of the act were set aside and evaded, and the overcharges which, in spite of Act of Union, and in spite of the remonstrances of Irish members, were made in the Irish accounts. I have also illustrated the enormous, fallacious additions which was made by Mr. Corry, in 1801, not only to the debt, but also to the interest which Ireland bore. But, even with all these, it is really wonderful to look at the amount of the debt charged to Ireland.

One of the conditions of the Act of Union required that Great Britain should raise special and separate taxes to pay the interest on the large debt which she owed in 1800; that debt was £457,188,665, the annual interest on which was

£17,805,074. The simple statement that Great Britain has not paid off any portion of the principal, and that she is now only raising £3,282,000 by special and separate taxes, shews at once the fraud that has been perpetrated on Ireland, it proves she has been called on to pay a portion of the interest on the debt of Great Britain. This has been accomplished by removing some of those duties which used to be paid exclusively in Great Britain—such as on soap, glass, bricks, etc. By extending others to Ireland, such as the income and property tax, and by increasing such duties as that on spirits, from the lower level imposed upon Irish whiskey, to the higher rate levied in Great Britain By these means the conditions of the Act of Union have been repealed or abrogated, and Ireland, forced to pay an undue and excessive taxation, has retrograded in almost every respect.

The manner in which the conditions of the Act of Union were subsequently set aside, (from 1801 to 1816,) is a striking episode in history, and it recalls vividly to mind the language of Chief Justice Bushe in the debate on the Union. He then said—

"I implore the House to consider what is the security for their performance ? I may be told the articles of the Union and the faith of nations. I hold a compact where one of the contracting parties covenants that he will cease to exist, to be an absurdity, when individuals contract with each other, the contract binds them and those who survive them : but who is the executor of a Parliament ? Who is to enforce the performance when this house is no more? National faith—a rotten security at the best, but British faith, the rottenest of all—punic faith. What! Britain talk of her faith in the very moment that she violates the compact of 1782 ? If ever there was a solemn league and covenant between nations, the settlement of 1782 was that transaction."

If the account of the two countries had been honestly stated, and fairly adjusted, Ireland might have realized the expectations of Pitt, and she might have advanced in civilization and wealth, at the same rate as Great Britain; but so great was the pressure of taxation that she receded; she lost what she had gained between 1782 and 1800, and, instead of advancing, she retrograded.

I now come to examine what was the amount of the debt contracted on *joint* account between 1800, and the time when the Exchequers were consolidated in 1816?

The return from which I before quoted (Parliamentary paper, 443, 1858), affords information as to the increase in the national debt each year since the Union, by which it appears:

That the entire amount of debt created for the United Kingdom, from 1801 to 1816, was £376,074,203, of which Ireland was charged with £103,459,432. I give the particulars of each year in the note at foot *

Ireland was at the utmost liable to be charged, say 2-17ths of these loans, which would be only £42,949,798. According to this account she was charged with nearly one-third of it ; but upon what principle these charges were made, or how they can be justified, according to the Act of Union, I am at an utter loss to decide.

In Mr. Speaker Foster's speech before the Union, when contrasting the amount of the British and Irish debt he shewed the difference between the position of Ireland in 1800, and what it would have been if the Union had taken place; he added the debts of Great Britain and Ireland together, and took as the Irish proportion, under the conditions of the Union at 2-17ths of the whole; and he shewed that it would have made the debt of Ireland £10,000,000 more than she had borrowed. His mode of calculating was not objected to, nay, it was assumed to be correct, and in accordance with the idea involved in the conditions of the treaty. If that con-

---

* Statement of the amount borrowed in each year, from 1801 to 1816, for the service of the United Kingdom, from the Parliamentary paper of 1858, and statement of the amount charged to Ireland, from 1801 to 1816, from the Parliamentary paper of 1848

Loans of United Kingdom, Parliamentary paper, 443, 1858.			Charged to Ireland, Parliamentary paper, 423, 1849.		
1801	...	£46,617,391	1801	...	£4,413,337
1802	...	20,141,237	1802	...	4,273,311
1803	...	10,079,788	1803	...	3,210,524
1804	...	23,398,522	1804	...	9,486,490
1805	...	28,733,529	1805	...	4,660,000
1806	...	21,226,836	1806	...	5,886,153
1807	...	12,729,729	1807	...	5,470,548
1808	...	9,729,471	1808	...	5,042,837
1809	...	10,915,428	1809	. .	4,984,615
1810	...	7,732,845	1810	...	7,585,971
1811	...	16,046,580	1811	...	2,770,154
1812	...	28,054,150	1812	...	9,329,538
1813	...	81,838,195	1813	...	12,415,985
1814	...	25,046,395	1814	...	10,687,454
1815	...	47,898,873	1815	...	16,567,385
Total	...	390,144,769	Total	...	106,809,794
Paid off, 1816,		14,170,565	Paid off, 1816,		3,350,362
		£376,074,204			£103,459,432

struction were carried out, in charging Ireland with the post-Union debt of the empire, she would have been liable to £42,492,798. This, I contend, was an excessive sum to charge Ireland with, but it was the extreme. She was charged with a much larger sum, and she was expected to raise the interest and sinking fund on this amount. The charges which were made, and which I have taken as above from a Parliamentary paper, are not *legal* charges. No Irish debt could be created but by Act of Parliament, and the amount of Irish debt created from 1801 to 1816 in this legal way, was only £22,800,000. The Exchequer of Great Britain was empowered to remit moneys to that of Ireland, but there is no proof that she did so; and the account between the two nations is in a most unsatisfactory position, and has never been settled. Ireland has been debited with large sums, without the sanction of Parliament. But any such debit is illegal, and ought to be inquired into. It is not only absurd, but irrational to suppose for a moment, that Ireland owed such a sum as she was charged with. The debt charged to Ireland *exceeds the entire amount of her chargeability* towards the general expenditure of the empire.

I will glance at some of the items, in order to shew the apparent whim which dictated the several debits to the Irish account, which is strikingly shewn when we come to examine some of the years separately ; thus in 1805, the increase in the national debt was £23,738,527, and of it £9,456,491, or one-third, was charged to Ireland. In 1800, the United Kingdom borrowed £7,732,645, and put £7,585,971, to Ireland's debit. Again in 1814, the amount added to the national debt was £25,046,405 ; but the Irish debt was loaded with £10,687,454, or nearly one half of the joint loan of that year ; again in 1808, the national debt was increased £10,915,428 of which Ireland was debited with £5,042,837, or nearly one-half ; but the grand *coup* was reserved for 1816, when, in order to facilitate the consolidation of the Exchequer, Ireland was debited with £16,567,375, ! ! How this marvellous result was accomplished is incomprehensible ; it is almost incredible were it not proved by the existence of Parliamentary papers.

I have stated the particulars with regard to the years 1801 and 1802. It would occupy too much space to go through the circumstances of each year, but I may refer to the last four years, because the statement in the Budget received confirmation in a somewhat curious manner.

On the 25th April, 1815, Mr. Bankes moved that the property and income tax should be extended to Ireland, and Mr. Vesey Fitzgerald, the Chancellor of the Exchequer, opposed the motion in his speech, see Hansard, vol 30, page 850; he adverted to the loans raised for Ireland, and said, " In the year 1812, £4,700,000 was raised in England, at a charge including the sinking fund of £7. 0s. 9d. per cent., and a loan was raised in Ireland of £1,500,000, at the lesser charge of £6. 4s. 0d.; in 1813, £6,500,000 was raised in England, at £7. 4s. 7d. per cent., and £2,000,000 in Ireland, at £6. 8s. 1d. and in 1814, £5,958,000 was raised in England, at £5. 18s. 9d., and £3,000,000 in Ireland, at £5. 11s. 9d. The entire charge for these years was, 1812, £422,000, in 1813, £595,000, and in 1814, £521,000, making in the aggregate for the three years, £1,545,000. The estimate of the taxes to meet this charge was, 1812, £468,0, 1813, £60000,000, 1814, £535,000, total, £1,605,000. He stated the increase in the revenues of 1815 over 1812, was £1,561,900, the Irish revenue was, in 1813, £6,616,488, 1814 £6,160,190, and in 1815, £6,716,056.

When introducing the budget, in 1815, the same gentleman gave the following statement of the ways and means in Irish currency.

Quota for 1815,	£10,574,215	Balance in Consolidated Fund	£686,807
Interest and charges for the Sinking Fund,	6,098,169	Produce of the Revenue	6,100,000
		Profit on Lotteries	125,000
		Repayment of sums advanced by Ireland for Military purposes	100,000
		2-17th old stores sold	90,305
		Loan raised in England for the service of Ireland £9,000,000 British equal to Irish.	9,750,000
Total	£16,672,384	Total	£16,584,112

The revenue for 1815, which was estimated at £6,100,000, yielded £6,805,573, but the account shews that £9,000,000 was to be borrowed, and that there was a balance to credit of £88,252. Strange to say, in that year the Irish debt which was created, was £16,587,385!! The difference between the

amounts authorised to be raised, and which Mr. Vesey Fitzgerald, in the speech above quoted, states, as the loans on
Irish accounts in the years 1812, 1813, and 1814, differ so
materially for the sums raised as to create a most unpleasant
feeling respecting the accuracy and truthfulness of the
accounts between the two nations; it stands thus:—

IRISH LOANS. Per Mr. Fitzgerald's speech, April 25, 1815.			PER RETURN OF 1819.		
1812. Raised in			1812. Debt created		£9,329,538
England	£4,700,000				
Ireland	1,500,000				
Total		6,200,000			
1813. Raised in			1813. " "		12,415,385
England	6,500,000				
Ireland	2,000,000				
		8,500,000			
1814. Raised in			1814. "		10,687,454
England	5,958,000				
Ireland	3,000,000				
		8,958,000			
1815. Per Budget		9,000,000	1815.		16,567,385
Total, four years		32,658,000			
Overcharge		16,341,762			
		£48,999,762			£48,999,762

At this lapse of time I am at a loss to conceive on what
principle Ireland was debited with such sums as above stated;
the Act of Union, provided that the debt contracted by the
United Kingdom, was to be one of undivided liability ; it was
a joint, or common debt, to which the property of the United
Kingdom was liable ; it could not be broken into fragments ;
but even if it were broken into fragments, Ireland was only
liable to 2-17ths of the amount borrowed, or £42,949,748,
instead of which she was charged with £103,720,818.

It is rather strange, but no less true, that wherever we
turn in the accounts between the two nations we are met
with inconsistency and difficulty. There is so much of mystification, and such apparent contradiction, that I cannot
account for it. For instance, in 1815, the Chancellor of the
Exchequer reported that he had raised a loan of £36,000,000,
of which £27,000,000 was for Great Britain, and £9,000,000
for Ireland; and he stated that the terms were £184 for each
£100. At this rate, the amount of debt created would have

been £66,240,000, but the increase in the national debt that
year was, according to the account of 1858, £47,898,873
As the portion of the debt for Ireland was, according to the
Chancellor's statement, one-fourth of the whole, she should
only be charged with £11,974,470, instead of which, she was
charged that year with £16,567,385; so that the operation
stands thus, on the shewing of the British Chancellor of the
Exchequer.

Ireland's portion of the loan
    was   £9,000,000,
       for which she had to pay   ... 16,567,385
Great Britain's portion,   27,000,000
       for which she had to pay   ... 31,331,498

    Total debt created in 1815   ... £47,898,873

Thus shewing the justice which was meted out to Ireland,
even in the matter of raising money! And this was done on
the eve of the consolidation of the Exchequers, and had the
effect of increasing the nominal Irish debt!

I do not think Parliament had any power to split up or
divide the debt which was contracted after the Union ; nor
can I discover that it was done by Parliament; it has been
managed by officials, in their bureaux; the debt was a joint
debt, but even if it be admitted that the Parliament of
the United Kingdom, in which the Irish members were
only one-sixth, had the power of arbitrarily charging Ireland
with such a portion of the *joint* debt as it might see fit, or
such taxes as it might see fit, there would be nothing to prevent their debiting Ireland with one-half of the revenue, and
considering the unpaid balance as a debt. If that be correct,
then the articles entered into by the Lords and Commons of
England and the Lords and Commons of Ireland, which were
laid before George III., and approved by him, were a sham
and a delusion, and the declarations of Lord Castlereagh in
introducing the act, were false and visionary, and the whole
proceeding was an intentional deception. I cannot adopt
that view, and I am forced to regard the Act of Union
either as a exposition of a fixed and definite decision, as the
expression of the bargain, which forms the articles of the treaty
it recites ; or as being wholly a sham. If the latter idea be
seriously entertained by any one, it may be asked under
what authority the Parliament of the United Kingdom sits
and acts ? Its sole authority is derived from this treaty
of Union, the acts of the British, and of the Irish Parliaments

in 1800 form its written constitution, and I hold that it is not competent for the Parliament of the United Kingdom to do anything contrary to those acts, without at the same time vitiating and nullifying the act which gave it existence.

That the Parliament of the United Kingdom did increase the separate debt of Ireland after the Union, is a matter of history—at least it raised £22,800,000 on Irish account—that it had the power to do it, is the question for consideration ; the amounts which were charged against Ireland, and nominally increased her debt, have not even the authority of Parliament; thus to bring the respective debts of both countries to that proportion which would enable Parliament to dispense with the restrictions imposed by the Act of Union, was contrary to the act itself. Those charges were made for a purpose, and that purpose was to increase the nominal debt and the taxation of Ireland, but this could not be fairly done under the Act of Union.* Now

* The following is the amount of the Irish debt and interest as stated in 1817, in order to justify the consolidation of the Exchequers, and enable Parliament to levy equal taxes in both countries : and of the debt and interest as stated in 1858, when the apparent necessity for such overcharge had ceased—the documents are accessible to all, and I quote from them to shew the great injustice which has been done to Ireland :– The amount stated in the return of 1819, is the redeemed and unredeemed debt, that of 1858 is the unredeemed debt.

	From session paper, No. 35, session, 1819.		From session paper, 443, session, 1858.	
	Irish debt.	Interest.	Irish debt.	Interest.
1800	£22,345,190	£950,698	£13,705,615	£777,875
1801	27,792,975	1,157,064	13,295,471	757,359
1802	32,226,313	1,274,227	13,379,051	787,299
1803	36,499,623	1,388,316	14,712,739	803,985
1804	39,740,146	1,467,674	14,949,185	815,307
1805	49,196,637	1,752,286	13,933,649	765,328
1806	53,856,637	1,941,961	16,114,570	839,984
1807	59,742,790	2,094,834	16,142,979	846,763
1808	65,213,338	2,229,015	17,955,622	929,453
1809	70,256,175	2,390,551	18,980,954	957,429
1810	75,240,790	2,523,102	17,891,428	884,847
1811	82,826,762	2,670,025	21,765,441	931,902
1812	85,596,915	2,697,201	23,738,535	1,101,868
1813	94,926,454	2,920,021	25,030,125	1,148,081
1814	107,311,839	3,268,148	27,593,154	1,261,358
1815	118,029,292	3,552,231	26,776,323	1,231,473
1816	134,596,677	3,963,284 *	28,701,246	1,313,795

* This is the amount of interest. I do no wish to overload my argument by considering the question of the contributions to the sinking fund.

that the purpose is served, these charges disappear from the national accounts, and the return which has been recently issued, (number 443, session 1858,) abandons those illusory charges, and places the Irish debt on a truer bases. I refer to the older paper merely as a matter of history, to shew how the approximation of the debts of both countries was accomplished. I do not wish to encumber my argument with the figures.

The debt of Ireland is stated, in the return of 1849, to have been, in 1817, £130,561,037, but of this £27,222,611 was redeemed debt—that is, the accumulation of the sinking und, which was contributed from the annual income of Ireland. The charge against Ireland is nearly one-third of the debt contracted, instead of being 2-17ths, and it is made up from two sources:—first, there were overcharges made in the annual accounts—that is, sums were considered separate charges on Ireland which really belonged to the debt of the empire, and she was expected to pay the entire of these amounts, instead of having to contribute only 2-17ths; and then the sums with which she was so charged were made to accumulate at compound interest. The interest charged against Ireland in the account of 1819, which I have given, was £37,300,970, whereas, sixteen years' interest of the separate debt she owed would be £18,522,029 ; the overcharge on this item alone is £18,878,946, or more than double.

A very general error prevails as to the debt of Ireland in 1816. Many persons suppose it was £130,000,000, and one public body has adopted this, as being the correct amount due; but in doing so they have failed to distinguish between the redeemed and unredeemed debt. The former was not a debt, it was stock which had been purchased by the Commissioners for the redemption of the National Debt, out of the annual contributions from the Irish revenue towards the sinking fund. This, as long as the sinking fund was in existence, was considered a debt, and the interest on it was paid, as well as the interest on the unredeemed debt, but the sum so raised was applied to the reduction of the unredeemed debt. The charge on Ireland for the sinking fund was, in 1815, £2,087,809; and, in looking at the budgets of each year, from the Union to 1816, we must remember that this charge for the sinking fund forms a part of the debt, and, as the Income was not sufficient, she was charged with debt to provide this fund.

Another reason for the magnitude in the debt of Ireland was the improvident system of borrowing. The British ministry of that day preferred raising a large capital, at a low rate of interest, than borrowing the amount at a higher rate. Money was then worth five per cent., and, in order to borrow at three per cent., it was necessary to issue a larger amount of capital. In 1805, the Hon. James Fitzgerald called attention to this improvidence. In 1810, Sir John Newport lamented the increase in the funded debt of Ireland, and urged " that if the debt of Ireland were raised, like the debt of England, within the country, a great part would be done away." In the debate on Mr. Bankes' motion to extend the property-tax to Ireland, the Irish Chancellor of the Exchequer boasted of the great advantage which had arisen from borrowing in Ireland, where the amount was borrowed on far more advantageous terms. We have a singular proof of the disadvantage of this system of borrowing in the loan of 1816. The Chancellor of the Exchequer reported to the House of Commons (see " Annual Register," 1815, page 191,) that he had raised £36,000,000, on the following terms:—£130-3 per cent. Reduced Stock, £18-4 per cent. Stock, and £44-3 per cent. Consols—in all, 184 for each £100 received. Speculators, in anticipation of this loan, forced down the funds. In January, 1815, they were 65; in April, when the loan was raised 56½; and in December 67—thus showing how disadvantageous it was to raise money at this low rate. The evil of this mode was pointed out by the Irish members at the time, and their views on finance have since been adopted by the ablest financiers.

The amount proposed to be raised on Irish account, and the amount of debt created, present a very great contrast; and I give them, page 94; they shew how the nominal debt of Ireland was swelled and puffed out from the improvident system of borrowing. This does not tell much on my argument, and I merely adduce it to shew the soundness of the views expressed by the Irish financiers of this day.

I base my case on a very broad foundation—so broad that it will support the structure I want to raise on it ; and it is simply this—according to the Act of Union, the separate debt of Ireland closed on the 31st December, 1800, and all debts contracted afterwards were joint debt. No addition could be made to the separate debt of Ireland. The Parliament of the United Kingdom might tax her, as they did tax her, in

L

order to make her pay the proportion, 2-17ths, for the twenty
years after the Union. If they did not raise sufficient to pay
the quota of Ireland, the balance was at the risk of Great Britain; but, in point of fact, the returns of revenue and expenditure alike show that Ireland did pay her quota
to the full; and, therefore, the pretence that she owed
£130,000,000 in 1817 as a monstrous fabrication.

I have been forced to discuss this question of debt, and the
previously stated subjects of revenue and expenditure, because the act of 1816 was based solely on the supposition
that Ireland owed such a sum, as made it competent for Parliament to consider whether they could consolidate the Exchequers, and get rid of all separate accounts. If Ireland did
not owe the amount which was charged against her, then it
was not at all competent for Parliament to consider the
consolidation of the Exchequers; and if it was not competent
for Parliament to consider the question, it could not be competent for it to legislate thereon. The immediate effect
of that legislation was to increase the proportionate taxation
of Ireland; and it is under that supposed power that Mr.
Gladstone has, since 1853, nearly doubled the taxation of
Ireland.

Therefore, it is absolutely necessary to look at the indebtedness of Ireland in 1816 in a fair, honest, and manly manner. It is necessary to have definite ideas on the subject of
the Irish liabilities; and I think the figures which I have
brought forward, from the highest authority within my
reach, must satisfy all impartial persons, that the account
against Ireland was greatly overcharged. Every authority
admits that the proportion fixed at the Union was too high;
I maintain that, high as it was, and unfair as it was, yet Ireland discharged it to the utmost; and having done so, it was
not competent for Parliament to have deprived her of the protection, which was so solemnly guaranteed to her by the Act
of Union.

LETTER IX.

A COMMITTEE was appointed in 1814, to consider the financial condition of Ireland. This committee seems to have laboured to arrange the accounts of the two countries, and in the 13th page of their report, which was ordered to be printed the 14th June, 1814, they say:—

"Your committee have employed a considerable portion of their time and attention in the investigation of the expenditure of the United Kingdom, with a view to the settlement of the account of proportionate contribution between the two countries. They have not yet the means of stating an account with so much exactness as to serve as the foundation of a definite settlement between Great Britain and Ireland, as the accounts which they have directed to be made up in Ireland, are not yet completed; while they have been in preparation, your committee have thought they could not be more usefully employed during several of their sittings, than in discussing and settling, subject to the final judgment of Parliament, the principles by which the account ought to be regulated, with respect to certain articles, as to which the sense of the Act of Union appears to admit of question. With respect to these points, your committee are of opinion, that in the adjustment of the payments made on account of the joint charge of Great Britain and Ireland, the payments made from the consolidated fund of Ireland, since the Union, under the act 40 Geo. III., cap. 34, (so far as relates to any compensation made to bodies corporate, or individuals in respect of any city or borough which may have ceased to send any member or members to Parliament, in consequence of the Union,) should not be considered as a joint charge.'

This is a point on which the Irish people naturally felt, and still feel very indignant. They never were convinced that the Union would be advantageous to them, they knew it was brought about by bribery and corruption; but it was hard indeed to expect they should pay for the rod used for their own chastisement. The Union was brought about to secure the strength of the British empire, and it was Britain which should pay the cost. It was an outrage on the feelings as well as the pockets of the Irish people, to force them to pay for bribing their representatives, to betray their country.

The committee of 1814, was followed by one in 1815, from whose report followed the legislation of 1816, which, in consolidating the Exchequers of the two countries, and putting an end to the separate budgets, and separate system of accounts, has given rise to the belief, that Ireland was deprived of the protection from excessive or undue taxation, guaranteed to her by the Union. I think an unfair construction has been put upon the act of 1816, but I shall treat of that hereafter. I am now dealing with the report of the select committee of 1815.

Even at the risk of seeming to repeat what I have quoted before, I must remind my readers of the condition of the two countries which the committee was bound to investigate, they had to consider—was Ireland taxed beyond her relative ability, as regards Great Britain ? As to the means of ascertaining this relative ability, I must again refer to Lord Castlereagh's speech in 1800. He said:—

" In respect to *past* expenses, Ireland was to have no concern whatever with the debt of Great Britain; but the two countries were to unite as to future expenses, *on a strict measure of mutual ability.*"

He then proceeds to shew that the course which had been followed with Scotland could not be pursued with regard to Ireland, and said—

" Such, however, is the disproportion between the debts of the two kingdoms, that a common system was then impossible ; nor could any system of equivalent, as in the case of Scotland, be applied for equalizing their contributions. It was therefore necessary that the debts of the two kingdoms should be kept distinct, and that, of course, their taxation should be *separate and proportionate.*"

Bearing in mind that Ireland was especially exempted from paying any portion of the charge for the British debt, and that she had received no compensation for doing so ; and remembering that the treaty of the Union was forced upon her against her wish, we are the better able to appreciate the full force of the report of the finance committee of 1815, which seems to have been appointed for the purpose, of finding some pretext for removing from Ireland, the protection to which she was entitled under the treaty of Union.

This report, (No. 214 of the Session of 1815,) does not state the names of the members who composed the committee, so that I am unable to say whether there was a *single Irish member* on it; nor does it contain the names of the witnesses who were examined, or the evidence which they gave. It is a one-sided, and most unfair document; nay, more, it is a singular tissue of falsehood and hypocrisy. It pretends to sympathise with Ireland; it praises her large contributions to the revenue, extols the sacrifices she has made, and professes a desire to relieve her; but, at the same time, shews the cloven hoof, by stating that, notwithstanding all Ireland had suffered from forced and excessive taxation, it had not been pushed to its extreme limits, as there were, to use its own words, "some important branches protected from any increase, before the year 1820, by the Act of Union;" and the committee, in order to get rid of this protection to Ireland, while it professes that its object was " to relieve Ireland from a burthen, which experience has proved to be too great; and at the same time, with the hope of rendering her resources more productive," they recommend the House of Commons by a declaration to remove the protection given by the Act of Union, and " to declare that all future expenditure, together with the interest and charges of the *joint* debt, shall be defrayed indiscriminately by equal taxation imposed upon the same articles in each."

We rarely see such undisguised hypocrisy; under cover of benefit, it seeks to effect an injury! Under guise of relieving this country, it removes its protection!! Under pretence of making her resources more productive, it increases the levy of additional taxation!!!

I must examine this report somewhat in detail, as it formed the basis for subsequent legislation of a most injurious character for Ireland.

It commences, (page 4,) with a very extraordinary account of the funded debt of Ireland, which it states was on the 25th March, 1800, £24,037,290, and on the 5th January, 1815, £127,865,037, Irish currency. It makes the interest and sinking fund in 1800, £1,315,277, and in 1815, £5,908,891; but it explains this statement with regard to the debt by saying, " It appears that the total amount of the public funded debt of Ireland was, on 5th January, 1815, £127,805,067, of which £22,455,155 had been purchased by the commissioners, for the redemption of the national debt, leaving a funded debt unredeemed of £105,409,613," (Irish currency.)

A subsequent return, on the motion of Viscount Goderich, (No. 443, session 1858,) makes the Irish debt, funded and unfunded, in 1800, £13,705,615, and in 1815, £26,776,323; and the interest in 1800 to have been £777,875, and in 1815, £1,231,473. The difference between the two accounts is striking and appalling. It is quite evident they are not both right. The report of 1815 does not give any account of the growth of the debt of Great Britain from 1800 to 1815, the time of which it treats, nor has it any information about the *joint debt.* The separate debt of Ireland was, according to the first paragraph of the seventh article of the treaty of Union, "the debt incurred before the Union;" and according to the third paragraph, the interest and charges of that debt, were to be defrayed as the first charge out of the Exchequer; this report does not say by what authority the separate debt of Ireland was increased from £24,037,290, in 1800, to £127,865,067, in 1815; and I assert the latter figures are false and fallacious. Ireland did not, in 1815, owe any such debt. The sixth paragraph of the seventh article enacts, "That all moneys raised after the Union by loan, in peace or war, were to be considered a joint debt," and this report has no statement whatever of the joint debt. It is thus evidently unfair and dishonest, and it proves its own unfairness, by shewing that the annual charge for the interest and sinking fund of the separate debts had increased from £1,315,277, in 1800, to £5,908,891 in 1815! I must here quote the commencement of the seventh article of Union—"That it be the seventh article of Union, that the charge arising from the payment of the interest and sinking fund, for the reduction of the principal of the debt incurred in either kingdom *before the Union* shall continue to be separately defrayed by Great Britain and Ireland;" and from the sixth paragraph, which says, "That all moneys be raised *after the Union* by loan, in peace or war, for the United Kingdom by the Parliament thereof, shall be considered to be a joint debt, and the charges thereof shall be borne by the respective countries in the proportion of their respective contributions." This shews that the increase in the separate debt of Ireland was a most mendacious statement, utterly opposed to the Act of Union, and evidently prepared to force on a foregone conclusion. The report

of 1815 next proceeds to give the permanent revenue
of Ireland, the gross receipts of which were, it says, in 1791,
£1,805,964; in 1800, £3,445,718; and in 1815, £6,937,558.
In 24 years they had increased nearly four-fold!! This table
is, however, like almost all the tables we have seen on Irish
revenue, grossly unfair. At the time of which it treats it
was the habit to make payments on account of the public
service, out of the customs and excise, before they were paid
into the Exchequer. Thus, in 1815, the payments for army
of reserve was £111,700; for navy and army half-pay,
£101,504; and for bounties for national objects £31,889,
making a total of payments of £245,093 before it reached
the Exchequer. The unfairness in the table before us lies in
the fact, that it does not give the net revenue applicable to
national objects, which it should do; but the net revenue paid
into the Exchequer. It then professes to give the expenditure
Ireland on the separate and joint account, and states that,
on the 5th January, 1815, there was a balance of £6,016,986
due by Ireland to Great Britain. The next portion of the
report is the trade and navigation returns; then follows an
extract from the Act of Union, and an estimate of the value
of the Irish debt, in comparison with that of Great Britain.
The report says:—

" Your Committee are aware that any strict and literal interpretation of
this article is attended with considerable difficulty ; but construing it with
reference to what must have been in the contemplation of both Parliaments,
when this article was adopted, as most distinctly appears from the spirit,
and from the context of the Act of Union—namely, *protection to the
country then least burthened with debt*, and least able to provide extraordinary resources."

We gladly accept this construction of the treaty. Ireland
was the country least burthened with debt at the time of the
Union, and the committee might naturally have inquired,
was it possible that the country least burthened with debt in
1800, could have been most heavily in debt in 1815,
especially when all debts contracted after the Union,
were, according to that act, joint debts, and the charges to be
borne in proportion to the respective contributions of each
country? The only charge on separate account recognised
by the Act of Union was, the interest on the debt due by
Ireland previous to the Union, which it states to have been
£1,315,274; yet the charge for separate account was, in 1802,
the very year after the Union, £3,316,266, and this separate

charge was so increased that it is put down, in 1815, at
£5,892,658. It really seems incredible that such open violation of the Act of Union—such apparent contempt of its
provisions, did not strike the mind of every man on the committee, the facts are so patent. Ireland was comparatively free
from debt in 1800; the treaty was meant, say the committee,
to " protect the country least burthened with debt." All debts
contracted after the Union were joint debts, and how, then,
could it be possible that the Irish debt was proportionately
larger than the British debt in 1815? It was a moral impos-
sibility that it could be so! It does not require the aid of
figures to demonstrate a truth so apparent; yet, the committee
adopt the strange hallucination, that the debt of Ireland,
which was in 1800, to that of Great Britain, in the same proportion of 1 to 18 according to this report; or as 1 to 32
according to Lord Goderich's returns, had swelled so much
that, in 1815, it was in relation to the British debt as 1 to 7.
Having thus, (as they thought,) established that the debt of
Ireland bore to that of Great Britain, the proportion of 2 to
15, though in truth, this condition was not reached; the
committee resolved, that Parliament was in a position that it
might avail itself of this circumstance, to consolidate the
Exchequer of the two countries, and deprive Ireland of the
shadow of this " protection," which, they say, " was afforded
to the country then least burthened with debt;" but which,
owing to the manner in which the national accounts were
kept, had become, (according to the public ledger,) the most
heavily burthened. The committee of 1815 proceed in their
report to say :—

" It remained then for your committee to consider whether or not, the
respective circumstances of the two countries would henceforth admit of
their contributing indiscriminately by equal taxes, etc.
" It is well known that Parliament has not hitherto deemed it expedient
to extend to Ireland the most productive of the taxes imposed in Great
Britain for raising by direct taxation the supplies within the year. In
other respects your committee have found the taxes of Ireland not fully
equalized with those of Great Britain, particularly in the excise, where
some important branches are protected from increase until 1820, by the
act of Union ; and as the stamps. But on the other great head of revenue—customs and assessed taxes—they have formed a very near approximation between the rates in both countries.
" And your committee cannot but remark, that for several years Ireland
has advanced in permanent taxation more rapidly than Great Britain
itself, notwithstanding the immense exertions of the latter country, and
including the extraordinary and war taxes. The permanent revenue of

Great Britain having increased from the year 1801, when the amounts of both countries were first made to correspond, in the proportion of 16½ to 10.

" The whole revenue of Great Britain, including war taxes, in the proportion of 21¼ to 10 ; and the revenues of Ireland in the proportion of 23 to 10.

" But in the 24 years referred to by your committee, the increase of Irish revenue has been in the proportion of 46¾ to 15."

This evidence is of the utmost importance, it is that of a committee selected for the purpose of finding a pretext to assimilate the taxes of the two countries; that is to sweep away the last vestige of protection which Ireland had under the Act of Union, and to enable the Parliament of the United Kingdom to levy indiscriminate taxes in both countries; in other words, to make Ireland responsible for the interest of the debt contracted by Britain previous to the Union; and yet this committee is forced to admit that the taxation of Ireland had advanced at a greater ratio than that of Great Britain, and it must be remembered that when Lord Castlereagh introduced the Act of Union, he urged its acceptance on the ground that the taxation of Ireland would be reduced.

The report of 1815, concludes thus:—

" It appears to your committee, from the whole tenor of the Act of Union, and from the very circumstance of both Parliaments having proposed and acquiesced in certain guards and temporary restrictions, calculated to prevent the too sudden imposition of burthens on the weaker country, before time had been allowed for the acquisition of at least equivalent benefits, that an Union as strict and perfect in matters of finance as that existing between England and Scotland, to the extent of consolidating the treasuries and the Exchequer, must have been contemplated by the two legislatures.

" On the whole, therefore, with a view to the clear advantage of all parts of the empire, to relieving Ireland from a burden which experience has proved to be too great, and at the same time, with the hope of rendering her resources more productive, your committee have come to the following resolution :—Resolved—'That it is the opinion of this committee, that it is now become expedient that Parliament should take into consideration so much of the seventh article of the Act of Union as respects the competence of Parliament, under certain circumstances therein stated, to declare that all further expenditure of the United Kingdom, together with all interest and charges of the joint debt incurred previous to such declaration, shall be defrayed indiscriminately by equal taxation imposed on the same articles in each.' "

This report was dated 19th June, 1815, and on its being laid before the House of Commons, Mr. Vesey Fitzgerald stated, that no legislation would be proposed until the following year.

On testing this extraordinary report by the information since supplied, I am forced to the opinion that that committee withheld from Parliament such a statement of the revenue of Great Britain and Ireland as would have enabled it to arrive at a correct opinion, whether it was competent for the Parliament of the United Kingdom to consolidate the Exchequers of both countries. I impugn, not only the accuracy, but also the honesty of that report; and I assert that the precedent conditions, required by the Act of Union, not having been fairly and legitimately arrived at, the act of 1816, which is based on the supposition that the conditions precedent had been reached, is, in itself null and void; and the Irish people are entitled to the same priveleges, protection, and immunities, as if that act had not been passed. I have no hesitation in declaring my opinion, that as the Act of Union required the previous payment, by Great Britain, of a large portion of the debt which she owed before the Union, before any consolidation of the Exchequers, and, as that liquidation has not taken place, Great Britain is still bound to provide every year for the payment of the interest of the debt which she owed at the Union; that interest was £17,845,075; during the last five years Great Britain has only raised by special taxes, about £3,180,000 per annum, so that she has shamefully violated the Act of Union, by forcing Ireland to pay interest on the debt which Great Britain owed in 1800.

I think the evidence which I have adduced, proves beyond dispute, that Ireland did not owe the amount which is here alleged against her. The investigation of the accounts seems to have revealed some rather extraordinary facts, one was, that the debt due by Ireland in 1797, had been all discharged, and that there was an available surplus. An act was passed in 1816, the 56 Geo. III., cap 70, to which I shall have to refer, which declares that this debt was all paid, and enacts, that the stock £5,829,156 13s. 4d. should be cancelled, and there was a balance over and above of £2,063,273 5s. 2d. to credit; this arose from funds which the Irish Parliament had provided, to pay off that loan, thus shewing their care and forethought. Another act was passed the same session, 56 Geo. III., cap. 89, for cancelling a further portion of the Irish debt, amounting to £4,378,186. This was done at a time when the English Chancellor of the Exchequer, violated the act with regard to the British sinking fund; and in order to save that country from taxation applied £7,000,000 out of the sinking fund, towards the expenses of the year.

The report of the finance committee of 1815 does not afford us any means of comparing the alleged debt of Ireland with the actual debt of the United Kingdom, it states that

The unredeemed capital of the Irish debt was,
(Irish currency) £105,400,613
Equal to Dutch Currency   96,625,497
The return of 1824 makes it to have been in
1815, (British Currency)   97,311,180

The two returns very nearly agree, indeed, so nearly, that we shall suppose them to be correct. The unredeemed debt of the United Kingdom, as given in the return of 1858, was on the 5th January, 1815, £861,039,049. According to the Act of Union the Amalgamation of the Exchequers, could not take place unless the two debts bore to each other the proportion of 17 to 2. This principle is conceded by the finance committee, who say, " Your committee have directed their attention maturely to consider whether it is still within the *competency* of the United Parliament to declare a consolidation of the debts and expenditures of the two countries, under the seventh article of the act of Union;" a simple computation of the relative amounts shew that 2-17ths of the unredeemed debt of the United Kingdom would have been £101,181,063, and as Ireland was alleged in the report only to owe the sum of £96,625,497 British, it was not competent for the Parliament of the United Kingdom to have availed itself of the condition of the seventh article of the treaty.

The Report of the Select Committee on the Irish Poor of 1830 states, that the loans raised on Irish account from 1801 to 1817 were £74,068,791; that the amount paid off was £17,608,086, leaving a balance of £56,459,983; this was the debt contracted by Ireland, and it does not make the Irish debt bear the proportion to the British required by the Act of Union.

I deny that Ireland owed £96,625,497 if the account was fairly stated, but even on the shewing of those who framed the report, her debt did not bring the subject within the purvey of Parliament, and therefore the necessary precedent conditions not having been arrived at, it was not competent for the Parliament of the United Kingdom to have legislated on it, and if it was not competent for it to have legislated, the legislation is invalid.

LETTER. X.

THE DEBT OF IRELAND.

I HAVE, in my previous letters, examined the Revenue, the Interest, and the Expenditure accounts of Ireland, and of Great Britain, and stated therefrom the proportion which Ireland contributed to the Revenue, and the amount of Interest and general Expenditure which, under the Act of Union, she might have been called upon to bear; and also pointed out the evident over-charges which were made; and I have shewn the manner in which the finance committee of 1815 dealt with the debt of Ireland. It is generally allowed that what a man does by his agent he does himself; this rule may be applied to states; but a distinction must be made between. the accounts of departments, or the reports of committees, and the Acts of *Parliament*. Parliament is a composite—a tri-partite body; its proceedings are *Acts* of Parliament, which embody the consent of the Crown, that of the House of Peers, and that of the House of Commons. All these are necessary to create a debt of the Empire, or to create a debt of any part of the Empire. The most rigid stickler for the omnipotence of Parliament only asserts that the *Acts* of Parliament, the deliberate and united decision of the three estates of the realm are the authority to which we must bow, that this the empire of law, the ascertained will of the people through their legislation, is what ought to govern us.

The natural duty of the finance committee of 1815, when it proceeded to examine the debt of Ireland, would have been to ascertain from the *Acts of Parliament* what was the debt which was created on the Irish account? Instead of doing so, they adopted, as the Irish debt, an amount *which was never authorized by Act of Parliament*, this they stated to be the debt of Ireland. Thus a fallacious and illusory impression was raised, that Ireland was largely in debt. Parliament was imposed upon by a statement which it too readily adopted as correct. The Irish members, though protesting, year after year, against the unfair and most ruinous load which was laid upon Ireland, seem to have been paralyzed at its immense amount; but a careful *examination of the Acts of Parliament which created the Irish debt, shews that the amount which was legally created was not one-fifth of that which was returned by the finance committee*, and their report, is, as far as relates to the IRISH DEBT, QUITE ILLUSORY. IRELAND DID NOT OWE THE IMMENSE SUM THEY STATE. These statements are so serious in their import, that they should not be rashly made, and I shall therefore assign the authority with which I support these assertions. It is under a sense of their importance, I approach the examination of the national accounts, and the first inquiry will be, what was the amount which was authorized by Parliament to be raised on Irish account? and what was the amount of Irish debt created? I must *in limine* remark that I do not admit the right to create any separate debt for Ireland, as I hold most strongly that all debts contracted after the Union, for the service of the United Kingdom, were joint debts, and that no addition could be made to the separate debt after the 31st December, 1800. One of the first acts relative to the Irish finances was passed in 1801. It was: the 41 Geo. III., cap. 84, which states that there was a balance in the Irish treasury of £1,566,061, being part of the supplies voted by the Irish Parliament in 1800, and it enacts that the same should be paid into the Treasury, as part of the supplies for the year 1801.

During the following years, I find that different acts were passed, creating an Irish debt.* I think these acts were not

---

*The amount authorized to be raised by acts of Parliament were as follows :—

					Irish Loan.
1801	41 Geo. III.,	cap.		3,	£2,500,000
1802	42	...	...	58,	1,500,000
1803	43	...	...	113,	1,000,000
1804	44	...	...	48,	1,250,000
1805	45	...	...	38,	1,500,000
1806	46		...	47,	2,000,000
1807	47	...	...	46,	1,500,000
1808	nil		—		
1809	49	...	...	78,	1,250,000
1810	50	...	...	68,	1,400,000
1811	51	...	...	62,	2,500,000
1812	52	...	...	70,	1,500,000
1813	53	...	...	61,	2,000,000
1814	54	...	...	74,	3,000,000

£22,800,000

in accordance with the Act of Union, and that no separate debt should have been created; but it is a matter of history that they were passed—they stand upon the statute-book. These acts, thirteen in number, became law in the different years from 1801 to 1816; and the amount which they authorized to be raised on the Irish account was £22,800,000. This is the whole amount of the Irish debt which was legally created, and is the extent of loans chargeable by act of Parliament to Irish account. The whole of these sums was not raised in Ireland; the amount of the Irish funded debt, on which the interest was payable in Ireland in 1801, was £11,859,688, and in 1817, £21,004,430, so that the increase of Irish investments in the 16 years was only £9,144,732.

The report of the select committee on the Irish Poor, of 1830, refers to the debt created on Irish account in the 16 years, *subsequent* to the Union. Its statement is very different from that which is published in the return of 1849; though it does not correspond with the Acts of Parliament according to its authority, (page 82.)

The Loans raised on Irish account from 1802 to 1817, were ; raised in Ireland	...	£15,900,367
Do. do. do. in Great Britain	...	58,168,426
		£74,078,793
Applied to the reduction of debt in Ireland £6,211,754		
Great Britain 11,397,057		17,608,811
		£56,359,982

This sum is in excess of the loans authorized by Acts of Parliament, to be raised on Irish account, but it is not much more than one-half of the debt stated, by the return of 1849, to have been created on Irish account.

I find, that by different acts of Parliament,* the Treasury of

* The sums which the English Exchequer was authorized to remit to the Irish Exchequer were as follows :—

1801	42 Geo. III.,	caps,	30 &	33,		£2,000,000
1803	43	...	...	65 &	68,	2,000,000
1804	44	...	...	47		4,500,000
1805	45	...	...	12		4,500,000
1806	46	...	...	32		2,000,000
1807	47	...	...	28		2,000,000
1809	49	...	...	69		3,000,000
1813	58	...	...	69 &	156,	6,000,000
1814	54	...	...	86		5.500,000
	Total		...			£30,500,000

Great Britain was empowered to remit to the Irish treasury part of the loans raised in Great Britain; and in the sixteen years, from 1801 to 1816, the amount so authorized was £30,500,000. There is no evidence that these remittances were made, but, on the contrary, I learn, from a return made in the year 1833, that remittances were made, but quite the other way.

The amount remitted from the Irish treasury to that of Great Britain, from 1801 to 1817, is stated in the return of 1833 at ‡ £15,569,262

And from the treasury of Great Britain to that of Ireland 2,279,834

The balance received from Ireland was ... £13,289,428

The report of the select committee of the House of Commons, with reference to the Irish Poor, 1830, makes this balance still greater, it states the remittances as follows, (page 83.)

Remitted from the Irish to theBritish Exchequer, from 1801 to 1817 ... ... £17,029,272
From the British to the Irish Exchequer 2,446,577

Balance remitted by Ireland £14,582,715

Thus shewing most decisively, that Ireland was raising by her revenue, larger sums than were required for her own

‡ The balance arising from the remittance of money to and from the Irish and British Exchequers from 1801 to 1816 :—

	Remitted from the British Exchequer to the Irish.			Remitted from the Irish Exchequer to the British.		
	£	s.	d.	£	s.	d.
1801	—		—	403,799	1	10
1803	461,000	0	0	—		—
1804	117,444	8	11¼	—		—
1805	39,000	0	0	—		—
1806	165,354	3	3	—		—
1807	295,709	10	0	276,000	0	0
1808	207,604	3	4	—		—
1809	114,169	10	4	—		—
1810	146,527	15	6	—		—
1811	174,416	13	3	1,270,000	0	0
1812	104,250	0	6	1,465,000	0	0
1813	116,500	0	0	1,656,276	0	0
1814	122,416	13	3	2,603,457	0	0
1815	117,194	8	9	2,466,545	0	0
1816	98,249	19	11	6,107,984	12	3¼
Total	£2,279,834	1	6	£15,569.262	14	1

service, and that she remitted them to Great Britain, in order
to enable her to pay the large expenses, arising from the state
of war, in which she was engaged.

The mere recital of these extraordinary facts is in itself
sufficient to shew the imposition, the wrong, the delusion,
which was attempted towards Ireland—nay, which was practised upon the Parliament of the United Kingdom; for, had
it known the true state of the Irish debt, it would never have
sanctioned the project of the minister, nor have deprived
Ireland of that protection which she was promised. The
dealings with the Irish debt were very curious, and I must
call attention to one or two facts, as stated in the Acts of
Parliament of 1812 and 1816.

In 1812, the irregularity respecting the Irish accounts was
so great, that an act was passed for auditing them; the
preamble states that it was necessary more effective provision should be made for the regular examination and audit
of the public accounts of Ireland, and it appoints a board
of commissioners for that purpose.

In 1816, a curious discovery was made with reference to
Irish finances, and this led to the passing of the 56 Geo. III.,
cap. 70; the preamble declares that the debt due by Ireland,
on the 25th March, 1797, was £5,829,156 13s. 4d., and that
provision was made for the payment of that debt by quarterly
payments to the "Commissioners for the reduction of the
National Debt of Ireland." It relates that the amount paid to
the commissioners, with interest, was £7,892,550, and that
the debt was all paid, and there was a balance of £2,063,373
over and above. It declares, "Whereas the public burthen
may at this period be greatly alleviated, and the whole of
the national debt of Ireland now existing may, nevertheless
be redeemed within forty-five years from the period of the
respective loans by which the same was created, and the
reduction thereof may be accelerated;" it enacts that the
capital debt of Ireland, existing March 25th, 1797, was
deemed discharged, and the stock placed to the credit of the
commissioners for the reduction of the national debt, and
that it be cancelled. Clause 3 requires the commissioners to
purchase public annuities equal to the debt which existed
previously to June 28th, 1802, and also to redeem the subsequent debt within 45 years.

Another cancelling of Irish debt took place, in 1816, under

the act of 56 Geo. III , cap. 89, by which loans to the following extent were cancelled—

£1,852,072,	5 per cent. Irish Stock.
294,530,	4 do. do.
2,231,914,	3 do. do.

Total £4,378,486

This does not look as if Ireland was in the position of a nation which was overburthened with debt!

The amount authorized to be raised, and the amount charged to Ireland, may be contrasted with some advantage ; it illustrates the manner in which Ireland was dealt with. The amount authorized by Parliament to be raised for the service of Ireland was £22,800,000. The amount which the British treasury was authorized to remit to Ireland was £30,500,000, making a total of £53,300,000, the amount borrowed on Irish account was stated in the return of 1849 to be £106,089,794.* I give the particulars at foot.

This return is at variance with several other Parliamentary papers, and strikingly in contrast with the report of the committee on the Irish poor of 1830, to which I have before referred, but it is so necessary that the reader should have the figures before him, that I re-quote them. Page 83 states

	* Irish Loan. per Acts of Parliament.		Amount which British Treasury might remit.		Irish Debt created per return of 1849.
1801	£2,500,000	...		..	£4,433,337
1802	1,500,000	...	£2,000,000	...	4,273,311
1803	1,000,000	...	2,000,000	...	3,210,524
1804	1,250,000	...	4,500,000	...	9,486,490
1805	1,500,000	...	2,500,000	...	4,660,000
1806	2,000,000	...	2,000,000	...	5,886,153
1807	1,500,000	...	2,000,000	...	5,470,538
1808		...		...	5,042,937
1809	1,250,000	...	3,000,000	...	4,984,615
1810	1,400,000	...		...	7,583,971
1811	2,500,000	...		...	2,770,154
1812	1,500,000	...		...	9,329,538
1813	2,000,000	...	6,000,000	...	12,415,385
1814	3,000,000	...	5,500,000	...	10,687,454
1815		...		...	16,587,386
1816		...		...	
	£22,800,000		£30,500,000		£106,809,794

M

that the loans raised on Irish account, in the period from 1801 to 1817, were as follows :—

Loans raised in Ireland		£15,900,367
„ Great Britain ...		58,168,426
Total debt created		£74,068,794
Debt paid off in Ireland	£6,211,754	
„ Great Britain	11,397,056	
Total debt paid off		17,608,811
Increase in Irish debt		£56,459,983
Remitted from Ireland to Great Britain	£17,029,272	
From Great Britain to Ireland	2,446,577	
Balance of remittance to Great Britain		14,582.715
Balance against Ireland ...		£41,877,268

This return gives a "recapitulation showing the balance of income and expenditure, and the manner in which the deficiency was supplied," and states

The expenditure of Ireland at	£105,254,897
Income	60,366,542
Expenditure over income ...	£44,888,355

which nearly corresponds with the amount of debt as above stated, and shows that the statement that the debt had been fairly increased by £106,809,794, is quite absurd and erroneous. As, therefore, no debt can be created legally but by act of Parliament, it is quite apparent that an attempt has been made to charge Ireland with a very large sum, which was never expended in her service, which was not necessary to make up her proportion of the charge under the Act of Union, which was not even created by act of Parliament; and therefore I am fully warranted in saying that a great and grievous wrong has been done to Ireland, and that she did not owe the amount which was charged against her. The legislation, since 1816, was based upon the assumption that Ireland owed upwards of £130,000,000 whereas she owed no such amount. It appears that the wrong which was done to her in the period from 1801 to 1816, was made the ground for the further wrong and injury, which has been perpetuated, and into which shall I now proceed to inquire.

LETTER XI.

PARLIAMENT, in 1815, received the report of the finance
committee, but gave no effect to it. In 1816 an act was
passed, (the 56 Geo. III., cap. 98,) entitled, " An Act to Consolidate into one Fund all the Public Revenues of *Great
Britain and Ireland,* and to provide for the application thereof, to the general service of the United Kingdom." The
preamble recites, " Whereas, it hath become expedient *for
carrying into effect the* provisions and purposes of two several
Acts for the Union of Great Britain and Ireland, (the one
made in the Parliament of Great Britain, in the 39th and
40th years of his present Majesty's reign, and the other in
the Parliament of Ireland, in the 40th year of his Majesty's
reign,) that all the public revenues of Great Britain and Ireland should be consolidated and applied to the service of
the United Kingdom." It enacts the mode in which this
should be done. In considering the effect of this act upon
the Act of Union, which it recites, it is necessary that my
readers should have some of its provisions before them, and,
even with the inconvenience of repeating what I quoted
before, I must recite two of the paragraphs of the seventh
article of the treaty.

The Act of Union provided that Ireland should pay a
fixed proportion for twenty years, and also enacted that at
the end of that time, the relative proportion which she should
contribute, should be changed and placed upon a different
basis. The condition to which I refer is as follows:—

" II. That for the space of twenty years after the Union shall take
place, the contribution of Great Britain and Ireland respectively, towards
the expenditure of the United Kingdom, in each year, shall be defrayed
in the proportion of fifteen parts for Great Britain and two for Ireland:
that at the expiration of the said twenty years, the future expenditure of
the United Kingdom (other than the interest and charges of the debt to
which either country shall be separately liable) shall be defrayed in such
proportion as the Parliament of the United Kingdom shall deem just and
reasonable, upon a comparison of the real value of the exports and imports
of the respective countries, upon an average of the three years next preceding the period of revision, or on a comparison of the value of the quantities of the following articles consumed, within the respective countries on

a similar average ; viz., beer, spirits, sugar, wine, tea, tobacco, and malt : or according to the aggregate proportion resulting from both these considerations combined, or on a comparison of the amount of income in each country, estimated from the produce for the same period of a general tax, if such shall have been imposed on the same descriptions of income in both countries. And that the Parliament of the United Kingdom shall afterwards proceed in like manner to raise and fix the said proportions according to the same rules, or any of them, at periods not more distant than twenty years, nor less than seven years from each other, unless previously to any such period, the Parliament of the United Kingdom shall have declared, as hereinafter provided, that the expenditure of the United Kingdom shall be defrayed indiscriminately by equal taxes imposed on the like articles in both countries."

Under it Ireland would have been entitled to a revision of her taxation at the end of the twenty years (that is in 1821); but the Parliament of the United Kingdom was in great haste to deprive Ireland of any prospective right to a diminution of taxation, and, having improperly increased the debt of Ireland, previously to 1816, it attempted to put in force the provisions of another clause in the treaty, which was as follows:—

" VII. That if at any future day the separate debt of each country respectively shall have been liquidated, or if the values of their respective debts (estimated according to the amount of the interest and annuities attending the same, and of the sinking fund applicable to the reduction thereof, and to the period within which the whole capital of such debt shall appear to be redeemable by such sinking fund,) shall be to each other in the same proportion with the respective contributions of each country respectively ; or, if the amount by which the value of the larger of such debts shall vary from such proportion shall not exceed one-hundreth part of the said value, and if it shall appear to the Parliament of the United Kingdom that the respective circumstances of the two countries will thenceforth admit of their contributing indiscriminately, by equal taxes imposed on the same articles in each, to the future expenditure of the entire kingdom, it shall be competent to the Parliament of the United Kingdom to declare that all future expense thenceforth to be incurred, together with the interest and charges of all *joint* debts contracted previous to such declaration, shall be defrayed indiscriminately by equal taxes imposed on the same articles in each country, and thenceforth from time to time, as circumstances may require, to impose and apply such taxes accordingly, subject only to such particular exemptions or abatements in Ireland, and in that part of Great Britain called Scotland, as circumstances may appear from time to time to demand."

It will be observed that the declaration which this clause of the Act of Union requires to be made is a declaration by the *Parliament* of the United Kingdom. Parliament is comprised of three estates of the realm—King or Queen, Lords, and Commons. It was this body—the Parliament of the

United Kingdom—which alone was competent to make the declaration referred to in the Treaty; but up to the present time no such declaration has been made by the Parliament of the United Kingdom.   It is quite true that a resolution of the House of Commons was passed in 1816, affirming the principle, but that resolution was not a declaration by Parliament.   To make such a declaration of legal force, it should have been embodied in an act of Parliament, which would have passed the three estates of the realm.   The act of 1816 consolidates the Exchequers of the two countries, and provides for the safe keeping of the funds; but it does not contain the declaration required by the Act of Union.   Nay more, up to the present time the taxes of the United Kingdom have not been indiscriminately levied; if they were, the Irish poor-rates and Grand Jury cess should be paid out of the Imperial Treasury.   This aspect of the question is one of great importance, because the absence of the declaration, which the Act of Union requires, is fatal to the supposition that the conditions of that Act are at an end.   My argument is two-fold.   It asserts—

First, that the condition as to the relative debt, of the two countries, was never such as to make it competent for Parliament, to deprive Ireland of the protection which she enjoyed under the Act of Union.

Second, that as Parliament has not made the declaration, " That the respective circumstances of the two countries will thenceforth admit of their contributing indiscriminately, by equal taxes imposed on the same article in each, to the future expenditure of the United Kingdom." It is not legal to enforce a larger quota from Ireland, than that which she was bound to pay by the Act of Union.

The equalization of the taxes has been attempted, piece by piece.   The Act of Union has not been formally annulled, but it has been partially abrogated; this abrogation is in defiance of rights as solemnly guaranteed as possible, and it affects the prosperity of a nation, which had once been great and powerful.   She has been deprived of her Parliament, and then of the very privileges which were promised to her, if she would give up her Parliament; until at length her people are forced from her shores in myriads; her manufactures are destroyed, her commerce sacrificed, and her wealth absorbed in EXCESSIVE TAXATION.   The continual force of the obligations of the Act of Union was admitted by many

leading British statesmen, amongst whom was the late Sir
Robert Peel, to whose speech, in 1842, I shall have occasion to
refer hereafter.

It cannot be too often repeated, that one of the leading
ideas of the Treaty of Union was the condition, that Ireland
should never be called on to pay the interest of the British
debt contracted before the Union, which interest was
£17,800,000 a year. Great Britain was bound by the contract to continue to raise this amount by "special" taxes,
levied solely in that country ; but she has evaded the performance of that condition, and forced Ireland to pay part
of that liability.

The other leading idea, is that which is so well expressed
in the preamble of the Irish Act, that is, "*to promote and secure the essential interests of Ireland,*" we must bear these two
conditions in mind when we come to deal with the provisions
of the Act of Union, and the manner in which it was carried
out.

The report of the finance committee of 1815, from which I
quoted in Letter IX., proposed, that there should be a radical
change of system of Irish taxation. It professed that the
object of the change was to relieve Ireland from burthen
which experience had shewn were too heavy for her.

I have brought down the comparison of the finances of
Great Britain and Ireland to 1816, as it was necessary to deal
with this portion of the subject separately, in order to ascertain what was the debt of Ireland in 1816, and to examine
whether the British debt had been so far liquidated as to warrant the Parliament of the United Kingdom in assuming that,
they might deprive Ireland of the protecting clauses of the
Act of Union. I think it can be most clearly shewn that
under an equitable settlement of the accounts of the two
kingdoms, the separate amount due by Ireland was only increased, (in the period from 1801 to 1817,) by £2,012,936, (see
Par. paper, No. 256, session 1824,) and that Ireland was
jointly liable with Great Britain for the interest and charge
of the debt contracted in that period; between 1815 and
1861, the national debt has decreased, the amount due in
1815 being £861,039,049; and in 1861, £799,949,807.
Therefore the debt has been lessened £61,090,242.

As the Act of Union required that the proportion of
2-17ths was to remain in force for 20 years, the remaining

four years must be calculated on the same scale. The revenue
during that period was as follows:

	Great Britain.		Ireland.	
	per return of 1824.	per return of 1841.	per return of 1824.	per return of 1841.
1818,	£49,740,779	£51,614,484	£4,877,694	£5,285,654
1819,	52,422,425	51,614,484	5,022,142	5,392,774
1820,	51,404,083	51,820,694	4,636,025	5,064,730
1821,	53,289,014	54,553,962	4,015,636	4,591,826
	£206,856,362	210,962,426	18,551,497	20,334,984

It is rather curious to note the change in the returns; up
to 1817, the return of 1841 made the Irish revenue invariably
less than that of 1824. After 1817, the variation is at the
other side.

The interest on the ante-Union debt of Ireland was reduced in 1816, by the payment of all she owed in 1797,
the cancelling of that stock, lessened the interest on this debt
by £341,277. The charge for the ante-Union debt was
further reduced by the payment on account of the debt contracted between 1797 and 1801, as stated in page 163.

The first charge on the revenue was the interest of the
debt due before the Union. If we add to the Irish revenue
three quarters of a million a-year for taxes received in Great
Britain on Irish account, and deduct from the revenue of each
country the interest on the ante-Union debt, it will shew
that the income available towards the general expenditure was:

Great Britain, four years, 1817 to 1821,					£136,742,176
Ireland ...	...	...	...	...	20,105,584
	Total	...	...	...	£156,757,760
Proportion for Great Britain, 15-17ths...		£138,303,906			
Ireland 2-17ths...		18,453,854			
					£156,757,760

Ireland, after paying the interest of her separate debt, had
revenue receipts to her credit to the extent of £20,105,584,
and her proportion 2-17ths would only have been £18,453,854,
so that, during these four years Ireland overpaid her proportion by £1,561,730. Taking the entire 20 years, from 1801
to 1821, Ireland paid in excess of her contribution of 2-17ths,
(judging by the return of 1858,) no less than £3,400,964;

judging by the return of 1849, the deficiency for the whole
20 years was only £3,000,000.

It was admitted by all competent authorities that the proportion, 2-17ths, laid on Ireland at the Union, was too great,
and even at the risk of appearing tedious, I shall re-quote
two or three authorities on the subject.

The finance committee report of 1815, (evidently a hostile
authority,) is forced to admit:

"That for several years Ireland had advanced in permanent taxation
more rapidly than Great Britain herself, notwithstanding the immense
exertions of the latter country, and including the extraordinary war taxes,
the whole revenue of Great Britain (including war taxes), had increased
from 1801 as 21¼ to 10, and the revenue of Ireland as 23 to 10."

Mr. Leslie Forster, speaking at this time, said:

"The taxation of Ireland at the Union was £2,440,000, and in 1810,
it had risen to £4,286,000, and in 1816, it was £5,700,000. In fact, taxation in that country had been carried almost to its *ne plus ultra*."

Lord Fitzgerald and Vesci, in 1816, speaking on the subject said:

"The necessity of reviewing the Act of Union has been caused by the
sacrifices Ireland has made, doing her best to keep pace with you—you
contracted with her for an expenditure she could not meet--she had been
led to hope that her expenditure would be less when united to you than
before. She has absolutely paid more in taxes since the Union than
£78,000,000, being £47,000,000 more than her revenue in the 15 years,
on which her contribution was calculated."

As I before remarked, the remedy for this admitted greiv-
ance would have been to reduce the proportion which Ireland
should contribute.   The remedy which was adopted did
away with her protection, and increased her proportion.
After the war the relief from taxation was mainly extended
to Great Britain, as is shewn at length in (Par. paper 361,
session 1842).   Mr. Vansittart, however, in proposing, in
1822, a reduction in the taxation of England, which would
give her a further relief of £2,000,000, offered a relief to
Ireland of £200,000, being in the proportion of 2 to 20, he
said:

"No choice was left as to a diminution of taxes, for Parliament was
bound to reduce duties in Ireland in the same proportion as they were
reduced in England."

This suggestion had not been regarded in previous reduc-
tions, for the relief extended to England, by reduced or repealed taxes, between 1815 and 1822, was, £23,589,359, and
to Ireland only £608,320. The amount paid in the 10 years,

from 1811 to 1820, both inclusive, presents the following contrasts (see Par. paper, 27th April, 1841):

	Revenue of Great Britain.	Ireland.	Proportion.
1811 to 1816,	£337,878,839	£28,924,312	1-13th.
1816 to 1821.	272,936,114	24,864,134	1 12th.
Reduction,	£64,942,725	4,060,178	1-16th.

Thus, though the report of the finance committee stated
that its object was " to relieve Ireland from a burthen which
experience proved was too heavy for her to bear," yet the
effect of adopting its recommendation, and the Act of 1816,
was to *increase* the proportion which Ireland should pay, and
to enable Great Britain, to reduce her taxation at the expense
of Ireland!

A little calculation makes this obvious; the reduction in
taxation was £69,000,000. If Ireland had been relieved at
the rate of 2-17ths her taxes should have been reduced
£8,000,000. Mr. Vansittart limited the reduction to 2-20ths,
(where he got this proportion I cannot tell,) but it should
have £6,900,000, instead of which the reduction was only
£4,000,000!

I think I have fully established, that the separate debts of
Ireland and Great Britain, (if the amounts charged to Ireland
were fairly stated, according to the Act of Union,) were not in
1816, brought to that proportion which was required by
the 7th paragraph of the treaty. To have accomplished
that result it would have been necessary for Great Britain to
have raised by taxation a sum of fully £200,000,000 over
and above her separate charges; and paid that amount in
discharge of a portion of her debt ; had she thus liquidated
or lessened the debt, she might then have claimed a consolidation of the Exchequer, and an equalization of taxation of
both countries; were this done, the annual charge for the
interest of the National Debt would have been reduced, and
Ireland would have had the advantage of it. The manner in
which the Irish debt was nominally increased, was at variance
with the Act of Union. Any enactment based upon this
error is equally adverse to the treaty ; and, in point of fact, it
tends to abrogate and annul it; because it imposes upon Ireland, that which the Act of Union was specially intended to
guard against, which was, the payment by Ireland, of interest
on the separate debt contracted by Great Britain, previous to
the Union; and further, the levying of indiscriminate taxes

upon Ireland and Great Britain, before the latter country
had performed her share of the bargain, and reduced her
separate debt to the proportion which the contributions of
Great Britain and Ireland were respectively fixed at, was un
just towards Ireland.

The Act of Union was a bad bargain for Ireland ; but,
nevertheless, Ireland fulfilled it.   It fixed the proportion that Ireland should bear for twenty years at 2-17ths of
the expenditure of the empire.   This was an unfair proportion—but Ireland has paid it.   But at the end of the twenty
years she was entitled to a re-adjustment of the proportion ;
and if we take the respective contributions to the Revenue
by each country, Ireland could not, in 1821, have been required to pay more than 1-13th. I shall hereafter shew the excessive amount which Ireland has paid; my present enquiry
is, whether the Parliament of the United Kingdom could, in
1816, legally—that is, according to the Act of Union—put
an end to its provisions?   The data I have produced shews
that the separate debt of Great Britain had not lessened since
1800; while Ireland had paid off all the debt which she owed
in 1797, and had also paid a portion of that contracted between
1797 and 1801—that the revenues of Ireland had been (according
to the return of 1858) in excess of her proportion, but fell short
of the charge on the country according to the return of 1849.
The deficit, if any, did not, according to the Act of Union,
constitute an addition to the separate debt of Ireland.   The
debt contracted subsequent to the Union was a *joint* debt;
but even if the separate debt of Ireland were increased by
adding to it the deficiency, if any, in the Irish revenue in
the sixteen years, from 1800 to 1816, and by further adding
to it the proportion of the joint debt on which Ireland was
chargeable with interest, still these united debts did not approach that proportion, under which, and under which alone,
the taxes could have been levied indiscriminately in each
country ; and hence, though the Consolidation Act of 1816, (the
56 George III., cap. 98,) was passed, it was, as stated in the preamble, for " further carrying into effect the provisions and
purposes of the two several acts for the Union of Great Britain and Ireland," it could not to have annulled and abrogated those acts; and therefore I am forced to consider
whether it was competent of the Parliament of the United
Kingdom to annul or abrogate the Act of Union?

It is asserted by some that the Consolidation Act of 1816

virtually annulled all the protective clauses of the 7th article of the Treaty of Union. They say that it, and the resolution of the House of Commons, meant to put an end to the separate debt of each country, and thus render Ireland liable to the interest of the debt due by Great Britain at the Union; that it meant to put an end to the provisions, by which Ireland was only to pay a fixed proportion to the Imperial income, and to increase the taxation of Ireland, by imposing upon this country, those taxes which were levied in Great Britain, but not in Ireland. These were, it is said, the objects aimed at in 1816, though, by a strange subtilty, a profession was made by the speakers, that it was intended " to relieve Ireland from taxation which she could not bear." The change thus made in 1816 obstructed Ireland, in claiming, in 1821, that revision of the proportion she should pay, which was laid down in the Act of Union, and which provision was based upon Lord Castlereagh's promise, " that Ireland should never be called on to pay any portion of the charge on the debt which Great Britain owed in 1800; and that the taxation of the two countries should be proportionate, and according to the relative ability of each country." These ideas are expressed in the preamble of the Act itself, in the statement that it was " to promote and secure the essential interests of Great Britain and Ireland." That the essential interests of Ireland were not promoted by this undue taxation is admitted by the finance committee of 1815. It was disproportionate, inasmuch as the taxation of Ireland had been increased at a greater ratio than that of Great Britain. Nor could the essential interests of Ireland be promoted by making her liable, without an equivalent, to the interest of the debt of Great Britain.

The British Parliament assumed the power to debit the separate debt of Ireland with such portion of the debt of the United Kingdom as it chose. This was not according to the Act of Union; having done so, contrary to that Act, it then took advantage of its own wrong doing, and made the charge, so improperly imposed, the excuse for abrogating the provisions of the Act of Union. Thus, Ireland has been deprived or those rights, privileges, and immunities, for which she covenanted. Thus were the conditions of the Act of Union evaded and set aside; and we are told by some, gravely told, that as there is a majority of British members in the House of Parliament, we have no redress. I claim for Ireland, that

her rights are secured by treaty, and that they cannot be set
aside by an act of Parliament. Vattell, the highest authority
upon the subject of the interpretation of treaties, thus lays
down this rule, at p. 249 of Chitty's translation :—

" All pitiful subtilties are overthrown by this unerring rule. When we
evidently see what is the sense that agrees with the intention of the
parties, it is not allowable to wrest their words to contrary meaning. The
intention, sufficiently known, furnishes the true matter of the convention—what it promised and accepted—demanded and granted. A violation of the treaty is rather a deviation from the intention which it sufficiently manifest, than from the terms in which it is worded, for the terms
are nothing without the intention by which they are dictated."

I cannot but think that a proper appeal to the good sense,
the known integrity, and good feeling of the British people,
would satisfy them that injustice has been done to Ireland;
and I am persuaded that Parliament, and the British nation,
would not object to a proper account being taken as to the
amount of the engagements to which Ireland is liable, and
the position which she ought to occupy with regard to taxation. I see that grievous wrong has been done to Ireland, in
the manner in which the accounts were stated; and I think
Parliament will not refuse to inquire into, and endeavour to
redress the grievance we complain of; especially when they
see that Ireland is over-taxed, and that it is this very over-
taxation, which is preventing the progress of this country.
Ireland complains that she has, by what Vattel describes as
" a pitiful subtilty," been deprived of the rights secured to her
by treaty. She complains that the separate accounts of the
Irish debt were unfairly surcharged with sums which she
had no right to pay. She complains that the treaty was
wrested to a forced and contrary meaning, and she urges
that Great Britain is bound, by duty and honour, to see that
this solemn act is not abrogated and nullified.

With regard to the prerogatives of the Parliament of the
United Kingdom, and the force of treaties, I quote the fol-
lowing from the report of a case in which the question was
raised, and very ably handled. I allude to the case of John
Jackson. His counsel, Mr. Ellis, thus defines the Treaty of
Union :—

" Parliament, I submit, is incompetent thus to annul the
articles of Union. First, because they are fundamental laws,
and parts of written constitution of this country."

" The fundamental regulations (says Vattel, p. 3,) that determines the
manner in which the public authority is to be executed is what forms the

constitution of the state ; and those laws which together form the constitution of the state are the fundamental laws.

"The treaty of Union is not only the fundamental regulation that determines the manner in which the public authority in Ireland is to be
executed, but it is also the sole source from which that authority is derived.
By force and effect of the treaty of Union alone the separate Parliament
of Great Britain and Ireland ceased to exist. By force and effect of the
treaty of Union alone a new Parliament, entitled the Parliament of the
United Kingdom of Great Britain and Ireland, was created and constituted.
The treaty of Union is the deed which grants to the United Parliment all
its authority in Ireland ; which marks out the limits of that authority,
and determines the manner in which it must be exercised. The United
Parliament has no ancient prerogatives--no prescriptive rights in Ireland.
It is the mere creature of the treaty of Union. That treaty is the sole
fountain of its power—the only legal source of its authority in Ireland.
Every ingredient of a written constitution is thus contained in the treaty
of Union. No quality of a written constitution is absent from it. The
treaty of Union is indeed the written constitution of Ireland, and its
covenants are our fundamental laws—the security of our rights—the bul-
warks of our liberties. The legislature, which is the mere creature of that
written constitution, and those fundamental laws, cannot abrogate or annul
that written constitution, and those fundamental laws; for, by doing so, it
would destroy the sources of its own authority. Common sense—common
reason points out this limit to the power of a legislature ; but we are not
left to establish the force of a fundamental law, by an appeal to common
sense and reason alone. No rule is laid down more positively by the
writers upon the law of nations than this—that fundamental laws cannot be
annulled by legislative acts. Appealing still to Vattell, the ablest arranger
and digester of the laws of nations, and who is himself an authority upon
that law, second to none, I find the incompetence of legislative acts to
annul fundamental laws thus clearly laid down by him, at page 10 of his
great work upon the law of nations :—

" ' Here again, a very important question presents itself. It essentially
belongs to the society to make laws both in relation to the manner in which
it desires to be governed, and to the conduct of the citizens ; this is called the
legislative power. The nation may intrust the exercise of it to the prince,
or to an assembly, or to that assembly and the Prince jointly, who have then
a right to make new laws and to repeal old ones. It is asked whether their
power extend to the fundamental laws, and whether they may change the
constitutions of the state? The principles we have laid down lead us to decide
with certainty that the authority of these legislatures does not extend so
far ; and that they ought to consider the fundamental laws as sacred, if the
nation has not in very express terms given them power to change them.
For the constitution of the state ought to possess stability ; and since that
was first established by the nation, which afterwards intrusted certain
persons with the legislative power, the fundamental laws are excepted from
their commission. It is visible that the society only intended to make
provision for having the state constantly furnished with laws, suited to the
particular conjunctures, and for that purpose gave the legislature the power
of abrogating the ancient civil and political laws, that were not fundamental, and of making new ones, but nothing leads us to think that it
meant to submit the constitution itself to their will. In short, it is from
the constitution that those legislators derive their power ; how, then, can
they change it without destroying the foundation of their own authorities?"

LETTER XII.

IRELAND AFTER THE UNION.

HER INDUSTRIAL POSITION.

THE mystification respecting the necessity for the introduction of ENGLISH CAPITAL into Ireland, to enable it to become a prosperous or manufacturing country, by which so many of our countrymen and of our most intelligent public writers have been duped, demands that I should give here an accurate definition of Capital, before quoting the admirable remarks of Adam Smith which follow, illustrative of the ruinous operations of heavy taxation. Capital stock, properly signifies the means of subsistence for man, and for the animals subservient to his use. The jurisconsults of former times expressed the idea by the words *res fungibiles*, by which they meant consumable commodities, or those things which are consumed in their use, for the supply of man's animal wants, as contradistinguished from unconsumable commodities, which, latter writers, by an extension of the term, in a figurative sense, have called *fixed* capital.

Fixed capital is, correctly speaking, the representative of, or substitute for capital, properly so called, whether that be gold, or silver, ships, houses, or machinery. Both are equally the products of labour ; in the one is found its means of subsistence, in the other the objects which it is employed to produce, and by which it is virtually replaced, or for which it is directly exchanged. National wealth consists in the abundance of both, and national poverty in their deficiency.

Hence it clearly appears, that Ireland produces annually, within itself, capital to an enormous amount, which, to an equally enormous amount, is abstracted from us, with consequent corresponding impoverishment and suffering. Adam Smith remarks, Wealth of Nations, vol. 2, chap. iii., pp. 466, 467:

" Land and Capital stock—are the two original sources of all revenue, both private and public. Capital stock pays the wages of productive labour, whether employed in agriculture, manufactures, or commerce. The management of those two original sources of revenue, belongs to two different sets of people; the proprietors of land, and the owners or employers of capital stock.

"The proprietor of land is interested for the sake of his own revenue to keep his estate in as good a condition as he can, by building and repairing his tenants' houses, by making and maintaining the necessary drains and enclosures, and all those other expensive improvements which it properly belongs to the landlord to make and maintain. But by different land taxes the revenue of the landlord may be so much diminished; and by different duties upon the necessaries and conveniencies of life, that diminished revenue may be rendered of so little real value, that he may find himself altogether unable to make or maintain those expensive improvements. When the landlord, however, ceases to do his part, it is altogether impossible that the tenant should continue to do his. As the distress of the landlord increases, the agriculture of the country must necessarily decline.

"When, by different taxes upon the necessaries and conveniences of life, the owners and employers of capital stock find that whatever revenue they derive from it, will not, in a particular country, purchase the same quantity of those necessaries and conveniences, which an equal revenue would in almost any other; they will be disposed to remove to some other. And when, in order to raise those taxes, all, or the greater part of merchants and manufacturers, that is, all, or the greatest part of the employers of great capital, come to be continually exposed to the mortifying and vexatious visits of the tax-gatherers, this disposition to remove will soon be changed into an actual removal, the industry of the country will necessarily fall with the removal of the capital which supported it, and the ruin of trade and manufacture will follow the declension of agriculture."

The above extract points, in clear, intelligible, unmistakable language to the result likely to arise from heavy taxation, and these results have taken place to a very great extent. We have seen the Irish people transfer their industry and their capital stock to other climes, thus realizing the truth that, "when, by different taxes upon the necessaries and conveniences of life, the owners and employers of capital stock find that whatever revenue they derive from it will not purchase those necessaries and conveniences which an equal revenue would in almost any other, they will be disposed to remove."

This is at once an ample and sufficient explanation of the reason of that emigration from Ireland which is so frequently termed the Irish Exodus, and which is an exemplification of Adam Smith's views.

I shall now glance at the effects produced upon Ireland by the excessive taxation which ensued after the Union, and shew how it affected the different branches of Irish industry, the consumption of those commodities, which are considered to indicate the condition of the people.

The returns which are before me do not give the particulars of the taxes upon each article in 1815 (at the time Ireland contributed the largest revenue), and I am, therefore, only able to contrast the consumption of 1800, 1810, 1820. It shews the great increase that took place in the duties on the various commodities, which are considered tests of the condition of the people. This aspect of the subject possesses great interest, because it shews us not only the operation of the system of taxation, but also the effects upon the social position of the people. The following statements, with reference to Irish Taxation, are pertinent to my subject.

In 1813, Mr. Vesey Fitzgerald stated that the Irish nation was about to contribute £16,000,000 to the common stock of the year, and to pay additional taxes, £610,000, which amounted to one-half of the addition to which rich and happy England was subjected.

In 1814, new taxes were imposed on all foreign articles— among which were tea, sugar, coffee, wine, tobacco, and foreign spirits, and an increase of duty on several articles used in the manufactures of Ireland. Sir John Newport contended that the proposed assimilation must have the effect of crushing Ireland.

In 1816, the Irish Chancellor of the Exchequer said, " in the fifteen years preceding the Union the expenditure of Ireland amounted to £41,000,000, but in the fifteen years of Union it swelled to the enormous sum of £148,000,000. The increase of her revenue would have more than discharged without the aid of loans, an expenditure greater than that of the fifteen years preceding 1801. Ireland has absolutely paid in taxes more than £78,000,000, being £17,000,000 more than her revenue in the fifteen years upon which her contribution had been calculated."

In May, 1824, Lord Althorp urged this view upon Parliament: he moved that a select committee be appointed to inquire into the state of Ireland, and report their observations and opinions thereon. The principal objects of his motion were, 1. the relation of landlord and tenant; 2. the want of capital and employment; 3. the repeal of taxes impeding the extension of manufactures; 4. the subject of grand jury presentments, etc., etc. He pressed for the repeal of taxes in Ireland as a measure mainly tending " to revive the manufactures of that country, and bring it into a more prosperous condition," but it was lost by 184 to 136.—See Hansard (new series), vol. 11. p. 659.

Sir John Newport, who was constant and untiring in his efforts to reduce the excessive taxation of Ireland, urged the same view. Speaking in 1824, he said—"Ever since the Union the Imperial Parliament had laboured to raise the scale of taxation in Ireland as high as it was in England, and had only relinquished it when it found that the attempt was wholly unproductive. For twelve years he had remonstrated against this scheme, and had foreseen the evils resulting from it—*a beggared gentry and ruined peasantry.*"

The *increase* in the taxes, and *decrease* in the consumption of various articles, is remarkable. I propose to give those of a few of the leading articles.

SUGAR.—The duty on British plantation sugar, in 1800, was 17s. 6d. per cwt., and on East India 2s. 6d. per cwt., and £40 19s. 3½d. per cent. *ad valorem ;* in 1820, the duty on the former was 27s. to 30s. per cwt., and on the latter 37s. to 40s. per cwt. The consumption had increased previous to the Union. In 1788, it was 196,633 cwt.; it increased in 1800 to 355,662, but in 1820, under the increased taxation, it had gone back to 320,783 cwt.

WINE.—The decrease in the consumption of wine is very striking. In 1800, the duty on Cape wine was 2s. 9½d. per gallon; on Madeira, Portuguese, and Spanish, 3s. 5d.; and on French, 5s. per gallon. In 1820, it was on Cape, 2s. 11½d.; on Madeira, Portuguese, and Spanish 9s. 1½d.; on Rhenish, 11s. 3d., and on French, 13s. 6½d. per gallon. The quantity entered for home consumption in 1788, was 1,219,970 gallons; in 1799, it was 2,588,156 gallons: and in 1820 it had fallen to 508,501 gallons—thus shewing, to use Sir John Newport's expression, " a beggared gentry," who had lessened the consumption of wine to less than *one-fifth* of that which they used at the Union.

FOREIGN SPIRITS.—The duty on rum, in 1800, was 4s. 3d. to 5s. 6d. per gallon, and on Brandy and Geneva, 5s. 11d. to 8s. 6d. per gallon. In 1820, it had increased. Rum paid 12s. 9d. per gallon, and Brandy and Geneva, 17s. 3½d. per gallon; and here also we find a diminution. In 1788, the consumption was 1,365,523 gallons; in 1800, it was 1,240,961 gallons; and in 1820, it had fallen to 30,434 gallons. The decrease in 1800 was accounted for by large increase in the consumption of home-made spirits; but the decrease between 1800 and 1820 is a further proof of the altered position of the upper classes.

N

HOME-MADE SPIRITS.—The duty on this article in 1800, was from 1s. 5½d, to 2s. 4½d. per gallon. In 1820, it was 5s. 7½d. per gallon; and, though there was a difference in 1800, of 4s. 6d. to 6s. 2d. per gallon, between the duty on home-made and foreign spirits, which was increased in 1820, to 11s. 8d. per gallon, and while the consumption of foreign spirits had greatly lessened, yet that of home-made spirits also lessened. In 1788, the consumption of home-made spirits was 2,599,176 gallons; in 1800, it had increased to 4,140,429 gallons; and in 1820, it had fallen to 3,849,298 gallons.

TEA.—The duty in 1800 was 4d to 6½d per lb. In 1820, it was increased to 96 per cent. *ad valorem*, when sold under 2s. per lb., and 100 per cent. *ad valorem*, when over 2s. per lb. The quantity consumed in 1788, was 1,545,000 lbs; it had nearly doubled in the twelve years, and in 1800 it was 2,926,166lbs. It had increased in 1820, to 3,150,844 lb., but this increase from 1800 to 1820 forms a very poor contrast beside the increase which took place between 1788 and 1800.

TOBACCO.—The duty on tobacco in 1800, was 7½d. to 1¹³/₄d. per lb; in 1820, it was 3s. to 4s. per lb. The consumption had increased from 3,120,043 lbs. in 1788, to 6,767,275 lbs. in 1800; fell off during the subsequent twenty years; and in in 1820, the consumption was 2,582,498 lbs., or less than in 1788 ! !

FLAX SEED.— The quantity of land under flax lessened from 1800 to 1820. In 1800, the flaxseed imported was 327,691 bushels, and in 1820, it was only 296,142 bushels. Thus shewing a decrease in the supply of home-grown flax. The decrease in the linen manufacture I shall refer to farther on.

COTTON.—Previous to the Union there was no duty on cotton. In 1820, the duty was 16s. 11d. per 100 lb. The cotton manufactures of Ireland were ruined from the operation of the system of drawbacks, under which, when the English market was dull, the Irish market was inundated with low-class goods—the manufacturers of which got the drawback immediately in cash, and the goods were sold at ruinously low prices, to the injury of the Irish manufacturer.

SILK.—The duty on raw silk, in 1800, was 9¾d. to 11d. per pound. In 1820, it raised from 3s. 9d. to 5s. 7½d. per lb. The silk trade was almost destroyed by the increased duty. In 1800, there were 2,300 broad looms in Dublin; in 1840, they were reduced to 250.

IRON.—At the Union, the duty on English and foreign iron was the same; it was from 9s. 8d. to 10s. 8d. per ton. The Imperial Parliament repealed the duty on English iron ; and, in order to force the best Swedish iron out of consumption, put a duty on it of £6 9s. 10d. per ton.

TIMBER AND DEALS.—The duty, in 1800, was 1s. 10½d. to 2s. per load; in 1820, it was £3 4s. 11d. per load. An even greater advance was made on the duty on deals, which, in 1800, paid 10s. 7d. to 11s. 9d. per 100; and, in 1820, £18 9s. 5d. per hundred.

In 1814, an act was passed for imposing a duty on glass in Ireland, and in the autumn session of the same year, it was admitted by Government that this was a blunder; and on November 14, 1815, Mr. W. Fitzgerald moved for leave to bring in a bill to repeal the Irish Glass Duty Act, passed in the same year. Mr. Ponsonby said he could not possibly object to the repeal of an act, which, in conjunction with the similar act respecting timber, had—although he was persuaded the hon. gentleman, in proposing it, had not apprehended such a consequence—been so injurious, that the best title which could be given to it would have been, an "Act to Prevent the further Improvement of Ireland." The right hon. gentleman said that the price of glass had been doubled. It had been trebled!

In the debate on the Irish Customs' Duties, on November 23, 1814, Sir John Newport called attention to the timber duties. He urged particularly the effect on the provision trade, from an advance, at one step, upon staves, from 7d. to 25s. "He was perfectly certain that if this assimilation system was pursued, they would find an increasing taxation, but a decreasing revenue. It was futile to think of a similarity of taxes without a similarity of advantages."

Mr. Ponsonby urged the impolicy of this tax and the glass tax, and said the habitations of the peasantry were known to be small and dirty. The gentry of Ireland had manifested a great disposition to remedy this evil; and it, therefore, was a matter of vast importance that so desirable an object should not be impeded by any additional tax upon an article so necessary to its success.

Mr. Courtenay declared that there was a great and radical objection to a tax of this nature; it not only prevented improvements in habitations, but also in agriculture and other branches of industry. There was a manifest spirit of im-

provement in Ireland, which this tax would check and diminish. No tax could be more injurious.

COALS.—The duty on coal was also increased; they paid
8d. per ton in 1800, and 1s. 7¼d. per ton in 1816. The increased duty on coals affected all the manufacturers who
used them. No duty was levied in England on coals consumed at home; and this increased duty was, in addition to
the freight, a heavy expense upon the Irish manufacturers—
in fact, it placed them upon most disadvantageous terms. It
was not removed until 1833, when the proprietors of flax and
cotton mills were once more enabled to meet their British
rivals on fairer and more equal terms.

Whether we consider those articles principally consumed
by the middle and upper classes, or those which are principally used by lower classes, we find that the gradually-in-
creasing consumption, which had taken place between 1788
and 1800, was checked in every article except tea. The returns prove that there was a decrease, even though the population had largely increased. Between 1800 and 1820,
the consumption of these various articles had lessened. View-
ing the consumption of these commodities as a test of the
condition of the people, we see a decrease in their comforts—
a retrogression in their habits. We see the consequences of
undue and excessive taxation.

LINEN TRADE.

I must now glance briefly at the effect which was produced
upon the industrial employments of the Irish people—and
first amongst them ranks the LINEN manufacture. This
manufacture was encouraged by Lord Stafford, in the reign
of Charles the First, when an effort was made to suppress the
woollen manufactures. The foreign linen trade was principally developed in the North, but a large domestic linen
trade was spread over various parts of Ireland. This important trade was mainly dependent for its raw material on
home-grown flax; and I have, in stating the decrease in the
importation of flaxseed, indicated the decline in the growth
of flax. The linen manufacture was in a rather languishing
state previous to 1782. In 1783, the exports were 16,039,705
yards, valued at £1,069,313; in 1796, they had grown to
46,705,319 yards, the value of which was £3,113,687. From
the pressure upon the industry of Ireland, the Irish linen
trade suffered, and the exports, in 1820, were reduced to

42,665,928 yards; the growth of flax had decreased in a much greater ratio, as is shewn in the reduction of the quantity of flaxseed.

WOOLLEN TRADE.

The WOOLLEN manufactures revived after the freedom of the Irish Parliament was achieved; and we have an account of the feelings of the English manufacturers towards Ireland in the debate which took place in each of the Houses of Parliament, on one of the resolutions on which the Treaty of Union was founded. On the 2nd May, 1800. Mr. Plumer, as counsel for certain petitioners against the commercial resolution which permitted the exportation of British wool to Ireland, addressed their lordships at considerable length, setting forth the danger which that staple manufacture would incur from repealing the prohibition act against the exportation of raw material, the House, however, agreed to the resolution. On the 28th April, 1800, the House of Commons went into committee on the resolutions, and Mr. Law and Mr. Plumer appeared as counsel at the bar. Mr. Law stated that nearly 3,000,000 of the inhabitants of that country were, directly or collaterally, concerned in the woollen trade—that a capital of no less a sum than £20,000,000 was engaged in it—and that if the resolutions now proposed were to pass into a law, this immense property would be nearly annihilated. The whole of the witnesses examined confirmed, by their evidence, the decrease and scarcity of wool, for some years past, in this kingdom and the borders of Scotland. On the 29th April, further evidence was taken, and in the debate which subsequently ensued, Mr. Wilberforce urged, " that wool had long sold at a higher price in Ireland than in England, which would operate as a strong inducement on its exportation." He added—" Ireland had by no means been inattentive to the encouragement of her woollen manufactures—premiums had been offered, institutions formed, and other measures adopted." He said he did not consider himself the representative merely of the opinions of the manufacturers, but he also represented the landed interest, and he urged the retention of the export duty of 10 per cent.

Mr. Pitt, in replying, said, that however anxious he was for an incorporate Union, and free commercial intercourse between both countries, yet, if he thought it would affect such an important interest as the woollen manufactures of Great

Britain, he could not hesitate to deviate from the principle; but he urged, if any change took place it would be gradual.' The resolution passed.

A great change took place in the woollen manufactures of Ireland—far greater than anything which occurred to the linen manufactures. I extract the following information respecting the woollen manufactures from a work published in 1843, entitled, " The Commercial Injustice of Ireland:—

	1800	1840
Master manufacturers in Dublin	91	12
Number of hands employed	4,936	682
Master WOOL-COMBERS	30	5
Hands employed	230	66
Master manufacturers of STUFF SERGE	25	11
Hands employed	1,491	131
Master manufacturers of CARPETS	13	1
Hands employed	120	12
Master manufacturers of BLANKETS, Kilkenny	56	12
Hands employed	3,000	925
Looms at work on FLANNELS in County Wicklow	1,000	0
Hands employed on RATTEENS and FRIEZES Roscrea	900	0

COTTON MANUFACTURES.

At the Union there were 100 cotton factories in Ireland—they were all knocked up by the course of trade after the Union. They were exposed to a ruinous competition from the system of drawbacks. The Irish cotton manufactures had suffered in consequence of the existence of the duty on printed goods in Great Britain, and of the consequent forced competition produced by the drawback system. Goods of the worst qualities were frequently thrown upon the Irish market, and were sometimes fraudulently made up for the sake of the drawback. This system was abandoned in 1833; but, previous to it, the cotton manufactures of Ireland had been nearly ruined. In the neighbourhood of Belfast there were, in 1800, 27,000 persons employed in the cotton manufactures; in 1839, the number occasionally employed was reduced to 12,000 to 15,000; but their wages were very miserable.

HOSIERY.

	1800.	1840.
Hosiery frames in Dublin	329	80
— Cork	200	12

The hosiery trade has become almost extinct in Belfast, Lisburn, Clonmel, Limerick, Waterford, Carrick, Kilkenny, Carlow, Portarlington, Maryborough, Newry, Dundalk, Armagh, and Drogheda.

THE SPIRIT TRADE.

The Spirit Trade affords a further and very striking instance of the commercial injustice which was done to Ireland. The debates are given at length in the *Annual Register*. I make the following extracts from them. I have previously referred to these discussions in pp. 106—108, as illustrating the manner in which the Act of Union was observed.

Notwithstanding that the Act of Union granted equal privileges to the commercial classes in both countries, yet, the English and Scotch distillers endeavoured to prevent the Irish distillers having equal rights with those which they enjoyed, and in 1809, a committee was appointed to inquire into the intercourse of spirits between Great Britain and Ireland. Several acts were passed, for short periods, to prevent that intercourse—thus securing a monopoly to the English and Scotch distillers. On April 6, 1814, the Chancellor of the Exchequer moved for the re-appointment of the committee. Sir John Newport said, " it was not his intention to oppose it, as he was anxious they should examine the subject fairly, as nothing was so improper as the temporary acts which had been passed, and *which were in direct violation of the first principles of the Act of Union*." In June, 1814, this subject was again before the House on a petition from some Scotch distillers, when Sir John Newport said, the prayer of the petition was to establish a permanent infringement of the Act of Union, by which the importation of Irish spirits into England was stipulated for. It would be a more manly course to move for its repeal altogether than to petition for the evasion of those parts which were beneficial to Ireland. It was true, that under the Act of Union the Irish spirits could come into the English markets at a price inferior to the spirits manufactured in Great Britain, but it was an advantage guaranteed them by the Act of Union—all suspensions of which he had always opposed, and he should oppose."

Mr. W. Fitzgerald, speaking on behalf of Government, said he agreed with the right hon. baronet (Sir John Newport), and observed, that " the measure of 1809, which the petition supported by its prayer) *had been acknowledged to be a violation of the Act of Union.* The petition could not be supported when its first prayer was for a continuance of the violation of that contract."

Mr. W. Smith " thought the matter of too much importance to be cursorily passed over ; and he must protest against the doctrine he had heard, that there was the slightest desire to interfere with the principle of the Union—such a false representation should not be suffered to go abroad."

The statement made by Sir John Newport was amply confirmed by Mr. Fitzgerald, who, speaking on the behalf of Government, admitted that from 1809 to 1814 the Irish spirit trade was deprived of the advantage secured to it by the Act of Union, and that there had been an acknowledged violation in the Act of Union for that long period.

On June 24, the subject was resumed, when the Scotch distillers were heard by counsel; the English members asked to be secured in greater advantages than were conceded to them by the Act of Union., and wished to make permanent the report of the committee of 1809.

Mr. Hawthorn said that the reason the report was not acted on was, that because it contained principles at variance with the articles of Union.

Mr. Grattan vigorously maintained the inviolability of that Act; his speech is given in page 108.

The Chancellor of the Exchequer spoke in favour of the bill, and it was carried by 63 to 41.

But the injury which was done to Irish distillers was very great. The number of them was seriously diminished, as they were deprived of the advantages to which they were entitled, in order to please their rivals in England and Scotland, while the consumption of home-made spirits in Ireland also decreased.

SILK.

This branch also experienced the effects of the increased duties. Raw silk, in 1800, paid 9¾d. to 11d. per lb.; in 1820, the duty was raised to 3s. 9d. to 5s. 7½d. per lb. The number of broad looms in Dublin, in 1800, was 2,500; in 1840, they were reduced to 250.

SOAP.

The soapboilers experienced the same unhealthy competition to which the cotton manufacturers were exposed, from the system of drawbacks. Large quantities of inferior soap was manufactured for the Irish market. The maker got six weeks to pay the duty, but got the drawback in cash upon production of the certificate of its landing in Ireland.

Thus, the system of taxation operated most injuriously upon Ireland, and deprived her of that employment which they enjoyed under her domestic legislature.

At the same time, the higher rates of duties levied subsequent to the Union lessened the consumption of most of the articles enumerated in the treaty as tests of the relative condition of the two countries.* Her people were starving amid abundance of food, and naked while exporting the materials for clothing, they were idle for want of employment. These were the effects from the excessive taxation of this period.

* The following statement shows the consumption of the following articles in Great Britain and Ireland.

		Great Britain.	Ireland.
1788	Tea	13,218,665lb	1,545,900 lb
1800	...	20,358,702	2,926,166
1820	...	22,452,052	3,150,344
1788	Tobacco	6,846,606 lb	3,120,048 lb
1800	...	11,796,415	6,737,275
1820	...	13,016,562	2,582,498
1788	Foreign Spirits	4,048,151 gals	1,365,523 gals
1800	...	4,805,555	1,240,961
1820	...	4,100,738	36,758
1788	Home-made Spirits	... ...	... 2,599,176
1800	... ...	... ...	... 4,140,429
1820	... ...	... ...	... 3,849,298
1788	Wine	6,761,403 gals	1,219,376 gals
1800	...	7,728.871	2,588,166
1820	...	5,019,960	508,501
1788	Sugar	1,775,681 cwt	196,633 cwt
1800	'...	1,506,921	355,662
1820	...	2,581,256	320,733
1788	Coffee	758,403 lb	38,458 lb
1800	...	823,590	120,985
1820	...	896,286	207,123

The only articles in which the consumption has increased in Ireland since the Union are tea and coffee, while in all other articles there is an increase in Great Britain; thus shewing the progress of one country and the retrogression of the other.

LETTER XIII.

IRELAND AFTER THE UNION.

HER SOCIAL CONDITION.

THE object of all government is the well-being of the people—" *Salus populi suprema lex.*" I have adduced, in letter II., facts fully sufficient to shew that the Irish Parliament, after attaining its independence in 1782, carried out that object, and that, under its rule, Ireland progressed most rapidly. To secure the welfare of society is the supreme law. and it governed the Irish Parliament in its legislation for Ireland. But the British minister forced the Act of Union upon the Irish Parliament, and deprived it of the power of legislation. Great Britain then adopted the responsibility of the new position in which she was placed; she was, therefore, bound to see that Ireland is governed in conformity with this great natural law, and to secure the well-being of the Irish people. It was on the grounds that the Union would conduce to this object, and make Ireland greater and happier, that it was pressed by Mr. Pitt and Lord Greville upon the British Houses of Parliament. This idea finds expression in the preamble of the Act of Union, which professes that it was passed " *to promote and secure the essential interests of Ireland*" as well as Great Britain. This responsibility becomes the more serious when we reflect that Ireland was deprived of the right of self-government, and that the change was, as regards her, from a free, well-balanced constitution of her own election, to an absolute government by a foreign nation, which distinction is very essentially described in the protest of Lords Blayney and Bellamont given in pp. 69, 70. The Parliament of the United Kingdom, in which the British members were nearly five-sixths of the whole, was bound by the law of nature, of which Grove, in his "System of Moral Philosophy," vol. ii. p. 61, note 5, says: " The law of nature is eternal and necessary; so that it always could and always did exist. It is universal, insomuch, that all mankind are born the subjects and objects of this law, notwithstanding the difference of climate, of government, of language, and of opinions and customs that have prevailed in different parts of the world. Moreover, the law of nature is immutable, for the divine nature is immutable." This law of nature demanded that legislation for Ireland should be of such a character as would promote her well-being. " As God," says Judge Blackstone, " when he created matter, endowed it with a principle of mobility, established certain rules for the perpetual direction of motion; so, when He created man, and endowed him with free will to conduct himself in all parts of life, he laid down certain immutable laws of human nature, whereby that free will is in some degree regulated and restrained, and gave him also the faculty of reason to discover those laws." The British nation took upon itself a great responsibility when it deprived Ireland of her Parliament. So long as Ireland was independent, her Parliament was responsible to God, and to the people, for the laws it enacted. It was bound to see that all its legislation was in accordance with that grand maxim, " Salus populi suprema lex." That duty now rests with the British people. The representatives of Ireland are in such a minority that their presence cannot relieve the British people and the British Parliament of the responsibility which, in forcibly depriving Ireland of her Parliament, they assumed.

It therefore becomes necessary to examine how has this duty been fulfilled? Has Ireland thriven and prospered? Have her people been raised and educated? Has the legislation of the Parliament of the United Kingdom been beneficial, or has it abused the trust, disregarded the responsibility? and, instead of proving an angel to raise, has she proved a minister of vengeance to distress and destroy? This inquiry is a serious task—a solemn duty—but I cannot avoid it—I am forced to consider the effects of the legislation—the taxation of Great Britain upon Ireland. I approach the subject with something of fear and distrust—with an earnest anxiety to be truthful and impartial. I have no wish to distort facts—no desire to create apprehension; but he who would deal wisely with the interests of a country must first satisfy himself as to the facts, and then endeavour to arrive at the remedy of its grievances

I shall first glance at the question of POPULATION; the Great Author of man's being, in placing him upon the earth, gave him the injunction to "increase and multiply;" thus, at the same time, giving a command and a blessing to the human race. A writer on this subject, in *Reece's Encyclopedia*, justly observes: "It is certain that the greater number of persons any country contains, the greater are the means it possesses of carrying on agriculture, manufacture, and commerce, and, likewise, of defending itself against any hostile attempts of other states; a high degree of population has, therefore, been generally considered as conducive to national prosperity and security." Adam Smith, in his *Wealth of Nations*, expresses this idea in somewhat different language. He says, vol. i., page 342: "The annual produce of the land and labour of any nation can be increased in its value by no other means but by increasing either the number of its productive labourers, or the productive power of those labourers who had before been employed." The number of its productive labourers, it is evident, can never be much increased, but, in consequence of an increase of capital or of the funds destined for maintaining them." The increase of capital is laid down by Adam Smith as a precedent necessity to the employment of productive labour; instead of capital, he might have used the more generally intelligible term " means of subsistence," in which Ireland has always abounded. I confine myself here to a consideration of the growth of population, which is justly regarded not only as a means of wealth, but also as a test of prosperity. Where employment exists, population increases, as Adam Smith observes: "It is in this manner that the demand for man, like that of any other commodity, necessarily regulates the production of men."

I propose to contrast the growth of the population of Ireland, in the interval which has passed since the Parliament of the United Kingdom legislated for Ireland, with that of other European kingdoms. I do not wish to confine or limit my inquiry, but to take the whole of Europe, and see, has the increase in the population of Ireland been equal to that of Europe, as a whole? or to that of the particular European states? The contrast presents some rather startling results, and it is naturally suggestive—the reasoning mind will seek to find some explanation for such singular results as are displayed in the contrast of the population of the European states in 1801 and 1861.

Population of European States in 1801 and 1861.

	1801.		1861.
Russia, ...	36,000,000	...	64,000,000
France, ...	26,000,000	...	36,650,000
French conquered provinces, including the Netherlands, Savoy, Nice, and German states, ...	10,345,000		
Germany, ...	24,000,000	...	44,000,000
Austria, ...	20,000,000	...	37,000,000
Italy, ...	12,000,000	...	24,000,000
Great Britain, ...	10,917,000	...	23,322,976
Spain, ...	10,341,000	...	13,000,000
Turkey, ...	8,500,000	* * *	15,000,000
		Greece,	1,100,000
Ireland, ...	5,395,000	...	5,764,543
Prussia, ...	5,200,000	...	17,000,000
Netherlands, ...	...	...	4,623,080
Denmark, ⎫ ...	2,750,000	Denmark,	2,500,000
Norway, ⎭ ...	... ...	Norway,	1,490,000
Portugal, ...	2,550,000	...	4,000,000
Holland, ...	2,220,000	...	3,543,775
Sweden, ...	2,000,000	...	3,639,322
Switzerland, ...	1,800,000	...	2,500,000
	Bavaria,	4,615,748	
	Saxony,	2,122,148	
	Hanover,	1,843,976	
	Wurtemburg,	1,690,898	
	Baden,	1,338,972	
Total,	179,112,650		270,000,000

The increase in the population of Ireland, during the 60 years, is less than that of any European state; next to her, in point of progress, comes Spain, whose misgovernment has become almost a proverb. The increase in the population of Europe has been 60 per cent., in that of Ireland it has been 8 per cent. Many of the European states have increased, in the 60 years, more than 100 per cent. In looking at this question, the thought at once occurs to the mind, how many states, with a smaller population than Ireland, are self-governed; and what reason was there that Ireland should have been deprived of the function which she enjoyed? The union of two Parliaments into one has been found to militate against the progress of the states thus united, as may be traced in the history of Arragon and Castile. As far as population is concerned, we are forced to the conclusion, that the end of good government has not been answered. Ireland has not progressed at all in the ratio of the sister kingdom, nor even in the ratio of other European states, in the growth of human labour, which is the basis of all wealth, she has not progressed, but has suffered the natural loss pointed out by Adam Smith and other writers.

The effect of population in producing wealth is thus described by Michael T. Sadler, M.P., in his work on the " Evils of Ireland," p. 90.—" Our old-fashioned natural economists calculated the wealth of the country, principally to consist of the number of its inhabitants; in the new school, human beings still continue to be valued, but as respects many of them, in a kind of negative sense. What, I would ask, is it that creates that capital, concerning the definition of which so great a stir is made, as to cause the thing itself to be nearly lost sight of ? Human labour. What then constitutes capital but men; and furthermore, what can alone give value to capital when created? Men." The report of the commissioners on the state of Ireland remarks, that where the population is the thinnest the demand for labour is the least, and, of course, the most unremunerative. The Netherlands, one of the most populous countries of the world, is one of the wealthiest, and we are told of it, " that the AGRICULTURE of the Netherlands, which even in the northern portion, that was formerly the Seven United Provinces, was MORE THE FOUNDATION OF ITS WEALTH THAN EITHER MANUFACTURES OR NAVIGATION, deserves the most close examination."* Jessop in his " Travels in Holland," assures us that " No country in Europe provides from its own soil so great a quantity of sustenance, not only for its own people, but so large a surplus of food for exportation, and such valuable commodities to exchange for articles of foreign growth, as Flanders."

We learn that the increase of population in Hannalt " was so great that it diminished the size of the farms, but *Proprietors, in dividing their estates, have almost doubled their value.*" Addison, speaking of Lucca, one of the most populous states of Italy, says: " It is very pleasant to see how the small territories of this little Republic are cultivated to the best advantage, so that one cannot find the least spot of ground that is not made to contribute its utmost to the owner. In all there appears an air of cheerfulness and plenty not often met with." Forsyth, a later traveller, wrote: " The little state of

* Encyclopedia Britannica.   Supplement, p. 60.

Lucca is so populous that very few acres, and those subject to inundation are allotted to each farmer in the place.   Hence their superior skill in agriculture and draining ; hence that variety of crops in every enclosure, which gives to the Vale of Suchio the economy and show of a large kitchen garden." He adds : " Every state in the Peninsula is productive, or otherwise, in proportion to the number of farmers on a given space of land equally good."   Chateauvieux, in his *Travels in Italy*," remarks of Piedmont, (where the population is 222 on the square mile, while in Ireland it is 145).

" The number of farms in Piedmont is surprising, yet this limited country, having a great part of its surface occupied by mountains, after satisfying its own wants, supplies the territory of Genoa, Nice, and even the port of Toulon, with corn and cattle."

How great is the contrast between these states and that of Ireland, which was thus described in the Report of the Committee of the Lords, in 1836 : " A greater portion of the labouring population are insufficiently provided, at any time, with the commonest necessaries of life.   Their habitations are wretched hovels; several of a family sleep together upon straw, or upon the bare ground, sometimes with a blanket, sometimes without even so much to cover them. Their food commonly consists of dry potatoes, and with these they are at times so scantily supplied as to be obliged to stint themselves to one spare meal in the day.   There are even instances of persons being driven by hunger to seek sustenance in wild herbs.   They sometimes get a herring, a little milk, but they never get meat, except at Christmas, Shrovetide, or Easter."

One of the earliest influences for evil which sprung from the Act of Union was the great increase of ABSENTEEISM. This was the necessary sequence of the transfer of the Parliament from Dublin to London.   The Peers of Parliament, the great Commoners, and the principal gentry removed their establishments from Dublin to London.   The drain on the resources of Ireland, which, previous to the Union, was about £1,000,000 a year, increased to £4,000,000 a year, and thus affected the imports, as well as the exports of this country.

The official value of the imports into Ireland in 1801 was, from Great Britain, £3,270,350, and from foreign parts £1,350,974 ; in 1821 it was, from Great Britain, £5,338,838, and from foreign parts £1,068,589 ; thus shewing a large

decrease in our foreign trade, and a large increase in our imports from Great Britain, arising from the destruction of
Irish manufactures. The total imports were, in 1801,
£4,621,344, and in 1821 £6,407,427, the increase being
£1,785,083.—In 1801 the exports of from Ireland to
Great Britain, £3,537,725 ; to foreign parts, £526,819,
making a total of £4,064,545. In 1821 the exports to Great
Britain were £7,117,452, and to foreign parts, £665,425,
making a total of £7,783,875; the increase being £3,118,330;
thus, shewing that the consequence of the destruction of our
native manufactures required an increased import of British
goods to the value of £2,068,488. The increased absentee
remittances, made to meet the payment of the landlords, was
equal to the difference between the value of our imports and
exports in 1801, and the difference between the value of our
imports and exports in 1821 ; in 1801, when our landlords
resided at home, and there was not so large a drain for absentee
rents, the imports into Ireland exceeded the exports from
Ireland by £556,799. In 1821 the value of the exports
exceeded the imports by £1,375,448, the increased drain is
the sum of these two sets of figures, or £1,932,247. It is
generally estimated that the amount of absentee rents drawn
from Ireland in 1800 was a million a-year, and that the effect
of the Union produced an increase of absenteeism equal to
£3,000,000, a year. The return before me (the Board of
Trade report for 1833), indicates a variation between the imports and exports of Ireland of nearly two millions a-year,
which would be a portion of the remittances to meet these
absentee claims. The impolicy of this drain, in relation to
the taxation is very apparent; when we contrast the taxation
of 1800, with that of 1821, we must remember that so long
as the absentee rents were spent at home, they contributed
to the revenue of Ireland; and when they were spent in
Great Britain, they contributed to the revenue of that country ;
and the Act of Union required the revenue to be adjusted
according to a comparative scale: Ireland could rightfully
claim credit for the contribution to the revenue of Great
Britain, which was consequent upon an expenditure of
Irish rents in that country.

The transfer of the House of Parliament from Dublin to
London necessarily increased absenteeism from Ireland.
There was a considerable increase in the drain from this
source, and that increase was met by larger exports, not of

manufactured goods, but of raw produce. As the manufactures of Ireland declined, so did the condition of the people; the consumption of articles of their own growth, decreased in the same ratio as those of foreign import ; the scale of living for the bulk of our population deteriorated. But as absentee rents, (which used to be spent at home, and thus afford employment and encouragement to manufactures, and also induced greater imports of teas, wines, and such articles,) increased, so did the exports of raw produce. This does not *per se* predicate an improvement in the condition of Ireland. The increase in the exports of raw produce from Ireland, does not prove any improvement in the condidition of the Irish. These statements will at once be appreciated by every intelligent mind ; but lest it should not, I will put the case thus—Supposing that the number of persons employed upon the woollen manufactures of Ireland in 1800, 20,000; and that their average earnings was £30 a year, it would represent earnings to the extent of £600,000 ; the money so earned would be principally spent at home, and upon the articles of agricultural produce. These manufactures being knocked up, it would be necessary to import woollen goods to supply the void thus created, by which the imports into Ireland would be increased; and to pay for them it would be necessary to export the agricultural produce which used to be consumed at home; and thus the exports would increase. But those who were employed in these manufactures, would sink from the position of skilled artisans to that of farm labourers, and the food on which they subsisted would deteriorate; therefore the increase in imports and exports is not a true index of the improvement in the internal condition of Ireland.

The effect of this *absenteeism* was two-fold—it was *material* and *mental:* in its *material* aspect, its effects were very marked ; the necessary remittance of rents, led to larger exports of raw produce, and also to non-consumption in Ireland, and non-employment of the people. We have latterly heard a great deal said of the advantage of the English market for our live stock, but it would be a far greater advantage to consume it at home. We are told that we get such good prices from the English for our live stock, and of the consequent benefit to Ireland, but this is rather fallacious; we hardly get back our own money. I will put a case, it is one of ordinary occurrence. His Grace the Duke of Many-boroughs has an

Irish estate which yields him an income of £100,000 a year; one of his tenants, paying a rent of £100 a year, when the half-year's rent falls due the tenant drives 10 head of cattle to the fair, and gets £50 for them, the buyer ships them to England, and probably gets £55, and every one exclaims what a valuable thing it is to have the English market; but the tenant goes to the bank and gets a letter of credit for the £50, and sends it to his Grace. He might as well have written to his landlord and said, " As my rent is due, I send you 10 head of cattle, worth £50, to pay it." His Grace does not give the cattle, but the money that represents them, to his butcher and baker, his tailor and his shoemaker. Now, if he resided in his castle in Ireland there would be no occasion to ship them; they would be wanted at home. His Grace would want some of the cattle for the use of his suite and his visiters. Then, his tradesmen would want meat, and thus we should see greater employment at home, greater wealth at home, and *less* exports. The constant outlay of £3,000,000 a year in Ireland, by the owners of property, would have an indirect as well as a direct bearing upon the state of the country. The tradesman, who is now only half employed, would be fully employed, and thus the expense of production would be lessened. The great reason of the progress of Great Britain arises from the subdivision of labour, and this is in consequence of the enlarged demand for the products of labour. I shall have to dwell upon the subject in detail hereafter.

The *mental* aspect of the effect of *absenteeism* deserves some consideration. The progress of society, and the increase of wealth, arises from the influence of mind upon matter. It is the mind which finds employment for the masses. Restless energy in the pursuit of wealth leads to those discoveries which stimulate production. The migration of those who are more educated—those whose influence tends to raise the tone of society—those who think—is an incalculable loss to Ireland. The East and the West are looking to Ireland to supply them with thinkers. Our colleges and schools are sending out large numbers of ardent-thinking, well-cultivated Irish minds, to contribute their agency in raising the condition of these several countries. But where is the sphere in Ireland for such talent? The Bar takes a few of her sons, but every other profession is almost closed against them. The Church can take only a small portion. In the medical profession, the highest capacity, wants opportunity.

There is no sphere in Ireland for mind; and we export unsparingly the flower of our youthful intellect, which has no employment where it ought to find its development, in raising the condition of its native land. Irish talent and intellect is to be found in the torrid and the frigid zones—everywhere but in Ireland.

A thoughtful writer thus depicts some of the evils from absenteeism:—" By means of our nobles and gentry deserting their own country, and spending all abroad, our people are left without employment, and are forced to shift to other countries, even to America, to get a livelihood. It is not to be wondered at that we grow poorer every day under such an unprofitable issue of money, which all the labour of the people and produce of the country, with every acquisition they can make, are not sufficient to supply. This is an evil long complained of. There is no country in Europe which produces and exports so great a quantity of beef, butter, tallow, hides, and wool, as Ireland does; and yet our common people are very poorly clothed, go bare-legged half the year, very rarely taste of that fresh meat, with which we so much abound. We pinch ourselves of every article of life, and *export more than we can spare*, with no other effect or advantage than to enable our gentlemen and ladies to live more luxuriantly abroad."*

The Hon. Judge Day, when examined before the Lords' Committee, in 1825, attributed the miseries of the Irish to " the want of employment, and the absence and non-residence of landlords, who might superintend, control, and advice."

Major Powell gave somewhat similar evidence, adding, " I do not think there is a single resident gentleman in the whole barony, and that is one of the most disturbed."

Mr. Sergeant Lloyd's evidence was:—" The parts with which I am acquainted the principal gentry have deserted: they have become absentees; and I am sure I ought not to have omitted to enumerate that, as a principal cause of the disorderly state of the disturbed counties."

The Rt. Hon. Francis Blackburne, Judge of Appeal, stated, " As to the state of Ireland, any view I suggest would be incomplete without stating the effects of absenteeism. My opinion is, that, independent of its abstraction from the country of so much of its wealth, it produces great mischief to the whole frame of society. In Ireland, I may say, there is the destitu-

* Prior's List of Absentees.

tion, the want of a distinct class. In ordinary times, the loss of influence and authority, and the control which belongs to education, to rank, and to property, must be deeply felt in any country; but when it becomes disturbed, I need not say that that which would form the barrier for the protection of the peace, is lost in Ireland; and I have now been administering the Insurrection Act in counties where the property of absentees is extensive."

The author of "Ireland; Its Evils and their Remedies," thus forcibly points out the effects of absenteeism: "The low and degrading poverty to which Ireland is thus reduced, though of itself a great evil, is, nevertheless, one of the very least which absenteeism inflicts And first, as to those which are caused by the total abandonment of the most important duties. Few, I think, who are advocates for the social system, and especially those who are placed at its summit, but must be eager to acknowledge that, the duties it imposes are reciprocal, and that their due discharge becomes the more important the more elevated and commanding the station occupied. What, then, I would ask, must be the certain consequence, when those whom civil institutions have placed in the highest rank, and invested with the most extensive influence totally abandon their proper sphere, and desert their numerous and degraded dependents? As to wealth being accumulated or diffused under such circumstances, the very idea is preposterous. There are none to give employment to those who, in an advanced state of society, are liberated from the drudgeries of life; none to excite the genius or reward merit; none to confer dignity and eloquence on society; to lead the march of civilization; to diffuse knowledge or dispense charity. Thus it is, wherever absenteeism prevails, there wealth shuns the labour by which it is fed, and the industry by which it is distinguished, rigorously exacting all its dues, fancied or real, and returning none to those to whom they are really, though not legally owing; carrying off the products of the vintage of nature, even to the very gleanings, to a far country, and leaving the refuse to those who cultivate the soil, and express the juice; muzzling the mouth of the ox that treadeth out the corn, which is fed with the husks, and goaded to desperation."

How truly descriptive of the evils of absenteeism! An evil which arose from, and was inherent in the dissolution of the Irish Parliament, and the removal of the legislature from

Dublin to London; an evil which was ably pointed out and forcibly dwelt upon when the Union was under discussion All the speeches against the Union, both in the British and Irish Parliament, dwelt upon the injurious effect which increased absenteeism must have upon the social condition of the Irish people. Nor was it confined to speeches. The noble band of dissentient Peers, extracts from whose protests I have given, pp. 69 to 73, and who, with pathetic dignity "called upon our latest posterity, to entreat that, in virtue of this our solemn declaration they will acquit us of having been in anywise instrumental to their degradation, and to the ruin of the country which they may hereafter inhabit," assign among the many reasons for which they protested against the Union, the following :—

"Because it does not proffer to this country any benefits of which she is not already in possession, or offer any remedy for any of the evils which it at present has reason to apprehend.

"Because, next to the protection of Divine Providence, we hold this country indebted for its protection to the vigilance of its RESIDENT PARLIAMENT AND THE LOYALTY OF ITS RESIDENT GENTRY, the former of whom the proposed measure necessarily removes from the country, and the latter of whom it must powerfully tend to withdraw."

In another of the protests of the same noble peers, after pointing out some of the probable results on the financial position of Ireland, they say :—

"It must end in drawing from her her last guinea, in totally annihilating her trade for want of capital, in rendering her taxes unproductive, and consequently in finally putting her into a state of bankruptcy. We think ourselves called upon to protest against a measure so ruinous to this country, and to place the responsibility for its consequences upon such persons as have brought it forward and support it."

That the consequences which these noble Peers so sagely foresaw, have come upon Ireland, no one who will examine into the history of the country can deny. The responsibility for her present social position rests with those who proposed it, and with the Legislature, which, having destroyed the Irish Parliament, proceeded to govern it. One of the earliest social effects of this measure was to engender agitation and to create disaffection. The King refused to sanction an act brought forward by his minister, to give full effect to the sixth article of the Treaty, which provided, that all the subjects of the Crown in Ireland, should have equal political and civil privileges with those in Great Britain. Thus, ere the Parliament of the United Kingdom had reached its second session, a flagrant breach of faith was committed; but it was not without its results. We trace them with deep emotion—the consequences were the downfall of the minister, the illness of the Sovereign, and the misery of Ireland. Then followed the insurrection of Emmett, the death of Lord Kilwarden, the inauguration of an agitation, which grew until it overshadowed the land—which retarded the social progress of Ireland, divided those who were anxious for the material progress of the country; diverted the minds of thinking men from measures of social advancement, to those for the attainment of civil and political rights, until, after an agitation more or less virulent, the ministers of Great Britain, quailing before the agitation of Ireland, conceded to fear, what they refused to justice; and that great Irish general, who never surrendered to the conqueror of the world, laid down his arms before a section of the Irish people, who imperatively demanded those social and civil rights guaranteed to them by the Treaty of Union, but withheld from them by the British Parliament.

The Act of Union, which was forced upon the Irish Parliament, created great social evils in Ireland. Has the subsequent government of this country been in conformity with that grand maxim—" *Salus populi suprema lex?*" If it has, why has not the *population* increased in the proportion of other European states? Why has not her *wealth* increased in the same ratio as Great Britain? Why has not employment extended as rapidly as in the sister country? Why, in short, is there such a manifest—such an essential difference between the social and material aspect of the two countries, which were joined at the Union, and which, under an equitable system of laws, ought each to have advanced at the same speed in the path of progress?

LETTER XIV.

IRELAND AFTER THE UNION.

HER GOVERNMENT.

The extreme taxation of any country tends to injure and depress it. The excessive drain on its annual produce prevents the accumulation of wealth. The removal of its capital stock, or means of subsistence, to another country, and the use of that capital stock, by those who took no part in raising or creating it, naturally produced poverty, disorganization, and crime. The continued export from Ireland of her capital stock, or means of subsistence, is sadly illustrative of the following passage from the writings of Adam Smith, (vol. i., p. 338.)

" The proportion between capital and revenue, therefore, seems everywhere to regulate the proportion between industry and idleness. Wherever capital predominates, industry prevails; wherever revenue, idleness. Every increase or diminution of capital, therefore, naturally tends to increase or diminish the real quantity of industry, the number of productive hands; and, consequently, the exchangeable value of the annual produce of the land and labour of the country, the real wealth and revenue of all its inhabitants."

How illustrative of the position of Ireland! She is improvidently exporting her capital stock, *res fungibiles*, those consumeable commodities which constitute capital, and ought, therefore, to be retained in the country as the source of real wealth and revenue to the inhabitants. Ireland is mainly an agricultural country ; and, with reference to such employment, the same author remarks, and his language ought to be ever present with those who legislate for Ireland:—

" No equal quantity of productive labour employed in manufacture can ever occasion so great a reproduction. In them nature does nothing; man does all: and the reproduction must always be in proportion to the strength of the agents that occasion it. The capital employed in agriculture, therefore, not only puts into motion a greater quantity of productive labour than any equal capital employed in manufacture; but in proportion to the quantity of productive labour which it employs, it adds a much greater value to the annual produce of the land and labour of the country, to the real wealth and revenue of its inhabitants. Of all the ways in which capital can be employed, it is by far the most advantageous to society."

Yet, Ireland is exporting her reproductive labour, and diminishing the sphere of employment, by abandoning a proper system of agriculture, and resorting to the more pastoral and less civilized method of cultivating the land. I must not dwell upon this phase of the subject, but hasten to shew the social effects which were produced by the excessive taxation of this country, and before depicting its condition, I must bring before my readers what were the just and reasonable demands which the Irish nation made on its own Parliament, and which its Parliament sought to fulfil; and, as she was deprived of the power of legislating for herself, the Parliament of the United Kingdom was bound to perform those duties which government owes to the people. These duties are reciprocal. The subject, owes allegiance to the state; the state, owes protection to the subject. LOCKE, in his *Essay on Government*, says: " Reason tells us, that all men have a right to their subsistence; and, consequently, to meat and drink, and such other things as nature affords for their preservation." " God has not left one man so at the mercy of another that he may starve him if he please. God, the Lord and Father of all, has given no one of his children such a property in his peculiar portion of the things of this world but that he has given his needy brother a right to the surplusage of his goods, so that it cannot justly be denied him when his pressing wants call for it."

PALEY, in his *Moral and Political Economy*, writes:

" When, therefore, the partition of property is rigidly maintained against the claims of impotence or distress, it is maintained in opposition to the intention of those who made it, and to His, who is the Supreme Proprietor of everything, and who has filled the world with plenteousness for the sustentation and comfort of *all* He sends into it."

ADAM SMITH, treating of labour, thus defines the rights of the labourer: "A man must always live by work, and his wages must at least be sufficient to maintain him. They must even, upon most occasions, be something more, otherwise it would be impossible for him to bring up a family, and the race of such workmen could not last beyond a generation. No equal capital puts in motion a greater quantity of productive labour than that of a farmer. Not only his labouring servants, but his labouring cattle, are productive labourers. In agriculture, too, nature labours along with man ; and though her labour costs no expense, its produce has its value as well as that of the most experienced workmen."

I might, in addition to these English authorities, quote pagan authors in confirmation of the rights of the people. Amongst the foreign Christian writers of eminence, Grotius Puffendorf, and others, maintain the same views. I must content myself with quoting one foreign writer. Montesquieu, in his " L'Esprit des Loix" says—" The state owes to every citizen a certain subsistence—a proper nourishment, convenient clothing, and a kind of life not incompatible with health."

I am obliged to examine, how far the government of Ireland, comported with these views of eminent British and foreign writers; and to ascertain what were the effects produced upon Ireland, by the heavy and excessive taxation which was raised in Ireland—a taxation which was disproportionate to her means and ability—which forcibly deprived her of her capital—compelled her to export her means of subsistence.

I have, in my previous letter, pointed out the state of happiness and comfort enjoyed by the most densely populated European countries—the people were contented, and there was no disaffection. If we are to judge of the condition of Ireland from her statute book, we must conclude that there was something radically wrong in her legislation—something that did not agree with the views propounded by the able writers whose views I have given above. Between 1801 and 1843, no less than *thirty* Acts of Parliament were passed to put down insurrection, and provide for the preservation of the peace. It is quite clear that if the Irish people were employed, happy, and contented, these acts would not have been required. We do not learn that they are necessary in the Netherlands, in Flanders, in Lucca, in Piedmont, where the system of small proprietory farmers and minute cultivation prevails ; and we must, therefore, regard these acts as the offspring of that system of government which overtaxed Ireland, and promoted social disorder.

Had Ireland been a conquered country—had she been won at the point of the sword—the responsibility to govern her so as to promote the welfare of her people would have devolved upon her rulers. This duty was the more cogent and forcible when the power over her was acquired by treaty. No one who reads the history of the Union can arrive at the conclusion that Ireland was a consenting party to the treaty which was forced upon her. Great Britain was morally as well as legally bound to see that Ireland was well governed, to see that her people were employed, that they were happy; this duty devolved upon her, the moment she assumed the government of Ireland. But the obligation to discharge that duty, increases with ten-fold force, when, in order to secure that power, her native legislature was destroyed, and an end was put to self-government. The rapid progress which Ireland made between 1782 and 1800 astonished the world. She was rapidly rising in wealth and in civilization. The Parliament of the United Kingdom entered upon its functions, not with a nation sunk in sloth and misery, but with a nation which had risen, and put forth its strength, to run the career of improvement. We all see what Ireland is, and has been; let us trace the records of Imperial legislation from the statute book, in order to examine whether the laws which have been passed are in accordance with those immutable principles laid down by the British writers, and thus decide whether the state of Ireland has arisen from ignorance, or from a flagrant disregard of those great truths, so ably expressed by many British and foreign writers, whose works should have been in the hands of British statesmen. Our statute book gives the following list of enactments:—

1801. An act to continue two former acts for the protection of the persons and properties of his Majesty's faithful subjects in Ireland.

...   An act to empower the Lord Lieutenant to apprehend and detain persons suspected for conspiring against government.

1803, July. A similar act.

...   An act for the suppression of rebellion, &c.

...   December. An act continuing former act of July, 1803.

...   ...   An act for continuing the act for the suppression of rebellion.

1805. An act for continuing the act of 1803.

1807. An act to suppress insurrection and prevent the disturbance of the public peace in Ireland.

...   An act to prevent improper persons having arms in Ireland.

1810.   An act to continue and amend the act of 1807.

1814.   An act to provide for the preserving and restoring of the peace
        in such parts of Ireland as may at any time be disturbed by
        seditious persons, or by persons entering into unlawful combi-
        nations or conspiracies.

1817.   An act for reviving the Arms' Act of 1807 and 1810.

1820.   An act for continuing the act of 1814.

1822.   An act to suppress insurrection and prevent the disturbance of
        the public peace in Ireland.

...   An act to empower the Lord Lieutenant to apprehend and detain
        such persons as he may suspect of conspiring.

...   An act for further continuing the former act.

1823.   An act to continue the acts of 1807 and 1810.

...   An act to continue the act of 1822.

1824.   An act to continue and amend the former act.

1825.   An act to amend certain acts relating to unlawful societies in
        Ireland.

1829.   An act for the suppression of dangerous associations or assemblies
        in Ireland.

...   An act to revive the Arms' Acts of 1807 and 1810.

1831.   An act to revive the three former acts, and to indemnify persons
        under same.

1833.   An act for the more effectual suppression of local disturbances
        and dangerous associations in Ireland.

...   An act to provide for the more impartial trial of offences in cer-
        tain cases in Ireland.

1834.   An act to continue the act of 1833.

...   An act to revive and continue the Arms' Acts of 1807 and 1810.

1835.   An act for the better prevention and more speedy punishment of
        offences endangering the peace.

1843.   Lord Elliott's famous arms' bill.

I need not continue the sad category of acts such as those
I have quoted, which are a dismal record. I doubt if any
country in the world can refer to such a record. It shews
how the provisions of the Act of Union, were carried into
effect, or rather, how the object stated in the preamble of
that act was so completely overlooked and forgotten. If the
legislation for Ireland, after the Union, had been of such a
character as to " secure and promote the material interests of
Ireland," such laws as I have quoted would have been
unnecessary.

Let us see what further evidence there is as to the government of Ireland.

In March, 1829, Sir Robert Peel, then prime minister, thus
describes the government of Ireland:—

" I apprehend that it is scarcely possible that we can change for the worse.
What is the melancholy fact? That scarcely one year during the period

that has elapsed since the Union has Ireland been governed by the ordinary course of law. In 1800, we find the Habeas Corpus Act suspended, and an Act for the Suppression of Rebellion in force. In 1801, they were continued ; in 1802, I believe, they expired. In 1803, the insurrection for which Emmett suffered broke out, Lord Kilwarden was murdered by a savage mob, and both Acts of Parliament were renewed ! In 1804 they were continued. In 1806, the west and south of Ireland were in a state of insubordination, which was with difficulty suppressed by the severest enforcements of the ordinary law. In 1807, in consequence chiefly of disorders that prevailed in 1806, the act called the Insurrection Act, was introduced ; it gave power to the Lord Lieutenant to place any district by proclamation out of the pale of ordinary law ; it suspended trial by jury, and made it a transportable offence to be out of door from sunset to sunrise. In 1807 this act continued in force, and in 1808, 1809, and to the close of the session of 1810. In 1814, the Insurrection Act was revived ; it was continued in 1815, 1816, and 1817. In 1822 it was again revived and continued during the years 1823, 1824, and 1825. The Act for the Suppression of Dangerous Associations was passed ; it continued during 1826 and 1827, and expired in 1828."

In 1833, Sir George Cornwall Lewis visited Ireland, and thus describes the legislation for this country :—

"Successive governments have apparently exhausted every means in their power to suppress the evil without success. The statute-books have been loaded with the severest laws ; the country has been covered with military and police ; capital punishment has been unsparingly inflicted ; Australia has been covered with transported convicts, and all to no purpose."

The Honourable Judge Day was examined before the Lords' Committee, in 1825 ; he was asked :—

"Have the disturbances in Ireland originated in religious differences, or in what other causes?" he replied, "The recent disturbances in Ireland have not had anything to do with religion. In what cause did they originate, in your opinion?—The want of employment ; the absence and non-residence of landlords, who might superintend, control, and advise ; the want of education, which leaves them in a semi-barbarous state, and incapable of judging for themselves. These are some of the various and combining causes which may be enumerated."

There is sad evidence of the manner in which the laws which I have quoted above were administered. The Honourable Judge Fletcher, in his charge to the Grand Jury of the county Waterford, in 1814, made the following fearful statement respecting the insurrection acts :—"I have seen times when persons, thinking the lives named in their tenant's leases were lasting *too long*, have, by the aid of such a law, found means to recommend a trip across the Atlantic to the persons thus unreasonably attached to life, and thus worked the downfall of a beneficial lease, and a comfortable *rise of their income*, in consequence. *Such things have occurred; I have known the fact.*"

George Bennet, K.C., father of the Munster Bar, was asked by the Lords' Committee, in 1825 :—

" In general, were persons convicted under the insurrection act, convicted on proof that they were out at night, or on proof that they had committed some outrage?—They were convicted on proof that they were out at night. It lay upon them to prove the lawful occasion they were out upon, and if they failed in proving that they were out on a lawful occasion, the conviction took place."

Major Wilcock describes the persons convicted as being " mostly poor and ignorant."

I shall not continue these extracts which are painful in the extreme, as shewing one of the phases of the post-Union government of Ireland; but shall turn to that which is, perhaps, more legitimately within the scope of my argument, i.e., the social condition of the the people, their state of comfort or happiness. If those laws, which are so well laid down by Adam Smith, had operated, they ought to have been comfortable and independent, because they had abundance of capital, of those consumable commodities which support productive labour. I turn to official documents, to ascertain the state of Ireland.

" The report of the Commons' Committee, 1830, states, (page 4,) " that a very considerable proportion of the population is considered to be out of employment; the number is estimated differently . . . . . *supposed* to be as much as one-fifth of the entire population . . . . . and is *calculated* to amount to one-fourth. . . . . . This, combined with the consequences of an *altered system of managing land*, is stated to produce MISERY AND SUFFRING WHICH NO LANGUAGE CAN POSSIBLY DESCRIBE, and which it is necessary to witness in order fully to estimate."

At page 8, in reference to the situation of the ejected tenantry, or of those who are obliged to give up their several holdings, in order to promote the consolidation of farms. The report says—" THEIR CONDITION IS NECESSARILY MOST DEPLORABLE. *It would be impossible for language to convey an idea of the state of distress to which the ejected tenantry have been reduced;* or of the disease, misery, and even vice which

they have propagated in the towns wherein they have settled;
so that not only they who have been ejected have been rendered miserable, but they have carried with them and propagated that misery. They have increased the stock of labour—
they have rendered the habitations of those who received
them more crowded—they have given occasion to the dis-
semination of disease—they have been obliged to resort to
theft, and all manner of vice and iniquity, to procure subsistence; but what is, perhaps, the most painful of all, A VAST
NUMBER OF THEM HAVE PERISHED OF WANT.

"Your committee," (adds the report, page 9,) "conceived
that it is the IMPERATIVE DUTY of individuals, of the government, and of the legislature, to consider what means can be
devised to diminish this mass of suffering; and at the same
time to secure for the country a better economic condition,
promoting a better management of estates, and REGULATING
THE RELATION BEWEEN LANDLORD AND TENANT ON RATIONAL
AND USEFUL PRINCIPLES.

The Devon Commission of 1845, referring to the previous
Report, which had been laid before Parliament, states—

"That the Irish peasant is still badly housed, badly fed,
badly clothed, and badly paid for his labour."

And again, speaking of the labouring population and cot-
tiers, the commissioners declare, (p. 35,)—"It would be impossible to describe adequately the privations which they
endure. It will be seen in the evidence that in many dis-
tricts their ONLY food is the potato—their only beverage,
water! that their cabins are seldom a protection against the
weather—that a bed or a blanket is a rare luxury—and in that
nearly all, their pig and manure heap constitute their only
property."

"When we consider this state of things, and the large
proportion of the population which comes under the desig-
nation of agricultural labourers, we have to REPEAT, that the
patient endurance which they exhibit is deserving of high
commendation, and entitles them to the best attention of Government and of Parliament."

"Their condition has engaged our most anxious consideration. Up to this period, any improvement that may have
taken place is attributable almost entirely to the habits of
TEMPERANCE in which they have so generally persevered—and
not, we grieve to say, to any increased demand for their labour."

" The obvious remedy for this state of things (says the Report, p. 11,) is to provide REMUNERATIVE EMPLOYMENT, which may at once increase the productive powers of the country, and improve the condition of the people."

The evidence which was given from time to time, and the suggestions which were made, demand greater consideration than they had received. I make a few extracts from a huge mass of evidence:—

Alexander Nimmo, Esq., civil engineer, (Lords' Committee, 1824, p. 226,)—" Your professional intercourse with Ireland has given you the means of general accurate information on the state of the peasantry of that country ?"

" I have seen a great deal of the peasantry; I have sometimes slept in their cabins, and had frequent intercourse with them, especially in the south and west of Ireland.

" I conceive the peasantry of Ireland to be, in general, in almost the *lowest possible state of existence;* their cabins are in the most miserable condition, and their food is POTATOES WITH WATER—very often without anything else, frequently without even salt; and I have frequently had occasion to meet persons, who begged of me, on their knees, for the love of God, to give them some *promise of employment*, that, from the credit of that, they might get the means of supporting themselves for a few months, until I could employ them."

W. H. W. Newenham, Esq., (Commons' Committee, p. 300,)—" Is the condition of the people very bad in respect to the means of subsistence, and houses, and dress?"

" Excepting where a gentleman's own residence is, particularly so. I have seen several countries, and I never saw any peasantry so badly off."

John O'Driscoll, Esq., barrister, (Commons' Committee, 1824, page 380)—" Will you describe to the committee, generally, the condition of the people, and their habits of living ?"

In the part of the country (county Cork,) that I am best acquainted with, the condition of the people *is the very worst that can possibly be.* Nothing can be worse than the condition of the lower classes of the labourers, and the farmers are not much better." Page 381—" They have nothing whatever, I think, but the *potatoes* and WATER. They seldom have salt."

Right Rev. Dr. Doyle (Commons' Committee, 1825, p.

205)—" What is the state of the lower order of the people in your diocese ?"

" I can safely state to the committee, that the extent and intensity of their distress is greater than any language can describe; and that I think the lives of many hundreds of them are very often shortened by this great distress; it also enervates their minds, and paralyzes their energies, and leaves them incapable of almost any useful exertion." (Page 206 describing the state in which some of the peasantry exist)—" Thus he drags out an existence which it were better were terminated in any way, than to be continued in the manner it is !"

R. De la Cour, Esq., county Cork (Commons' Committee, 1825, p. 548)—" What is the condition of the peasantry ?— Wretched in the extreme." P. 549—" Are the habitations of the people in that country exceedingly miserable ?— *Miserable, with very few exceptions.*"

The records of the misery and wretchedness of the Irish people are fearful to peruse, and they do not apply to one district or locality. They shew that they were insufficiently fed with food of the lowest character, and sometimes were forced to live upon the charlock or wild mustard—a most unwholesome article of diet—that they frequently had to fast for long intervals for want of food or fuel—that their cottages, or cabins were hovels of the most wretched description—that they were rarely supplied with any of that furniture required by human beings—that their fuel was of the very worst description, and quite insufficient to warm them—that their clothing was scanty in the extreme. This was the state of Ireland, under a system of laws which taxed her excessively, and under which the capital stock of the country, the consumable commodities which ought to have been used by her people, were largely exported. Grain more than sufficient to feed them, and meat of all kinds, were shipped in large quantities. Wool and leather, more than sufficient to clothe and shoe them, were also exported. They starved, in the midst of abundance. The products of their hands, was to be untasted by their lips—a fate worse than that of Tantalus was the doom of the Irish nation. This was the consequence of neglecting to follow those laws of nature which should have governed the legislature of the United Kingdom.

I do not wish to overload this subject with evidence, but I must make room for two extracts—one is from Mr. Nicholls, an Englishman, the introducer of the Poor Law system into Ireland. In the Second Report, p. 81, he says : "There was no employment in Donegal for the young people, nor relief for the aged, nor means nor opportunity for removing their surplus numbers to some more eligible spot; they could only, therefore, live on, hoping as they said that times might mend, and their landlords would sooner or later do something for them. Yet, with all this suffering no disturbance or act of violence has occurred in Donegal. During the severe privations of the last summer, when numbers were actually in want of sustenance, there was no dishonesty, no plundering. The people starved, but they would not steal, and although their little stock of cattle and moveables has been notoriously lessened these last few years, and especially in the last year, which seems to have swallowed up nearly all their visible means, they have yet paid their rents. The occupier's share of the produce has been insufficient for his support, yet the landlord's share has been generally paid in full."

The other is from the Report of the Devon Commission, page 12:—" Our personal experience and observations during our inquiry have afforded us a melancholy confirmation of these statements. And we cannot forbear expressing, our strong sense of the patient endurance which the labouring classes have generally exhibited, under sufferings greater, we believe, than the people of any other country in Europe have sustained."

Who can read these records without coming to the conclusion that there must have been something radically wrong in the system of Government of Ireland, the responsibility of which, rests with the British Parliament, or exclaiming in the language of the inspired writer?—" This is a people robbed and spoiled."

LETTER XV.

THE TAXATION OF IRELAND FROM 1821 AND ITS EFFECTS.

In considering questions of a political nature, our first duty should be, to ascertain the principles, and to indictate the course which should be pursued. It was therefore necessary, to enquire into the principles which govern the financial measures, of the United Kingdom, and to learn their operation, and, having done so, in the preceding letters it remains to examine the mode in which these principles were carried out, in the period which has elapsed since 1821.

The Finance Committee of 1815 hypocritically avowed that the object they had in view in proposing the consolidation of the Exchequers was, " to relieve Ireland of a burthen which experience had shewn was too heavy for her to bear." History tells us how this was done—as soon as peace was proclaimed, Parliament took care to relieve Great Britain of its burthens, but poor Ireland was left to bear hers, as best she could. I have given, page 170, the revenue of the five years ending 1816 and the five years ending 1821, it proves that in the former period, Ireland paid one-thirteenth of the whole, and that in the latter, her proportion was raised to one-twelfth. A reduction took place in the revenue, but Great Britain appropriated 15-16ths of it and Ireland got only 1-16th.

The relief afforded up to 1822, shews the great anxiety which Parliament felt, to carry out the recommendation of the Finance Committee, and "relieve Ireland from a burthen which experience proved was too heavy for her to bear!" it was as follows!—

Taxes diminished or repealed	Great Britain.	Ireland.
Assessed Taxes ...	£808,484	£40,112
Property Tax ...	14,617,823	
Hearth and Window Tax		297,000
Customs	255,356	55,273
Excise	7,559,934	312,600
Taxes	347,762	216,079
Stamps		24,368
Total	£23,589,359	£915,432

Ireland got about a twenty-fourth part of the reduction! though she had increased her contribution at a greater ratio than Great Britain.

The re-cuperative power of British taxation is shewn in the fact, that though the remission of taxation was $23\frac{1}{2}$ millions, the falling off in the revenue was only 5 millions, while in Ireland, the revenue fell off nearly to the extent of the remission. Parliament at this time relieved the British taxpayer at the expense of the Irish; had the principle avowed by Mr. Vansittart, (Chancellor of the Exchequer,) been fairly carried out, Ireland should have been relieved at the same ratio as Great Britain, but this was not the case.

In 1833, Mr. Spring Rice, (now Lord Monteagle,) in answering O'Connell's Repeal speech, said—"The members who attack England, for her conduct towards Ireland, do not recollect the separate taxation which England has paid and still pays. From all the taxes which have pressed, and still press, most severely upon England, Ireland not only claims, but enjoys exemption. I will state to the House some facts which will shew the extent to which the separate taxation of Great Britain has proceeded.

England has paid ; Taxes on property since 1801 £152,285,710
Produce of land and assessed taxes from
1823. when those taxes were repealed
in Ireland, ... 50,120,425
Beer 82,483,583
Soap 24,934,544
Candles, ... 10,294,980
Printed cottons, ... 13,549,607

Making a total of separate taxation on ————
Great Britain, ... £333,641,851

In referring to these facts, I am not arguing against my country, for I believe I am not a worse Irishman, in endeavouring to do justice to the·conduct of the people of England. It would, I admit, have been most unjust in the Imperial Parliament to have imposed heavier taxes upon Ireland; but, at the same time, I will contend that the fact of not having done so, must be taken as a proof of regard for Irish interests."

I fancy if Mr. Spring Rice could have discovered any other special tax paid by Great Britain, he would have added it, and have swelled this grand total of British payments.

I have to thank him for unconsciously doing two things. He has proved,

First, that there was no declaration by Parliament—at least up to 1833—that all taxes were to be levied indiscriminately; and,

Second, he has proved that Great Britain did not, up to 1833, contribute, by separate taxation, the amount which she was bound to do under the Act of Union.

He did not mean to prove either of these very important facts, but he has done so. I shall not dwell upon the first, because it is quite obvious; but I will illustrate the second, in order to shew the injustice done to Ireland, and also, that what he deems a matter of favour towards Ireland was, according to our contract, and that the separate payments made by Great Britain, instead of exceeding the amount which that country was bound to pay, really fell far short of it. The charge for interest on the debt of Great Britain, in 1800 was, £17,805,375. The Act of Union says—

"That it be the seventh article of the Union, that the charge arising from the payment of the interest and sinking fund, for the reduction of the principal of the debt, incurred in either kingdom, before the Union, shall continue to be separately defrayed by Great Britain and Ireland respectively."

Mr. Spring Rice spoke in 1833—that is, 33 years after the Union—and according to the conditions of the Act of Union, Great Britain was bound to raise by separate taxation, sufficient to pay the interest on the debt due at the Union. Did she pay this sum? or did she require Ireland to pay part of it? Let Mr. Spring Rice answer this question.

The interest on the debt of Great Britain for 33 years, at £17,805,375, per annum was	...	£587,576,375
The separate taxation of Great Britain, per Mr. Spring Rice, in 33 years ...	...	333,648,851
Deficiency of Great Britain,	...	£253,927,524

Thus the amount which Great Britain raised by special taxes was less by £253,927,522, than the sum which she was bound to pay, and therefore Ireland contributed her quota towards this balance, which was over a million a-year for the 33 years!! This large sum was levied off poor Ireland, to pay the interest on the debt which rich England owed at the Union. If each year's account was taken separately, as was done in the Irish accounts, and interest charged on the balance, and that it went on accumulating, then the amount of the deficiency of Great Britain would have more than doubled, inasmuch as the average receipts from special taxes in Great Britain was only *ten millions* a year, whereas, according to the Act of Union, she was bound to raise by separate taxes the full amount of the interest on the debt she owed previous to the Union, which was nearly *eighteen* millions a year. The debt of Great Britain, for interest alone, would in 1816 have been £168,436,419 ; and had it been carried on at the same rate to 1833, it would have been over £500,000,000, as will be seen by the following :—

1802.			£62,425,455
Annual interest,..	£17,800,000	Deduct paid, ...	10,000,000
Deduct paid,...	10,000,000		
		1808—Balance.	£52,425,455
1803—Balance	£ 7,800,000	Interest on same,	2,621,272
Interest on same,	390,000	Annual interest,	17,800,000
Annual interest,	17,800,000		
			£72,846,727
	£25,990,000	Deduct paid, ...	10,000,000
Deduct paid, ...	10,000,000		
		1809—Balance,	£62,846,727
1804—Balance	£15,990,000	Interest on same,	3,142,336
Interest on same,	799,500	Annual interest,	17,800,000
Annual interest,	17,800,000		
			£83,789,063
	34,589,500	Deduct paid, ...	10,000,000
Deduct paid, ...	10,000,000		
		1810—Balance,	£73,789,063
1805—Balance,	£24,592,500	Interest on same,	3,689,453
Interest on same,	1,229,975	Annual interest,	17,800,000
Annual interest,	17,800,000		
			£95,278,616
	£43,619,475	Deduct paid, ...	10,000,000
Deduct paid, ...	10,000,000		
		1811—Balance,	£85,278,606
1806—Balance,	£33,619.475	Interest on same,	4,263,931
Interest on same,	1,680,978	Annual interest,	17,800,000
Annual interest,	17,800,000		
			£197,342,547
	£52,500,455	Deduct paid, ...	10,000,000
Deduct paid, ...	10,000,000		
		1812—Balance,	£97,342,547
1807—Balance,	42,500,453	Interest on same,	4,867,127
Interest on same,	2,125,002	Annual interest,	17,800,000
Annual interest,	17,800,000		
			£120,009,674
	£62,425,455	Deduct paid, ...	10,000,000
		1813—Balance.	110,089,674

Interest on same,	5,500,483	Interest on same,	6,863,783
Annual interest,	17,800,000	Annual interest,	17,800,000
	£133,310,157		£163,939,447
Deduct paid,	10,000,000	Deduct paid, ...	10,000,000
1814—Balance,	123,310,157	1816—Balance,	153,939,447
Interest on same,	6,165,507	Interest on same,	7,696,972
Annual interest,	17,800,000	Annual interest,	17,000,000
	£147,275,664		£178,436,419
Deduct paid,	10,000,000	Deduct paid, ...	10,000,000
1815—Balance,	137,275,664	Balance, ...	£168,436,419

According to the statement made by Mr. Spring Rice in 1833, the amount due by Great Britain in 1816, for INTEREST on her separate account, was £168,436,419.

The enactment which obliged Ireland to pay 2-17th ceased in 1821, and under the Union the proportion would have been revised. I shall not detain you by going into a minute calculation of the amount which Ireland should then pay; it is enough for my purpose to assume, as the basis of calculation, that in the five years ending 1821, her condition, so far as trade and consumption of the articles prescribed in the Act of Union, was worse than it was in 1801, while the consumption of Great Britain had increased. The relative condition of each country had changed so much in 1821, that Great Britain's wealth was to Ireland in the ratio of 12 to 1; in 1861 it is proved by the income tax returns, that the property of Great Britain was to that of Ireland as 14 to 1. For the entire forty years, from 1821 to 1861, I shall adopt the ratio of 13 to 1. Great Britain and Ireland should, according to the Union, in the first instance, provide for the interest on the separate debt, due by each country before the Union, and then provide for the general expenditure in the proportion of 12-13ths for Great Britain, and 1-13th for Ireland. It can be proved, upon data, which cannot be controverted, that Great Britain has not performed her portion of the contract She has not raised by separate taxes, a sufficient sum to pay the interest on her separate debt, and the account against Great Britain, without charging interest each year, was, in 1833, no less than £253,927,124; if interest were charged each year the deficiency would then have been about £500,000,000, and it would have doubled since; nevertheless, she has gradually lessened her contribution, and the special taxes which were raised in Great Britain last year, were only £3,140,405, so that Great Britain last year evaded the payment of special taxes to the extent of £14,640,000, and she forced Ireland to pay her portion of that sum contrary to the equity of the case, and in defiance of the Act of Union.

The comparison of the British and Irish revenues to 1821, when that enactment of the Act of Union, which required Ireland to pay two-seventeenths of the general expenditure ceased, is given, ante page 170. According to the condition of each country, the Irish proportion of of the general expenditure should not then have exceeded *one-thirteenth*. I wish to be clearly understood, that it was not to be *one-thirteenth* of the total income of the United Kingdom, but *one-thirteenth* of the general expenditure, after Great Britain and Ireland had each, by special taxes, raised sufficient to pay the interest of the debt which they respectively owed before the Union, and which alone required £17,800,000 per annum from Great Britain, and £816,000 from Ireland. In the twenty years which followed the Union, Great Britain had not lessened her debt, but Ireland had done so. The 56th George III., cap. 70, declares that " the Irish capital debt, existing March 25, 1797, which was £5,829,156 13s. 4d., was discharged, and the stock placed to the credit of the Commissioners, for the reduction of the National Debt, was cancelled ;" and that a balance of £2,063,375, 5s. 2d. over and above remained to the credit of Ireland. The interest on this debt was £341,277; and in any calculations as to the relative payments, this sum must be deducted from the interest of the Irish debt.

The revenue of Great Britain and Ireland is given in lustrums ; in that from 1806 to 1811 the Irish contribution was equal to *one-fourteenth* of that of the United Kingdom ; in the next lustrum, ending in 1816, it was *one-thirteenth*. The reduction which took place after the peace was not so fair to Ireland as to Great Britain, and the Irish proportion was raised to *one-twelfth*. In the decade from 1821 to 1831, it was restored to *one-thirteenth* ; in that from 1831 to 1841, it was *one-twelfth*. Sir Robert Peel reduced the Irish proportion ; and in 1842, when he made the great financial changes, he recognised the validity of the Act of Union, and the necessity of regulating the finances of Ireland according to it. He then said, (see Annual Register for 1842, page 75,) " In case of war he should deem it reasonable, that Ireland should bear

her proportion of this (the income) tax ; but during peace,
and for a limited period, and in the absence of all machinery
in Ireland for collection, he should prefer raising the *quota*
of that country by other means. He thought he could do
so consistently with the Act of Union." This recognition of
the principle for which I contend, by one of the most eminent statesmen of the present century, is most valuable; it
shews that the taxation of Ireland should be in accordance
with the Act of Union, and that Ireland should raise her
quota—that is, her proportion according to a given scale. The
admission of this principle proves all that I ask. Since 1821,
the credited taxation of Ireland and of Great Britain is as
follows:—

Five years ending	Great Britain.	Ireland.	Proportion of Ireland.
1826	... £270,038,808	£22,538,098	1-13th.
1831	... 270,607,111	22,298,321	1-13th.

The taxation of Great Britain was then reduced, but that
of Ireland remained stationary, and during the following ten
years it was:—

Five years ending.	Great Britain.	Ireland.	Proportion of Ireland.
1836	... 244,074,356	22,096,998	1-12th.
1841	... 242,422,560	22,668,098	1-12th.

Then came Sir Robert Peel's policy, which lessened the
proportion which Ireland contributed.

Five years ending.	Great Briain.	Ireland.	Proportion of Ireland.
1846	... 254,092,727	22,484,700	nearly 1-13th.
1851	... 260,599,150	21,947,763	,, 1-13th.

Mr. Gladstone's policy has been essentially unjust to Ireland, and has altered the proportions, and in the past decade
the payments have been:—

Five years ending.	Great Britain.	Ireland.	Proportion of Ireland.
1856	... 302,644,809	30,055,544	,, 1-11th.
1861	... 305,671,563	33,583,382	1-10th.

During the past five years Ireland has paid *more* by nearly
18 per cent. than she did in those ending in 1816, while Great
Britain has paid *less* by nearly 10 per cent. than she did in

that period, thus shewing how essentially unfair has been the recent policy.

The injustice to Ireland, which had arisen from the non-observance of that portion of the Act of Union, which required Great Britain to pay the interest on her separate debt, which appears from the language of Mr. Spring Rice, in his speech in 1833, has not been obviated or lessened by subsequent legislation. Some Chancellors of the Exchequer have admitted that the Union ratio between British and Irish taxation should be preserved. In 1822, Mr. Vansittart, in his speech, asserted that Irish taxes should be taken off in the same ratio as British. In the six years previous, the relief to the British tax payer, was much greater than to the Irish. One of the greatest financiers of modern times—Sir Robert Peel—admitted this principle and carried it out to its full extent when he imposed the income tax on Great Britain in 1842; he did not do so to Ireland. He reduced the existing proportion and lessened the Irish contribution. The results of his policy was favourable to Ireland, as is amply proved by contrasting the amount of revenue collected in Great Britain in 1842, and in 1847 with the amount collected in Ireland in those years. The receipts in each year being as follows, see par. paper, No. 355, sess. 1863:—

	1842.	1847.
Revenue of Great Britain.	£46,041,934	£51,469,546
„ Ireland,	4,208,691	4,454,437
United Kingdom,	£50,250,625	55,923,981

In 1842, Ireland paid about the twelfth part of the Revenue of the empire; in 1847, she did not pay quite one-thirteenth, so that the change produced by the adoption of Sir Robert Peel's policy, was favourable to Ireland. It recognised the principle of separate taxation in Great Britain, and of proportionate increases. This policy has been abandoned by degrees within the last ten years. Taxes, which used to be specially levied in Great Britain, such as those on soap, bricks, &c., have been abolished in toto, without Ireland deriving any advantage. Taxes which used to be levied at a higher rate in Great Britain than in Ireland have been raised in Ireland to the same level as Great Britain—thus imposing additional taxation upon Ireland without a corresponding benefit; the spirit duty exemplifies this change—it has been quadrupled; while taxes, which used to be levied in Britain and not Ireland—such as the property and income tax—have been extended to Ireland. By the operation of these three methods, Great Britain has got rid of her separate taxes; she has evaded the payment of interest on her separate debt, due before the Union, and the only separate taxation now levied in Great Britain is the assessed taxes, which do not much exceed £3,000,000 a year.

I do not think the British people are aware of, or appreciate the fact, that their relief from Taxation has been partly purchased at the expense of the Irish people, and that it has been the means of inflicting serious injury upon Ireland. I am perfectly satisfied that if the provisions of the Act of Union were clearly explained to the British public ; if they were told, that they were bound to pay the interest on the debt which they owed before the Union; that their contract with the Irish people, at the time of the Union, was that they would always discharge that liability themselves. They would at once say—"we are able and willing to pay our own debts— this is a British debt, and we will never call upon Ireland to pay one penny of it." I am thoroughly convinced that if the matter were explained to the British people, and that the length and breadth of the land were polled, that ninety-nine out of every hundred would support the view which I put forward.

The British public are not aware of the extent to which Ireland has been taxed, nor are they aware of the effect of this taxation upon the industry of Ireland. They are not aware that in ten years, from 1842 to 1852, the Irish contributions to the Exchequer were £44,432,463 ; and in the ten years, from 1852 to 1862, they had increased to £63,723,051. Nor do they consider that the nineteen millions so raised in the past ten years in excess of the ten years from June 1842 to 1852, has gone into their pockets, inasmuch as they have so much less to pay by that large sum.

If Mr. Gladstone were to follow Mr. Spring Rice (Lord Monteagle,) in his calculation, and gave us a statement of the special taxes paid by Great Britain since 1833, we should find that the separate contributions which Mr. Spring Rice stated at about £10,000,000 a-year, when they should have been £18,000,000, had been greatly reduced. I doubt, if since 1833, they have averaged £8,000,000. So that rich England is only paying *ten shillings in the pound* of her separate liability. If an estimate were made, for the period since the

Union, of the amount which Great Britain raised by special taxes, and that she were charged year by year, with the interest on the amount which falls short of the sum which she contracted to pay, I believe the sum would be so large as to astonish every person. I think it would exceed the total amount of the present National Debt. Had no Union taken place, and had Ireland contributed towards the war expenses, in the ratio which she gave before the Union, Great Britain must have provided for the interest of this debt, and she would have been compelled, either to have maintained a much higher scale of taxation, or she would very largly have increased her debt. I need not dilate on this subject ; it is not my object to create animosity or ill-feeling, but to try, if possible, to obtain for Ireland, that system of taxation secured to her at the Union, and to which she is fully entitled ; not alone by the contract, but by the efforts she made, and the sacrifices she underwent, in order to fulfil to the utmost, the conditions of the union—conditions which were not proposed by her—nor even voluntarily accepted by her—but conditions, which, though her Parliament refused to consider them, were placed on record on the rolls of the British Parliament ; and their adoption was forced upon Ireland by corrupting her senators, by bribing her re-presentatives, and by preventing the expression of feeling by her people.—Those who made the offer, and forced Ireland to accept it, are bound by the strongest ties of duty and moral obligation, to see that it is enforced.

I have already shewn, that as far as revenue is concerned, the amount which Ireland raised in the period from 1801 to 1821 (the twenty years during which she was bound to pay 2-17ths of the expenditure of the empire) discharged per liability. I gave the data upon which I concluded that the fair proportion for Ireland to have paid at the first revision of the scale of taxation, would have been one-thirteenth; and I shall proceed upon this data to examine whether she overpaid this proportion? and if so, to what extent? A return published by the treasury in 1841, supplies the amount of revenue paid by Great Britain and Ireland in lustrums, and these periods are convenient for reference. I shall in this investigation, pursue the course I have already adopted, of deducting from the revenue of each country the separate interest due at the Union, and then ascertain what Ireland should have paid.

The over payments by Ireland were as follows:—

1821 to 1826—Overpayment by Ireland	...	...	£8,220,503
1826 to 1831—Five years' interest on same	...	...	1,646,100
— — Overpayment by Ireland	...	...	7,954,585
Total in 1831	...	...	17,821,188
1831 to 1836—Five years' interest on same	...	...	3,564,237
— — Overpayment by Ireland	...	...	9,809,746
Total in 1836	...	...	31,125,171
1836 to 1841—Five years' interest on same	...	...	6,239,034
— — Overpayment by Ireland	...	...	10,463,950
Total in 1841	...	...	47,898,155
1841 to 1846—Five years' interest on same	...	...	9,579,631
— — Overpayment by Ireland	..	...	7,832,465
Total in 1846	...	...	65,310,251
1846 to 1851—Five years' interest on same	...	..	13,062,050
— — Overpayment by Ireland	...	...	7,658,396
Total in 1851	...	...	86,030,697
1851 to 1856—Five years' interest on same	...	...	17,206,139
— — Overpayment by Ireland	...	...	9,425,516
Total in 1856	...	...	112,662,342
1856 to 1861—Five years' interest on same	...	...	22,532,468
— — Overpayment by Ireland	...	...	15,597,795
Total in 1861	...	... £150,792,405

On a fair adjustment of the account there would in 1861 be no less that *One Hundred and Fifty Millions* due to Ireland, that being the amount of her over payments since 1821.

Comment is superfluous ! !

This state of things was produced by the breach of that important provision in the treaty of Union, under which Great Britain was bound to raise by special taxes, each, and every year, the sum of £17,800,000 to pay the interest on her debt due before the Union. This provision is plain and positive ; it stands out at the head of the 7th article of the treaty of Union. I shall re-quote it here.

" That it be the seventh article of Union, that the charge arising from the payment of the interest, and the sinking fund for the reduction of the principal of the debt incurred in either kingdom before the Union, shall continue to be separately defrayed by Great Britain and Ireland respectively."

This principle was recognised by Sir Robert Peel, who levied separate taxes on Great Britain to a greater extent than in Ireland.

In 1853, when Mr. Gladstone brought forward the Budget, he said he proposed to charge Ireland with the income tax and the duty on spirits, but the said government had come to the determination to relieve her from the consolidated annuities, amounting to £4,500,000.

Mr. Fegan opposed the extension of the income tax to Ireland, and pleaded the act of the Union.

Colonel Dunne moved for a select committee " to consider the fiscal and political relations and relative taxation of Great Britain and Ireland, and to report whether the latter does not bear her fair share of Imperial Taxation."

Sir John Pakington pointed out the injustice which was attempted toward Ireland, he said Government abandoned the consolidated annuities, which were £250,000 a year, and im-posed the income tax which was £460,000; and spirit duties which were £198,000, and succession taxes, from £60,000 to £300,000 a year

Mr. E. Ball described " Ireland as one new risen from the grave, reeling with weakness, her cere clothes scarce shaken off, and then asking whether Government would not give her strength; instead of this, here is the Chancellor of the Exchequer diluting her, bleeding her, purging her, and when she asked for bread giving her a stone. Unhappy Ireland, hardly recovered from one plague, that of famine, is now to be visited with another plague, that of locusts."

The gallant Colonel's motion for a committee was refused.

The injustice pointed out by Sir John Pakington, who, on this occasion, shewed that the Conservative party recognised in 1853 the just policy of Sir Robert Peel, of 1842, was very great. Mr. Gladstone took credit for surrendering the con-solidated annuities of £4,500,000, which were repayable in 20 years; but he has obtained from Ireland income tax to the amount of nearly £7,000,000; spirit duties to the amount of £10,000,000, and the succession duties to the amount of £1,000,000; making a total against Ireland of £18,000,000 or more than four times the amount of the consolidated annuities.

I have brought my subject down to the present time, and thus historically closed the " Case of Ireland." I have depicted the manner in which the Union was carried, the provisions of the treaty, and the mode in which it was carried out; they alike illustrate the sad tale too often repeated, of " might overcoming right." The Union was carried by bribery and intimidation—its conditions were hard and unjust. As long as they operated against Ireland they were observed; but as soon as they were likely to turn in favor of Ireland, they were set aside. From 1801 to 1821, Ireland ruined herself by her efforts to pay the amount put upon her by the Union. Since 1821, she has overpaid her account by no less than £150,000,000. Great Britain, gained by the Union, the advantage of placing a large share of the debt arising from her Continental policy, upon the Irish people; but she has not fulfilled the requirements of her part of the treaty, inasmuch as she has not raised by special taxes a sufficient sum to pay the interest of her debt due previous to the Union. Had she done so, she must have raised an amount, which with compound interest, would be more than the entire of the National Debt of the empire.

The present aspect of the taxation question may be compressed into a small, compass and stated as follows:—

The interest on the debt due by Great Britain at the Union, was £17,800,000; that sum she was, and is bound to raise by special and separate taxes. She is now, and has for some time been raising less than 3¼ millions. Ireland is over taxed, to make up her share of the balance. Look at some of the effects.

On the motion for reading the Seditious Meetings Bill in the House of Lord, July 27, 1814,

The Earl of Careysfort gave the following picture of Ireland, he said " The benefits or advantages of the real constitution of England had never been fairly or fully extended to Ireland. The common people were more estranged than than any other from the nobility, and this arose from the necessary situation in which they were placed. When contrasted with the lower orders in this country, the people of Ireland appeared only like slaves. There was not a man in England who did not know that the fruits of his labour was protected, and if he fell into calamity, he was assisted ; but the state of Ireland on the contrary could not be described by any other name but that of slavery. They had neither dwellings, clothes to cover them, property to support then, nor even liberty.

Earl Stanhope, descanted on the hardships to which the lower classes in Ireland were subjected, particularly the poor tenantry ; the last taker of land being liable to be distrained by all the men above him ; he considered it scandalous on the part of the government, that nothing was done to relieve the people from such horrible oppression.   He urged that they should begin by taking off oppressive taxes, and abolishing other grievances, and thus bring the people of Ireland into good humour.

Lord Redesdale, thought, that the higher orders did not do their duties, with so much of that patriotism which he conceived would be proper and becoming ; not, that he meant to say that the higher orders in Ireland did not feel as patriotically as any men, but that mainly from mistaken views, they did not act with so much zeal, as, in his opinion, they ought to do.   The cure for this evil, would be the introduction of riches and change of habits.

In 1816 the Marquess of Buckinghamshire deemed it his duty to bring the state of Ireland under the attention of the House of Lords, and after describing the evils which arose from disunion in consequence of refusing to grant the Roman Catholics those civil rights to which they were entitled.   He proceeded to picture her financial position, and the great increase of the Irish debt.   He said, "almost every tax has been doubled, the assessed taxes have been trebled ; in short every exertion has been made to screw up the taxes of Ireland to the utmost.   What could this be called but a state of National Bankruptcy? There was also apparently a falling off in the linen manufacture, the staple of Ireland.   In 1792 the exports of Irish linens amounted to 49,000,000 yards almost entirely in England ; in 1815 the exports only amounted to 39,000,000 yards.   The exports of woollens from England into Ireland had also materially diminished."

The debate was taken part in by Lords Stanhope, Danley, Blessington, Carnarvon, Holland, and Greville, who supported the views of the Marquess of Buckinghamshire.—It was opposed by Lords Liverpool, Redesdale, and Sidmouth who, while they admitted the grievance did not see a practical remedy, but there was no denial of the accuracy of Lord Buckinghamshire's representation as to the state of Ireland, and it seems to me that this arose from the manner in which the treaty of Union was violated—by charging Ireland, with a larger portion of the debt contracted after the Union, than she agreed to, or she was able to bear.

The effects of this excessive taxation have been to prevent the progress of Ireland ; it has obstructed the growth of capital stock, and thus deprived the people of employment. When Great Britain set aside the Irish Parliament, and took upon herself the government of Ireland, she accepted the duties inherent in government. Foremost among which is that of feeding the people; Ireland possesses in abundance capital stock, or means of subsistence. The elements for supporting labour are largely exported out of this country, to be consumed elsewhere; and the people, who ought to consume them in Ireland, are exported in myriads, to enrich other climes. To secure the prosperity of Ireland three things are necessary:—

First—The diminution of taxation.

Second—The employment of her people.

Third—The consumption in Ireland of the means of subsistence which she raises.

The two latter seem to me contingent on the former. I have endeavoured to shew the relation between prosperity and taxation. Ireland, when lightly taxed under her own Parliament, progressed rapidly. Ireland, over-taxed by the Parliament of the United Kingdom, has receded.

The subject on which I have attempted to treat is a very large one, and I could wish that the task of treating it had fallen upon one possessed of greater abilities. I have been very particular to quote the statistics, I have laid before you from the highest authorities—the reports submitted to Parliament. The question of taxation is neither a party nor a sectarian question, it is, in the broadest significance of the word, an Irish question. I have endeavoured to treat it in the same spirit, and having laid " the case of Ireland" before you, the Irish people, it remains for you to act thereupon in a way which will secure to you and your children the rights to which, by justice, as well as by agreement and contract, you are entitled. You should press your case upon the attention of Parliament—you should call upon your representatives to demand the adjustment of the public burthens, in such a way as to relieve Ireland from undue taxation. You should make the question essentially a national one, and pursue it with vigour and determination, until you accomplish this object, and you will find your reward in the advancement of your native land. If I can aid the Irish people in any well directed effort to bring back to our country that prosperity which she once enjoyed, and to which she is so fully entitled, I shall feel that I am only discharging the duty which every Irishman owes to his native land.

LETTER XVI.

CONCLUSION.

To the Irish People—

Having been asked to prepare a condensed *resumé* of my statement of the "Case of Ireland" and to present the salient points with as little detail as possible, I have made the following brief summary of the contents of my letters.

Letter I. shews that the Act of Union was based upon a Treaty, and that such Treaty is governed by the Law of Nations; and, according to the dicta of writers of the highest authority, it is not competent of the Parliament of the United Kingdom, which owes its existence to that Act, to abrogate its conditions.

Letter II. is a condensed history of the financial and industrial progress of Ireland, from 1788 to 1800, during which time the Irish nation had made such great progress, as to astonish all who examine into her condition. Her Parliament was independent, and promoted her interests; her manufactures flourished—her wealth increased—her taxation was light—while the large consumption of those articles, which indicate the improved condition of her people, prove their advance in civilization and refinement.

Letter III. is devoted to a sketch of the debates on the projected Union, in the British and in the Irish Houses of Parliament in 1799; and Letter IV. to those of 1800. These debates shew the views of those, who proposed, and carried, the treaty of Union. The following extract, from the protest of the dissentient Peers, evinces their sentiments; they say:—

" It appears to us that, if this kingdom should take upon herself irrevocably, the payment of 2-17ths of the expenses of the empire, she will not have the means to perform her engagement, unless by charging her landed property with twelve to thirteen shillings in the pound. It must end in drawing from her her last guinea, in totally annihilating her trade for want of capital, in rendering the taxes unproductive, and consequently in finally putting her into a state of bankruptcy. We think ourselves called upon to protest against a measure so ruinous to this country. Calling upon our latest posterity, to entreat that, in virtue of this our solemn declaration, they will acquit us of having been in anywise instrumental to their degradation, and to the ruin of the country which they may hereafter inhabit."

These gloomy anticipations have been confirmed in every respect. Taxation has increased; manufactures have been destroyed; even the gold has left the country. In 1797, it was estimated that Ireland had 5,000,000 guineas; now, the gold held by the Bankers, and in circulation, is hardly one-half that amount.

Letter V. gives the text of the 7th article of the treaty of Union, the construction which each paragraph bears; and Letter VI., the manner in which it was carried out. Documents of the highest authority, prove, that the spirit and letter of the treaty and Act of Union, have been systematically violated.

Letter VII. is an examination of the Revenue and Expenditure of Ireland, from 1801 to 1816. The Revenue of Ireland, in that period, was at least £95,944,942; it was in excess of her proportion (2-17ths) by £2,940,234. The Irish proportion of the Expenditure (two-seventeenths) was £81,214,171; her Revenue, after payment of interest on the debt due at the Union, was £83,549,942, being £2,335,771 in excess of her proportion of expenditure.

Letter VIII. discusses the alleged debt of Ireland in 1816, and proves that the allegation that she had contracted a debt of £103,459,432, is a monstrous fraud, and that the Parliamentary returns, which refer to this debt, are conflicting and contradictory.

Letter IX. deals with the report of the Finance Committee of 1815, and shews the falsehood and hypocrisy of that document, which, under the pretence of "relieving Ireland from burthens which were too heavy for her," laid the ground for increasing them.

Letter X. states the amount borrowed on Irish account from 1801 to 1816, on the authority of Acts of Parliament—it was £22,800,000. The English Exchequer was, by other acts, authorized to remit to the Irish Exchequer £30,500,000; but the balance of remittances was the other way. Ireland remitted to England in this period £14,582,715, and the acts of Parliament shew that a portion of the ante-Union debt of Ireland was paid off and the stock cancelled. The allegation, that the Irish debt bore, in 1815, to the British debt the proportion of 2 to 15, is untrue.   The consolidation of the Exchequers was based upon this fallacy.

The effect of this measure is traced in Letter XI.   Great Britain from 1816 to 1822 was relieved of taxes to the extent of £64,942,725 while the reduction in the taxation of Ireland was only £4,060,178.   The declaration, that the respective countries were in a condition to contribute indiscriminately equal taxes, which was required by the Act of Union, was never made by Parliament.

The condition of Ireland after the Union, is the subject of Letters XII., XIII., and XIV.   They shew that her industry has been paralyzed, her manufactures destroyed, her people miserable.   She was misgoverned and it engendered crime and disaffection, and caused destitution.   The history of Ireland, from 1802 to 1840, as found in the laws of the empire, may be said to be written in blood   Since 1840, more than one-fourth of her people have fled from her shores.   Thus amply vindicating the almost prophetic anticipations of the dissentient Peers, in 1800.

Letter XV. proves that Great Britain has not fulfilled her share of the conditions proposed by herself.   She has not paid the separate interest of the debt she owed at the Union, and her share of the general expenditure of the empire. Had she paid her quota, it would, with interest, have formed a larger sum than the entire National Debt.   While she has thus evaded the payment of her share, she has compelled Ireland to pay more than her proportion, and these over-payments, with interest, make in the last 40 years, the enormous sum of £150,000,000, which has been raised in Ireland, over and above her rightful and just proportion.

It is morally impossible that Ireland can prosper while she is drained of her wealth—Her social and industrial position mainly depend upon her material condition.   Those who desire the prosperity of Ireland which is the interest of all Irishmen—must labour to get rid of a burthen which grinds her to the dust, and which prevents her filling that place in the scale of nations which her insular and geographical position, the intelligence, sobriety, and industry of her people, and her former fame, alike entitle her to occupy.

It is a pleasure to look back on the proud position which Ireland once filled; she was recognised as the intellectual head of Europe.   The whole civilized world, looked to Erin, for instruction in all that tended to raise man, and to dignify human nature; but it is sad to turn to the present—to see her people flying from her shores in myriads—her trade destroyed, and manufactures (except in one district) quite uprooted. The ills which afflict Ireland, proceed from the non-fulfilment of the conditions of a treaty, which was forced upon her. Great Britain may be said to have purchased Ireland at the Union, and to have evaded payment of the price.

The question which naturally arises is this. Is there any redress? Are we to continue year after year to bewail the calamities which oppress us, and the injuries which destroy our hopes? Are we to continue to see our people banished, our industry paralyzed, our commerce destroyed? These questions will occur to every Irishman, and all will say " No." Is there, then, no way to alter this pernicious system? Yes. All depends upon our own energies and determination; if we resolve to get rid of the undue taxation which presses upon us, and that we unite for the purpose, we must succeed, because OUR CLAIMS are JUST and RIGHT.

The DEBT with which Ireland has been charged is *illegal*— the TAXATION with which Ireland has been loaded is *illegal*— the BURTHENS which have been laid on her shoulders are *illegal*. I do not speak here of the violation of the Divine law; but I speak of illegality in its legal sense. Any Act of Parliament, which is in opposition to the spirit and letter of the Act of Union, must be null and void, because the former is based on the LAW OF NATIONS, and cannot be changed or varied. You can test the question, (which has not yet been tried) in a court of law, by subscribing and raising a fund to try the legality of the taxation of Ireland. This was done in England, when John Hampden tried the legality of ship-money, in the reign of Charles the First. This question of legality hangs on two points: 1st. The construction to be put upon the Act of Union. 2nd. The validity and effect of the Act of 1816. If the Act of Union bears the construction which I put upon it, Ireland should now only pay *one-fourteenth* of the general expenditure of the empire (after Great Britain has paid the interest of her debt previous to the Union). This would make the Irish taxation only £3,500,000 a year. whereas last year she paid £6,792,606. Ireland can also claim the repayment of £150,000,000, which she has paid, to her own wrong, since 1820. These questions may be raised upon appeal to our legal tribunals, who, I feel confident, will, from the authorities decide that any Act of Parliament contrary to the Act of Union is invalid and of no force.

Ireland may look for an equivalent, in lieu of some of the taxation which has been heaped upon her within the past ten years. The Income tax may be repealed as far as Ireland is concerned. This tax was levied in Great Britain for many years, during which it was not levied in Ireland, and that course may be resumed.

Another source of increased Irish taxation is from the advanced spirit duties, which has lessened the consumption of duty-paid spirits, the revenue and consumption as follows:—

	Gallons Consumed.		Duty Paid.
1842	...	...	7,401,051	...	...	£ 936,132
1852	...	...	8,208,256	...	...	1,098,434
1862	...	...	5,020,834	...	...	2,511,420

This indicates lessened comfort in the smaller consumption, though there has been an increase in the revenue of about £1,500,000. If it is necessary on fiscal grounds that the duty per gallon should be equal in Great Britain and Ireland, there is nothing to prevent the application of this increased revenue to relieve local taxation. Sir Robert Peel transferred the burthen of the Constabulary in Ireland, which was about £140,000 per annum, from the Grand Jury cess to the Revenue; and if the same principle were applied to the spirit duties, the support of the gaols, penitentiaries, reformatories, bridewells, and lunatic asylums, might be paid out of the increased revenue paid on Irish whiskey. Nay, more; it would provide a sufficient fund to pay the entire of the charges on the county-rate, and would thus relieve the agriculturists of this country.

If the income tax, which was imposed in lieu of the consolidated annuities, and which has already realized more than double the fund, which it was meant to pay, were given up, and that the increased spirit duties were applied to the payment of the charges now met by the county-rate, Ireland would then be paying about £1,500,000 a year more than her proportion under the Act of Union; and it would be open to Great Britain to offer her an equivalent, as was done in the case of Scotland, and pay such sum as would be proportioned to the liability Ireland undertakes.

You, the Irish people, should obtain the best legal advice on the following points:—

1st. Have the conditions of the 7th article of the Act of

Union been abrogated, or is it competent for Parliament to repeal or alter them, except in accordance with the Act of Union?

2nd. As the amount raised by a tax levied upon the incomes of each country shews that the relative ability of Ireland is to that of the United Kingdom as 1 to 14. Is it legal, according to the Act of Union, to require from her a larger proportion?

3rd. If the taxation of Ireland be in excess of her proportion, under the Act of Union, is there any legal means of obtaining redress? Would an appeal against the income tax be sustainable on the ground that it was contrary to the Act of Union? or would a replevin suit, in case the goods were distrained, be maintainable if based upon the plea that the taxation of Ireland exceeds the proportion to which she is liable under the Act of Union?

The Irish people have Representatives in Parliament, they can urge these Representatives to do their duty; if their wrongs and grievances were fairly stated in the Parliament of the United Kingdom, I have that faith in the honesty of the British people, to believe that they will cast aside a policy which taxes Ireland to save their own pockets.

I therefore urge my fellow-countrymen of all classes, creeds, and professions, to unite in endeavouring to get rid of the Excessive Taxation which has been placed upon Ireland. I call them to union, in behalf of their country, they have right and justice, truth and equity on their side, and if they will calmly, peacefully, and unitedly, stand for the cause of Ireland, whose case I lay before the whole world, they will find that those eternal principles of justice, which are immutable, must prevail—that an end must come to the wrong and injustice, that has been inflicted upon this country.

ERRATA.

The nature of the subject and the length of time occupied in the publication of the letters will be an excuse for the reiteration of the arguments.   The exceeding great discrepancy in the Parliamentary returns which have been examined, will explain the difference between some of the statements.

Page	86,	line	26,	for	"identified"	read	"identical."
	106,	„	39	„	April,	„	January.
	141,	„	25	„	1805,	„	1804.
	„	„	28	„	1800,	„	1810.
	„	„	33	„	£10,915,428,	.,	£9,729,471.
	142,	„	18	„	£486,0,	„	£486,000.
	„	„	„	„	£6000,0000,	„	£600,000.
	157,	„	9	„	Dutch,	„	British.

171, lines 19 to 23 should read thus :—
" Both are equally the products of labour, in the former are found its means of subsistence, and in the latter the other objects which it is employed to produce, and by which it is virtually replaced, or for which it is directly replaced."

APPENDIX.

SINCE these letters have been in the printer's hands, Sir Edward Grogan, Bart., M.P., has, at my request, obtained two returns relative to the taxation of Ireland; they are Nos. 355 and 356, of the session of 1863. From them, and other Parliamentary papers, it appears that the relative position of Great Britain and Ireland is as follows, viz :—

1801.

	Great Britain.	Ireland.
Population	10,500,956	5,216,331
Gross Revenue	£35,218,525	£2,919,217
Amount of Revenue per head of Population	£3 7s. 0d.	£0 11s. 2d.

1861.

	Great Britain.	Ireland.
Population	23,128,518	5,798,967
Gross Revenue	£61,360,749	£6,792,606
Amount of Revenue per head of Population	£2 13s. 0d.	£1 3s. 5d.
Property Assessed to Income Tax	£278,599,523	£22,746,523
do. do. per head of population	£12 1s. 0d.	£3 16s. 0d.
Taxation on each £1 of Income	£0 4s. 5d.	£0 6s. 4d.

Since the Union, the revenue of Great Britain has been reduced from £3.750 per head of the population in 1800, to £2 13s. 0d., the diminution being 14s. per head. The revenue of Ireland has been raised from 11s. 2d. per head of the population in 1801; to £1. 3s. 5d. in 1861; the increase being 12s. 3d. per head. In 1800, each person in Great Britain paid six times as much as each person in Ireland; now it is only twice as much. This has been done in disregard of the condition of the Treaty of Union, which requires that the taxation of each country should be according to their "*relative ability.*" The relative ability, is, if absentee remittances are excluded, only as 4 to 1, though the taxation is as 2 to 1. Ireland now pays *six shillings and four pence* in the pound, while Great Britain pays *four shillings and five pence* in the pound; if the absentee rents were deducted from the Irish Income, her taxes would be over *eight shillings in the pound.*

If the taxation of Ireland had been reduced at the same rates as that of Great Britain, Ireland should now be paying only 9s. 0d. per head of population. The payment in Great Britain has been lessened, in consequence of the increase in Ireland.

The decrease in the population and the increase in the taxation of Ireland, is shewn by a contrast of 1841 with 1861.

Population in 1841	8,175,124	Revenue in Ten years, 1841 to 1851	£44,423,463
Population in 1861	5,764,543	Revenue in Ten years 1851 to 1861	63,723,051
Decrease,	2,410,581	Increase,	£19,290,588

PROSPECTUS.

In the Press, and will Shortly be Published,

Price One Shilling; by Post, Fourteenpence.

A few Copies bound, at TWO SHILLINGS.

HOW
Ireland may be Saved;

OR,

THE INJURIOUS EFFECTS

OF THE

PRESENT SYSTEM OF AGRICULTURE

ON THE

PROSPERITY OF IRELAND, AND THE SOCIAL
POSITION OF THE IRISH PEOPLE.

BY

JOSEPH FISHER,

AUTHOR OF "TAXATION OF IRELAND," "IRELAND PAST AND PRESENT,"
&c., &c.

"The Ireland of the present seems hardly the same as the Ireland of the past."—*The* LORD LIEUTENANT'S *Speech at the Royal Agricultural Show in Limerick,* 1862.

LONDON: RIDGWAY, PICCADILLY.
SOLD BY W. H. SMITH & SON, LONDON AND DUBLIN,
AND ALL BOOKSELLERS.

INTRODUCTION.

THE Population of Ireland is diminishing! and the wealth or capital of the country is decreasing!! Is this to continue? How can the downward tendency be checked? How can Ireland be saved?

The people of Ireland are mainly dependent upon agriculture. It is the produce of the land which gives to all classes not only the command of luxuries, but the very means of support. The landowner, the professional man, the merchant, the tradesman, and the artizan, all rely on the productive power of the soil for income; the railway proprietor and the steam-boat owner, are also equally interested in its profitable cultivation.

The reduction in the area under tillage has had a very serious action, not alone upon the employment of the mere labourer, but also upon the small class of farmers, from both of which sections, numbers have been forced to emigrate. It has also diminished the income of the nation. The estimated value of the crops of Ireland in 1841, was *Fifty* Millions sterling: in 1851 it was reduced to *Forty-three* Millions sterling: and in 1861 it had further fallen to *Thirty-five* Millions sterling. Under a proper system of tillage the annual value of the crops would be *Seventy Millions* sterling per annum.

From 1811 to 1841, the population of Ireland increased in the same ratio as that of England and Scotland. Since 1841 these countries have continued to increase their population, while that of Ireland has diminished, England and Scotland have gone on increasing their wealth, but Ireland has lessened her resources and capital.

The deportation of the Irish people has been followed by an almost total cessation in the export of grain, and Ireland has become a large importer of corn. In 1860 and 1861 the value of the imports of foreign grain exceeded that of the exports by £7,477,700.

It is a singular anomaly to find an agricultural country unable to produce food for the support of its own population, and to find it obliged to become an importer of cereals.

Many suppose that the decrease in the export of cereals is made up by an increase in the exports of cattle, sheep, pigs, and butter; such an assumption has no solid foundation. The value of the exports of cattle, butter, sheep, and pigs from Ireland in 1861, exceeded those of 1847 by £750,000, but the value of the cereal crops of Ireland, in 1861, was less than those of 1847, by £13,000,000, thus showing a loss, in the latter year, of £12,250,000!

The live stock of Ireland increased at a greater ratio in the ten years, from 1841 to 1851, than it has done in the ten years from 1851 to 1861, though the famine swept over the land in the former period.

Emigration from Ireland was also greater in the ten years, from 1851 to 1861, than in the former decade, showing that we must look to other causes than the potato blight for an explanation of this emigration.

The fertility of the soil has lessened in even a greater ratio than the reduction in the population. The average produce per acre, in 1861, was hardly half what it was in 1851. Notwithstanding these disadvantages the taxation of Ireland has (since the accession of Mr. Gladstone to office in 1853) been largely increased. Since 1841 the increase of taxation has been about 150 per cent for each person in Ireland, while in Great Britain the average payment has been reduced; there it was less in 1861 than in 1841. Ireland is now most unfairly taxed.

The Lord Lieutenant (LORD CARLISLE) has for years been using his high position to discourage tillage in Ireland, thus diminishing the employment of the Irish people, and rendering emigration a necessity. He has at length been forced to admit that his anticipations have not been realised. In his annual oration to the Royal Agricultural Society (in Limerick), he thus admits that Ireland has not progressed under the non-tillage régime: he said—"The

Ireland of the present seems hardly the same as the Ireland of the past, and there were hardly any limits to the glowing anticipations we might form respecting the Ireland of the future."

The writer of these letters holds with Solomon, that "there is much wealth in the tillage of the soil," and he believes the real improvement of Ireland will be found to lie in the employment of the Irish people in the art of husbandry. The erroneous ideas which prevailed in England respecting the condition of Ireland, led to the publication of these letters in one of the leading English journals (*The Morning Herald*), and they are now republished, by request, in a collected form. Four diagrams have been compiled to assist in a proper comprehension of the changes which have taken place; 1st, in the population of the country; 2nd, the area under tillage; 3rd, the quantity of live stock; and 4th, the relative yield of the crops. They could not have been published in the newspapers.

During the publication of the letters an avalanche of crime has fallen on some parts of Ireland. This has been one of the results of the non-tillage policy. Those who, in more prosperous times, paid their rents without difficulty, have fallen into arrear. The outlet of emigration to America is closed by the fratricidal war; the occupants of small farms hear ringing in their ears the Lord Lieutenant's advice to landowners, "to consolidate their farms and reduce the number of holdings." Driven to desperation, they add but "guilt to woe," and seem reckless as to what abyss they fall into.

A true appreciation of the necessities of Ireland and the Irish people, would have prevented this ascerbity of feeling. The interests of Ireland and of the British Empire would have been served by encouraging husbandry in Ireland, and thus obviating the necessity of emigration on so large a scale. There is abundant occupation for a larger population than Ireland ever possessed, and an almost unlimited field for the profitable employment of capital.

The writer begs to thank the Press for the kind manner in which the letters were noticed as they appeared, and he trusts it will continue to aid him in bringing this important subject permanently under public notice; and he avails himself of this opportunity of thanking many gentlemen (who are personally unknown to him) for the encouraging commendations which he has received during the appearance of the letters. If their publication aids in promoting the wealth and prosperity of Ireland (which is an important portion of the British Empire), the object he has at heart will be attained.

Waterford, Oct., 1862.

OPINIONS OF THE PRESS.

Mr. Blake, M.P. in the House of Commons.

From " Hansard's Parliamentary Debates."

" For the information which he was about to furnish the House, he was indebted to the admirable letters addressed to the Lord Lieutenant, by Mr Fisher, which were published in some London journals, and in which he clearly proved, by statistics, arranged with great care and ability, that Ireland, in an agricultural point of view, was retrograding instead of advancing."

From the " Morning Herald."

" We used to talk a great deal about a poor and impoverishing people, but the Ireland which has cleared itself of the burden of their consumption, is probably hundreds of millions sterling poorer without them, than it was with them. Mr. Fisher has shown, *in his admirable letters*, that there were 5,343,272 quarters of grain grown, in 1860, less than in 1847 ; and that this reduction was no accident of seasons is proved by the fact that in 1860 there were 774,173 acres under cereal crops less than in 1847. In 1861 matters grew still worse. In addition to a further decrease in the acres given to cereal cultivation, there was a falling off in the value of the live stock."

From the " Standard."

" Truly there is some executive weakness in our Irish system which demands remedies of a more efficacious character than any which have been proposed since Lord George Bentinck propounded his views on a re-construction of the Irish industrial system. The rose-water plan of Lord Carlisle, however gracefully manipulated, has no aptitude for the exigency. If Irishmen have no other industry but that in the land to make them remain in their country and enrich it with their labour, the land must be looked to to meet the requirement. This is no Irish question. The Empire cannot afford to see Ireland drained of the manhood it may want we know not how soon, that she may be turned into a sort of Australian pasture ground, for breeding cattle for the London markets, and raising men for the labour fields of America."

From the " Morning News," Dublin.

" We hope every possible publicity will be given Mr. Fisher's letters in this country. He has taken care to give them a good start in England (by publishing them in the *Standard* and *Herald*). It is for the friends of truth in Ireland to disseminate them now."

From the " Nation," Dublin.

" We find, in the *Morning Herald*, another of Mr. Fisher's letters to His Excellency on the Irish Property question. It is one of a series devoted to a vigorous exposition of the actual state of Ireland, agriculturally and commercially, and to a refutation of the monstrous untruths with which the world around has been drugged by our rulers ; and this exposition of truth and fact, and refutation of error, comes from the pen of an Irishman, and the letters have been so conceived and issued that they cannot but come before tens of thousands of Englishmen, who would not otherwise have the smallest chance of seeing or knowing the truth with reference to this maligned country ; and what is more, we have reason to believe that most important modifications of opinion have been produced in England. We hope Mr. Fisher's labours will receive, in the country in whose interest they have been written, that encouragement which they so eminently deserve."

From the " Cork Examiner."

" Mr. Fisher has addressed a series of valuable letters to the *Morning Herald*. He affords the readers an accurate and valuable picture of Ireland. We are happy to learn that it is the intention of Mr. Fisher to reproduce them in the form of a pamphlet, for we doubt if a more useful little work on a very grave and important subject could be placed in the hands of intelligent readers. Mr. Fisher relies on the statistics of Mr. Donnelly, and the returns of the Census, the information afforded by which he presents in a popular and attractive form, and by so doing makes intelligible, and therefore useful, what, in their official form, would be a puzzle to ninety-nine out of every hundred of the community."

From the " Western Star."

" Mr. Fisher has addressed a series of letters to His Excellency the Lord Lieutenant, on Irish agriculture. The subject is one of the utmost importance, and should be pressed on the consideration of Parliament. The last letter of the series is before us, and from the statistics addressed in it, some very startling facts may be culled."

From the " Western Times," Scotland.

" The English newspaper reading public have been quite astounded by the facts and figures, illustrative of the state of Irish agriculture and commerce, which have lately been given by Mr. Fisher, in a series of letters addressed to the Lord Lieutenant of Ireland, and published in the *Morning Herald*. These letters are painfully suggestive and instructive, and well worthy being weighed by others than the rulers and people of Ireland."